Business Administration P720

TABLE OF CONTENTS
& ACKNOWLEDGEMENTS

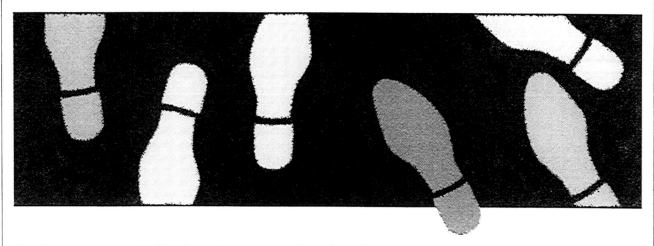

I. Operational Effectiveness Is Not Strategy

For almost two decades, managers have been learning to play by a new set of rules. Companies must be flexible to respond rapidly to competitive and market changes. They must benchmark continuously to achieve best practice. They must outsource aggressively to gain efficiencies. And they must nurture a few core competencies in the race to stay ahead of rivals.

What Is Strategy?

by Michael E. Porter

Positioning – once the heart of strategy – is rejected as too static for today's dynamic markets and changing technologies. According to the new dogma, rivals can quickly copy any market position, and competitive advantage is, at best, temporary.

But those beliefs are dangerous half-truths, and they are leading more and more companies down the path of mutually destructive competition. True, some barriers to competition are falling as regulation eases and markets become global. True, companies have properly invested energy in becoming leaner and more nimble. In many industries, however, what some call *hypercompetition* is a self-inflicted wound, not the inevitable outcome of a changing paradigm of competition.

The root of the problem is the failure to distinguish between operational effectiveness and strategy. The quest for productivity, quality, and speed has spawned a remarkable number of management tools and techniques: total quality management, benchmarking, time-based competition, outsourcing, partnering, reengineering, change management. Although the resulting operational improvements have often been dramatic, many companies have been frustrated by their inability to translate those gains into sustainable profitability. And bit by bit, almost imperceptibly, management tools have taken the place of strategy. As managers push to improve on all fronts, they move farther away from viable competitive positions.

Operational Effectiveness: Necessary but Not Sufficient

Operational effectiveness and strategy are both essential to superior performance, which, after all, is the primary goal of any enterprise. But they work in very different ways.

Michael E. Porter is the C. Roland Christensen Professor of Business Administration at the Harvard Business School in Boston, Massachusetts.

A company can outperform rivals only if it can establish a difference that it can preserve. It must deliver greater value to customers or create comparable value at a lower cost, or do both. The arithmetic of superior profitability then follows: delivering greater value allows a company to charge higher average unit prices; greater efficiency results in lower average unit costs.

Ultimately, all differences between companies in cost or price derive from the hundreds of activities required to create, produce, sell, and deliver their products or services, such as calling on customers, assembling final products, and training employees. Cost is generated by performing activities, and cost advantage arises from performing particular activities more efficiently than competitors. Similarly, differentiation arises from both the choice of activities and how they are performed. Activities, then, are the basic units of competitive advantage. Overall advantage or disadvantage results from all a company's activities, not only a few.[1]

Operational effectiveness (OE) means performing similar activities *better* than rivals perform them. Operational effectiveness includes but is not limited to efficiency. It refers to any number of practices that allow a company to better utilize its inputs by, for example, reducing defects in products or developing better products faster. In contrast, strategic positioning means performing *different* activities from rivals' or performing similar activities in *different ways.*

Differences in operational effectiveness among companies are pervasive. Some companies are able

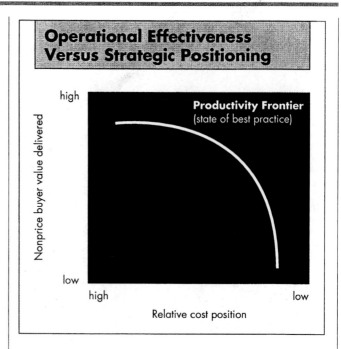

Operational Effectiveness Versus Strategic Positioning

Nonprice buyer value delivered (vertical axis, high to low)

Relative cost position (horizontal axis, high to low)

Productivity Frontier (state of best practice)

tional effectiveness are an important source of differences in profitability among competitors because they directly affect relative cost positions and levels of differentiation.

Differences in operational effectiveness were at the heart of the Japanese challenge to Western companies in the 1980s. The Japanese were so far ahead of rivals in operational effectiveness that they could offer lower cost and superior quality at the same time. It is worth dwelling on this point, because so much recent thinking about competition depends on it. Imagine for a moment a *productivity frontier* that constitutes the sum of all existing best practices at any given time. Think of it as the maximum value that a company delivering a particular product or service can create at a given cost, using the best available technologies, skills, management techniques, and purchased inputs. The productivity frontier can apply to individual activities, to groups of linked activities such as order processing and manufacturing, and to an entire company's activities. When a company improves its operational effectiveness, it moves toward the frontier. Doing so may require capital investment, different personnel, or simply new ways of managing.

The productivity frontier is constantly shifting outward as new technologies and management approaches are developed and as new inputs become available. Laptop computers, mobile communications, the Internet, and software such as Lotus Notes, for example, have redefined the productivity

A company can outperform rivals only if it can establish a difference that it can preserve.

to get more out of their inputs than others because they eliminate wasted effort, employ more advanced technology, motivate employees better, or have greater insight into managing particular activities or sets of activities. Such differences in opera-

This article has benefited greatly from the assistance of many individuals and companies. The author gives special thanks to Jan Rivkin, the coauthor of a related paper. Substantial research contributions have been made by Nicolaj Siggelkow, Dawn Sylvester, and Lucia Marshall. Tarun Khanna, Roger Martin, and Anita McGahan have provided especially extensive comments.

2

frontier for sales-force operations and created rich possibilities for linking sales with such activities as order processing and after-sales support. Similarly, lean production, which involves a family of activities, has allowed substantial improvements in manufacturing productivity and asset utilization.

For at least the past decade, managers have been preoccupied with improving operational effectiveness. Through programs such as TQM, time-based competition, and benchmarking, they have changed how they perform activities in order to eliminate inefficiencies, improve customer satisfaction, and achieve best practice. Hoping to keep up with shifts in the productivity frontier, managers have embraced continuous improvement, empowerment, change management, and the so-called learning organization. The popularity of outsourcing and the virtual corporation reflect the growing recognition that it is difficult to perform all activities as productively as specialists.

As companies move to the frontier, they can often improve on multiple dimensions of performance at the same time. For example, manufacturers that adopted the Japanese practice of rapid changeovers in the 1980s were able to lower cost and improve differentiation simultaneously. What were once believed to be real trade-offs – between defects and costs, for example – turned out to be illusions created by poor operational effectiveness. Managers have learned to reject such false trade-offs.

Constant improvement in operational effectiveness is necessary to achieve superior profitability. However, it is not usually sufficient. Few companies have competed successfully on the basis of operational effectiveness over an extended period, and staying ahead of rivals gets harder every day. The most obvious reason for that is the rapid diffusion of best practices. Competitors can quickly imitate management techniques, new technologies, input improvements, and superior ways of meeting customers' needs. The most generic solutions – those that can be used in multiple settings – diffuse the fastest. Witness the proliferation of OE techniques accelerated by support from consultants.

OE competition shifts the productivity frontier outward, effectively raising the bar for everyone. But although such competition produces absolute improvement in operational effectiveness, it leads to relative improvement for no one. Consider the $5 billion-plus U.S. commercial-printing industry. The major players – R.R. Donnelley & Sons Company, Quebecor, World Color Press, and Big Flower Press – are competing head to head, serving all types of customers, offering the same array of printing technologies (gravure and web offset), investing heavily in the same new equipment, running their presses faster, and reducing crew sizes. But the resulting major productivity gains are being captured by customers and equipment suppliers, not retained in superior profitability. Even industry-

Japanese Companies Rarely Have Strategies

The Japanese triggered a global revolution in operational effectiveness in the 1970s and 1980s, pioneering practices such as total quality management and continuous improvement. As a result, Japanese manufacturers enjoyed substantial cost and quality advantages for many years.

But Japanese companies rarely developed distinct strategic positions of the kind discussed in this article. Those that did – Sony, Canon, and Sega, for example – were the exception rather than the rule. Most Japanese companies imitate and emulate one another. All rivals offer most if not all product varieties, features, and services; they employ all channels and match one anothers' plant configurations.

The dangers of Japanese-style competition are now becoming easier to recognize. In the 1980s, with rivals operating far from the productivity frontier, it seemed possible to win on both cost and quality indefinitely. Japanese companies were all able to grow in an expanding domestic economy and by penetrating global markets. They appeared unstoppable. But as the gap in operational effectiveness narrows, Japanese companies are increasingly caught in a trap of their own making. If they are to escape the mutually destructive battles now ravaging their performance, Japanese companies will have to learn strategy.

To do so, they may have to overcome strong cultural barriers. Japan is notoriously consensus oriented, and companies have a strong tendency to mediate differences among individuals rather than accentuate them. Strategy, on the other hand, requires hard choices. The Japanese also have a deeply ingrained service tradition that predisposes them to go to great lengths to satisfy any need a customer expresses. Companies that compete in that way end up blurring their distinct positioning, becoming all things to all customers.

This discussion of Japan is drawn from the author's research with Hirotaka Takeuchi, with help from Mariko Sakakibara.

leader Donnelley's profit margin, consistently higher than 7% in the 1980s, fell to less than 4.6% in 1995. This pattern is playing itself out in industry after industry. Even the Japanese, pioneers of the new competition, suffer from persistently low profits. (See the insert "Japanese Companies Rarely Have Strategies.")

The second reason that improved operational effectiveness is insufficient – competitive convergence – is more subtle and insidious. The more benchmarking companies do, the more they look alike. The more that rivals outsource activities to efficient third parties, often the same ones, the more generic those activities become. As rivals imitate one another's improvements in quality, cycle times, or supplier partnerships, strategies converge and competition becomes a series of races down identical paths that no one can win. Competition based on operational effectiveness alone is mutu-

ally destructive, leading to wars of attrition that can be arrested only by limiting competition.

The recent wave of industry consolidation through mergers makes sense in the context of OE competition. Driven by performance pressures but lacking strategic vision, company after company has had no better idea than to buy up its rivals. The competitors left standing are often those that outlasted others, not companies with real advantage.

After a decade of impressive gains in operational effectiveness, many companies are facing diminishing returns. Continuous improvement has been etched on managers' brains. But its tools unwittingly draw companies toward imitation and homogeneity. Gradually, managers have let operational effectiveness supplant strategy. The result is zero-sum competition, static or declining prices, and pressures on costs that compromise companies' ability to invest in the business for the long term.

II. Strategy Rests on Unique Activities

Competitive strategy is about being different. It means deliberately choosing a different set of activities to deliver a unique mix of value.

Southwest Airlines Company, for example, offers short-haul, low-cost, point-to-point service between midsize cities and secondary airports in large cities. Southwest avoids large airports and does not fly great distances. Its customers include business travelers, families, and students. Southwest's frequent departures and low fares attract price-sensitive customers who otherwise would travel by bus or car, and convenience-oriented travelers who would choose a full-service airline on other routes.

Most managers describe strategic positioning in terms of their customers: "Southwest Airlines serves price- and convenience-sensitive travelers,"

The essence of strategy is choosing to perform activities differently than rivals do.

for example. But the essence of strategy is in the activities – choosing to perform activities differently or to perform different activities than rivals. Otherwise, a strategy is nothing more than a marketing slogan that will not withstand competition.

A full-service airline is configured to get passengers from almost any point A to any point B. To reach a large number of destinations and serve passengers with connecting flights, full-service airlines employ a hub-and-spoke system centered on major airports. To attract passengers who desire more comfort, they offer first-class or business-class service. To accommodate passengers who must change planes, they coordinate schedules and check and transfer baggage. Because some passengers will be traveling for many hours, full-service airlines serve meals.

Southwest, in contrast, tailors all its activities to deliver low-cost, convenient service on its particular type of route. Through fast turnarounds at the gate of only 15 minutes, Southwest is able to keep planes flying longer hours than rivals and provide frequent departures with fewer aircraft. Southwest does not offer meals, assigned seats, interline baggage checking, or premium classes of service. Automated ticketing at the gate encourages customers to bypass travel agents, allowing Southwest to avoid their commissions. A standardized fleet of 737 aircraft boosts the efficiency of maintenance.

Southwest has staked out a unique and valuable strategic position based on a tailored set of activities. On the routes served by Southwest, a full-

4

service airline could never be as convenient or as low cost.

Ikea, the global furniture retailer based in Sweden, also has a clear strategic positioning. Ikea targets young furniture buyers who want style at low cost. What turns this marketing concept into a strategic positioning is the tailored set of activities that make it work. Like Southwest, Ikea has chosen to perform activities differently from its rivals.

Consider the typical furniture store. Showrooms display samples of the merchandise. One area might contain 25 sofas; another will display five dining tables. But those items represent only a fraction of the choices available to customers. Dozens of books displaying fabric swatches or wood samples or alternate styles offer customers thousands of product varieties to choose from. Salespeople often escort customers through the store, answering questions and helping them navigate this maze of choices. Once a customer makes a selection, the order is relayed to a third-party manufacturer. With luck, the furniture will be delivered to the customer's home within six to eight weeks. This is a value chain that maximizes customization and service but does so at high cost.

In contrast, Ikea serves customers who are happy to trade off service for cost. Instead of having a sales associate trail customers around the store, Ikea uses a self-service model based on clear, in-store displays. Rather than rely solely on third-party manufacturers, Ikea designs its own low-cost, modular, ready-to-assemble furniture to fit its positioning. In huge stores, Ikea displays every product it sells in room-like settings, so customers don't need a decorator to help them imagine how to put the pieces together. Adjacent to the furnished showrooms is a warehouse section with the products in boxes on pallets. Customers are expected to do their own pickup and delivery, and Ikea will even sell you a roof rack for your car that you can return for a refund on your next visit.

Although much of its low-cost position comes from having customers "do it themselves," Ikea offers a number of extra services that its competitors do not. In-store child care is one. Extended hours are another. Those services are uniquely aligned with the needs of its customers, who are young, not wealthy, likely to have children (but no nanny), and, because they work for a living, have a need to shop at odd hours.

The Origins of Strategic Positions

Strategic positions emerge from three distinct sources, which are not mutually exclusive and often overlap. First, positioning can be based on

Finding New Positions: The Entrepreneurial Edge

Strategic competition can be thought of as the process of perceiving new positions that woo customers from established positions or draw new customers into the market. For example, superstores offering depth of merchandise in a single product category take market share from broad-line department stores offering a more limited selection in many categories. Mail-order catalogs pick off customers who crave convenience. In principle, incumbents and entrepreneurs face the same challenges in finding new strategic positions. In practice, new entrants often have the edge.

Strategic positionings are often not obvious, and finding them requires creativity and insight. New entrants often discover unique positions that have been available but simply overlooked by established competitors. Ikea, for example, recognized a customer group that had been ignored or served poorly. Circuit City Stores' entry into used cars, CarMax, is based on a new way of performing activities – extensive refurbishing of cars, product guarantees, no-haggle pricing,

sophisticated use of in-house customer financing – that has long been open to incumbents.

New entrants can prosper by occupying a position that a competitor once held but has ceded through years of imitation and straddling. And entrants coming from other industries can create new positions because of distinctive activities drawn from their other businesses. CarMax borrows heavily from Circuit City's expertise in inventory management, credit, and other activities in consumer electronics retailing.

Most commonly, however, new positions open up because of change. New customer groups or purchase occasions arise; new needs emerge as societies evolve; new distribution channels appear; new technologies are developed; new machinery or information systems become available. When such changes happen, new entrants, unencumbered by a long history in the industry, can often more easily perceive the potential for a new way of competing. Unlike incumbents, newcomers can be more flexible because they face no trade-offs with their existing activities.

5

producing a subset of an industry's products or services. I call this *variety-based positioning* because it is based on the choice of product or service varieties rather than customer segments. Variety-based positioning makes economic sense when a company can best produce particular products or services using distinctive sets of activities.

Jiffy Lube International, for instance, specializes in automotive lubricants and does not offer other

Strategic positions can be based on customers' needs, customers' accessibility, or the variety of a company's products or services.

car repair or maintenance services. Its value chain produces faster service at a lower cost than broader line repair shops, a combination so attractive that many customers subdivide their purchases, buying oil changes from the focused competitor, Jiffy Lube, and going to rivals for other services.

The Vanguard Group, a leader in the mutual fund industry, is another example of variety-based positioning. Vanguard provides an array of common stock, bond, and money market funds that offer predictable performance and rock-bottom expenses. The company's investment approach deliberately sacrifices the possibility of extraordinary performance in any one year for good relative performance in every year. Vanguard is known, for example, for its index funds. It avoids making bets on interest rates and steers clear of narrow stock groups. Fund managers keep trading levels low, which holds expenses down; in addition, the company discourages customers from rapid buying and selling because doing so drives up costs and can force a fund manager to trade in order to deploy new capital and raise cash for redemptions. Vanguard also takes a consistent low-cost approach to managing distribution, customer service, and marketing. Many investors include one or more Vanguard funds in their portfolio, while buying aggressively managed or specialized funds from competitors.

The people who use Vanguard or Jiffy Lube are responding to a superior value chain for a particular type of service. A variety-based positioning can serve a wide array of customers, but for most it will meet only a subset of their needs.

A second basis for positioning is that of serving most or all the needs of a particular group of cus-

tomers. I call this *needs-based positioning*, which comes closer to traditional thinking about targeting a segment of customers. It arises when there are groups of customers with differing needs, and when a tailored set of activities can serve those needs best. Some groups of customers are more price sensitive than others, demand different product features, and need varying amounts of information, support, and services. Ikea's customers are a good example of such a group. Ikea seeks to meet all the home furnishing needs of its target customers, not just a subset of them.

A variant of needs-based positioning arises when the same customer has different needs on different occasions or for different types of transactions. The same person, for example, may have different needs when traveling on business than when traveling for pleasure with the family. Buyers of cans – beverage companies, for example – will likely have different needs from their primary supplier than from their secondary source.

It is intuitive for most managers to conceive of their business in terms of the customers' needs they are meeting. But a critical element of needs-based positioning is not at all intuitive and is often overlooked. Differences in needs will not translate into meaningful positions unless the best set of activities to satisfy them *also* differs. If that were not the case, every competitor could meet those same needs, and there would be nothing unique or valuable about the positioning.

In private banking, for example, Bessemer Trust Company targets families with a minimum of $5 million in investable assets who want capital preservation combined with wealth accumulation. By assigning one sophisticated account officer for every 14 families, Bessemer has configured its activities for personalized service. Meetings, for example, are more likely to be held at a client's ranch or yacht than in the office. Bessemer offers a wide array of customized services, including investment management and estate administration, oversight of oil and gas investments, and accounting for racehorses and aircraft. Loans, a staple of most private banks, are rarely needed by Bessemer's clients and make up a tiny fraction of its client balances and income. Despite the most generous compensation of account officers and the highest personnel cost as a percentage of operating expenses, Bessemer's differentiation with its target families produces a return on equity estimated to be the highest of any private banking competitor.

Citibank's private bank, on the other hand, serves clients with minimum assets of about $250,000 who, in contrast to Bessemer's clients, want convenient access to loans—from jumbo mortgages to deal financing. Citibank's account managers are primarily lenders. When clients need other services, their account manager refers them to other Citibank specialists, each of whom handles prepackaged products. Citibank's system is less customized than Bessemer's and allows it to have a lower manager-to-client ratio of 1:125. Biannual office meetings are offered only for the largest clients. Both Bessemer and Citibank have tailored their activities to meet the needs of a different group of private banking customers. The same value chain cannot profitably meet the needs of both groups.

The third basis for positioning is that of segmenting customers who are accessible in different ways. Although their needs are similar to those of other customers, the best configuration of activities to reach them is different. I call this *access-based positioning*. Access can be a function of customer geography or customer scale—or of anything that requires a different set of activities to reach customers in the best way.

Segmenting by access is less common and less well understood than the other two bases. Carmike Cinemas, for example, operates movie theaters exclusively in cities and towns with populations under 200,000. How does Carmike make money in markets that are not only small but also won't support big-city ticket prices? It does so through a set of activities that result in a lean cost structure. Carmike's small-town customers can be served through standardized, low-cost theater complexes requiring fewer screens and less sophisticated projection technology than big-city theaters. The company's proprietary information system and management process eliminate the need for local administrative staff beyond a single theater manager. Carmike also reaps advantages from centralized purchasing, lower rent and payroll costs (because of its locations), and rock-bottom corporate overhead of 2% (the industry average is 5%). Operating in small communities also allows Carmike to practice a highly personal form of marketing in which the theater manager knows patrons and promotes attendance through personal contacts. By being the dominant if not the only theater in its markets—the main competition is often the high school football team—Carmike is also able to get its pick of films and negotiate better terms with distributors.

Rural versus urban-based customers are one example of access driving differences in activities. Serving small rather than large customers or densely rather than sparsely situated customers are other examples in which the best way to configure marketing, order processing, logistics, and after-sale service activities to meet the similar needs of distinct groups will often differ.

Positioning is not only about carving out a niche. A position emerging from any of the sources can be broad or narrow. A focused competitor, such as Ikea, targets the special needs of a subset of customers and designs its activities accordingly. Focused competitors thrive on groups of customers who are overserved (and hence overpriced) by more broadly targeted competitors, or underserved (and hence underpriced). A broadly targeted competitor—for example, Vanguard or Delta Air Lines—serves a wide array of customers, performing a set of activities designed to meet their common needs. It

The Connection with Generic Strategies

In *Competitive Strategy* (The Free Press, 1985), I introduced the concept of generic strategies – cost leadership, differentiation, and focus – to represent the alternative strategic positions in an industry. The generic strategies remain useful to characterize strategic positions at the simplest and broadest level. Vanguard, for instance, is an example of a cost leadership strategy, whereas Ikea, with its narrow customer group, is an example of cost-based focus. Neutrogena is a focused differentiator. The bases for positioning – varieties, needs, and access – carry the understanding of those generic strategies to a greater level of specificity. Ikea and Southwest are both cost-based focusers, for example, but Ikea's focus is based on the needs of a customer group, and Southwest's is based on offering a particular service variety.

The generic strategies framework introduced the need to choose in order to avoid becoming caught between what I then described as the inherent contradictions of different strategies. Trade-offs between the activities of incompatible positions explain those contradictions. Witness Continental Lite, which tried and failed to compete in two ways at once.

ignores or meets only partially the more idiosyncratic needs of particular customer groups.

Whatever the basis – variety, needs, access, or some combination of the three – positioning requires a tailored set of activities because it is always a function of differences on the supply side; that is, of differences in activities. However, positioning is not always a function of differences on the demand, or customer, side. Variety and access positionings, in particular, do not rely on *any* customer differences. In practice, however, variety or access differences often accompany needs differences. The tastes – that is, the needs – of Carmike's small-town customers, for instance, run more toward comedies, Westerns, action films, and family

entertainment. Carmike does not run any films rated NC-17.

Having defined positioning, we can now begin to answer the question, "What is strategy?" Strategy is the creation of a unique and valuable position, involving a different set of activities. If there were only one ideal position, there would be no need for strategy. Companies would face a simple imperative – win the race to discover and preempt it. The essence of strategic positioning is to choose activities that are different from rivals'. If the same set of activities were best to produce all varieties, meet all needs, and access all customers, companies could easily shift among them and operational effectiveness would determine performance.

III. A Sustainable Strategic Position Requires Trade-offs

Choosing a unique position, however, is not enough to guarantee a sustainable advantage. A valuable position will attract imitation by incumbents, who are likely to copy it in one of two ways.

First, a competitor can reposition itself to match the superior performer. J.C. Penney, for instance, has been repositioning itself from a Sears clone to a more upscale, fashion-oriented, soft-goods retailer. A second and far more common type of imitation is straddling. The straddler seeks to match the benefits of a successful position while maintaining its existing position. It grafts new features, services, or technologies onto the activities it already performs.

For those who argue that competitors can copy any market position, the airline industry is a perfect test case. It would seem that nearly any competitor could imitate any other airline's activities. Any airline can buy the same planes, lease the gates, and match the menus and ticketing and baggage handling services offered by other airlines.

Continental Airlines saw how well Southwest was doing and decided to straddle. While maintaining its position as a full-service airline, Continental also set out to match Southwest on a number of point-to-point routes. The airline dubbed the new service Continental Lite. It eliminated meals and first-class service, increased departure frequency, lowered fares, and shortened turnaround time at the gate. Because Continental remained a full-service airline on other routes, it continued to use travel agents and its mixed fleet of planes and to provide baggage checking and seat assignments.

But a strategic position is not sustainable unless there are trade-offs with other positions. Trade-offs

occur when activities are incompatible. Simply put, a trade-off means that more of one thing necessitates less of another. An airline can choose to serve meals – adding cost and slowing turnaround time at the gate – or it can choose not to, but it cannot do both without bearing major inefficiencies.

Trade-offs create the need for choice and protect against repositioners and straddlers. Consider Neutrogena soap. Neutrogena Corporation's variety-based positioning is built on a "kind to the skin," residue-free soap formulated for pH balance. With a large detail force calling on dermatologists, Neutrogena's marketing strategy looks more like a drug company's than a soap maker's. It advertises in medical journals, sends direct mail to doctors, attends medical conferences, and performs research at its own Skincare Institute. To reinforce its positioning, Neutrogena originally focused its distribution on drugstores and avoided price promotions. Neutrogena uses a slow, more expensive manufacturing process to mold its fragile soap.

In choosing this position, Neutrogena said no to the deodorants and skin softeners that many customers desire in their soap. It gave up the large-volume potential of selling through supermarkets and using price promotions. It sacrificed manufacturing efficiencies to achieve the soap's desired attributes. In its original positioning, Neutrogena made a whole raft of trade-offs like those, trade-offs that protected the company from imitators.

Trade-offs arise for three reasons. The first is inconsistencies in image or reputation. A company known for delivering one kind of value may lack credibility and confuse customers – or even undermine its reputation – if it delivers another kind of value or attempts to deliver two inconsistent things at the same time. For example, Ivory soap, with its position as a basic, inexpensive everyday soap would have a hard time reshaping its image to match Neutrogena's premium "medical" reputation. Efforts to create a new image typically cost tens or even hundreds of millions of dollars in a major industry – a powerful barrier to imitation.

Second, and more important, trade-offs arise from activities themselves. Different positions (with their tailored activities) require different product configurations, different equipment, different employee behavior, different skills, and different management systems. Many trade-offs reflect inflexibilities in machinery, people, or systems. The more Ikea has configured its activities to lower costs by having its customers do their own assembly and delivery, the less able it is to satisfy customers who require higher levels of service.

However, trade-offs can be even more basic. In general, value is destroyed if an activity is overdesigned or underdesigned for its use. For example, even if a given salesperson were capable of providing a high level of assistance to one customer and none to another, the salesperson's talent (and some of his or her cost) would be wasted on the second customer. Moreover, productivity can improve when variation of an activity is limited. By providing a high level of assistance all the time, the salesperson and the entire sales activity can often achieve efficiencies of learning and scale.

Finally, trade-offs arise from limits on internal coordination and control. By clearly choosing to compete in one way and not another, senior management makes organizational priorities clear. Companies that try to be all things to all customers, in contrast, risk confusion in the trenches as employees attempt to make day-to-day operating decisions without a clear framework.

Positioning trade-offs are pervasive in competition and essential to strategy. They create the need for choice and purposefully limit what a company offers. They deter straddling or repositioning, because competitors that engage in those approaches undermine their strategies and degrade the value of their existing activities.

Trade-offs ultimately grounded Continental Lite. The airline lost hundreds of millions of dollars, and the CEO lost his job. Its planes were delayed leaving congested hub cities or slowed at the gate by baggage transfers. Late flights and cancellations generated a thousand complaints a day. Continental Lite could not afford to compete on price and still pay standard travel-agent commissions, but neither could it do without agents for its full-service business. The airline compromised by cutting commissions for all Continental flights across the board. Similarly, it could not afford to offer the same frequent-flier benefits to travelers paying the much lower ticket prices for Lite service. It compromised again by lowering the rewards of Continental's entire frequent-flier program. The results: angry travel agents and full-service customers.

Continental tried to compete in two ways at once. In trying to be low cost on some routes and full service on others, Continental paid an enormous straddling penalty. If there were no trade-offs between the two positions, Continental could have succeeded. But the absence of trade-offs is a dangerous half-truth that managers must unlearn. Quality is not always free. Southwest's convenience, one kind of high quality, happens to be consistent with low costs because its frequent departures are facilitated by a number of low-cost practices – fast gate turnarounds and automated ticketing, for example. However, other dimensions of airline quality – an assigned seat, a meal, or baggage transfer – require costs to provide.

In general, false trade-offs between cost and quality occur primarily when there is redundant or wasted effort, poor control or accuracy, or weak coordination. Simultaneous improvement of cost and differentiation is possible only when a company begins far behind the productivity frontier or when the frontier shifts outward. At the frontier, where

Trade-offs are essential to strategy. They create the need for choice and purposefully limit what a company offers.

companies have achieved current best practice, the trade-off between cost and differentiation is very real indeed.

After a decade of enjoying productivity advantages, Honda Motor Company and Toyota Motor Corporation recently bumped up against the frontier. In 1995, faced with increasing customer resistance to higher automobile prices, Honda found that the only way to produce a less-expensive car was to skimp on features. In the United States, it replaced the rear disk brakes on the Civic with lower-cost drum brakes and used cheaper fabric for the back seat, hoping customers would not notice. Toyota tried to sell a version of its best-selling Corolla in Japan with unpainted bumpers and cheaper seats. In Toyota's case, customers rebelled, and the company quickly dropped the new model.

For the past decade, as managers have improved operational effectiveness greatly, they have internalized the idea that eliminating trade-offs is a good thing. But if there are no trade-offs companies will never achieve a sustainable advantage. They will have to run faster and faster just to stay in place.

As we return to the question, What is strategy? we see that trade-offs add a new dimension to the answer. Strategy is making trade-offs in competing. The essence of strategy is choosing what *not* to do. Without trade-offs, there would be no need for choice and thus no need for strategy. Any good idea could and would be quickly imitated. Again, performance would once again depend wholly on operational effectiveness.

IV. Fit Drives Both Competitive Advantage and Sustainability

Positioning choices determine not only which activities a company will perform and how it will configure individual activities but also how activities relate to one another. While operational effectiveness is about achieving excellence in individual activities, or functions, strategy is about *combining* activities.

Southwest's rapid gate turnaround, which allows frequent departures and greater use of aircraft, is essential to its high-convenience, low-cost positioning. But how does Southwest achieve it? Part of the answer lies in the company's well-paid gate and ground crews, whose productivity in turnarounds is enhanced by flexible union rules. But the bigger part of the answer lies in how Southwest performs other activities. With no meals, no seat assignment, and no interline baggage transfers, Southwest avoids having to perform activities that slow down other airlines. It selects airports and routes to avoid congestion that introduces delays. Southwest's strict limits on the type and length of routes make standardized aircraft possible: every aircraft Southwest turns is a Boeing 737.

Fit locks out imitators by creating a chain that is as strong as its strongest link.

What is Southwest's core competence? Its key success factors? The correct answer is that everything matters. Southwest's strategy involves a whole system of activities, not a collection of parts. Its competitive advantage comes from the way its activities fit and reinforce one another.

Fit locks out imitators by creating a chain that is as strong as its *strongest* link. As in most companies with good strategies, Southwest's activities complement one another in ways that create real economic value. One activity's cost, for example, is lowered because of the way other activities are performed. Similarly, one activity's value to customers can be enhanced by a company's other activities. That is the way strategic fit creates competitive advantage and superior profitability.

Types of Fit

The importance of fit among functional policies is one of the oldest ideas in strategy. Gradually, however, it has been supplanted on the management agenda. Rather than seeing the company as a whole, managers have turned to "core" competencies, "critical" resources, and "key" success factors. In fact, fit is a far more central component of competitive advantage than most realize.

Fit is important because discrete activities often affect one another. A sophisticated sales force, for example, confers a greater advantage when the company's product embodies premium technology and its marketing approach emphasizes customer assistance and support. A production line with high levels of model variety is more valuable when combined with an inventory and order processing system that minimizes the need for stocking finished goods, a sales process equipped to explain and encourage customization, and an advertising theme that stresses the benefits of product variations that meet a customer's special needs. Such complementarities are pervasive in strategy. Although some fit among activities is generic and applies to many companies, the most valuable fit is strategy-specific because it enhances a position's uniqueness and amplifies trade-offs.[2]

There are three types of fit, although they are not mutually exclusive. First-order fit is *simple consistency* between each activity (function) and the overall strategy. Vanguard, for example, aligns all activities with its low-cost strategy. It minimizes portfolio turnover and does not need highly compensated money managers. The company distributes its funds directly, avoiding commissions to brokers. It also limits advertising, relying instead on public relations and word-of-mouth recommendations. Vanguard ties its employees' bonuses to cost savings.

Consistency ensures that the competitive advantages of activities cumulate and do not erode or cancel themselves out. It makes the strategy easier to communicate to customers, employees, and shareholders, and improves implementation through single-mindedness in the corporation.

Second-order fit occurs when *activities are reinforcing.* Neutrogena, for example, markets to upscale hotels eager to offer their guests a soap recommended by dermatologists. Hotels grant Neutrogena the privilege of using its customary packaging while requiring other soaps to feature the hotel's name. Once guests have tried Neutrogena in a luxury hotel, they are more likely to purchase it at the drugstore or ask their doctor about it. Thus Neutrogena's medical and hotel marketing activities reinforce one another, lowering total marketing costs.

In another example, Bic Corporation sells a narrow line of standard, low-priced pens to virtually all major customer markets (retail, commercial, promotional, and giveaway) through virtually all available channels. As with any variety-based positioning serving a broad group of customers, Bic emphasizes a common need (low price for an acceptable pen) and uses marketing approaches with a broad reach (a large sales force and heavy television advertising). Bic gains the benefits of consis-

Mapping Activity Systems

Activity-system maps, such as this one for Ikea, show how a company's strategic position is contained in a set of tailored activities designed to deliver it. In companies with a clear strategic position, a number of higher-order strategic themes (in dark purple) can be identified and implemented through clusters of tightly linked activities (in light purple).

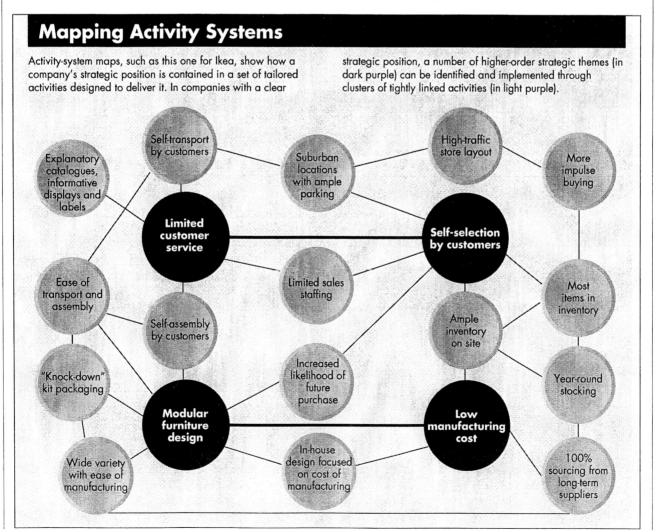

11

Activity-system maps can be useful for examining and strengthening strategic fit. A set of basic questions should guide the process. First, is each activity consistent with the overall positioning – the varieties produced, the needs served, and the type of customers accessed? Ask those responsible for each activity to identify how other activities within the company improve or detract from their performance. Second, are there ways to strengthen how activities and groups of activities reinforce one another? Finally, could changes in one activity eliminate the need to perform others?

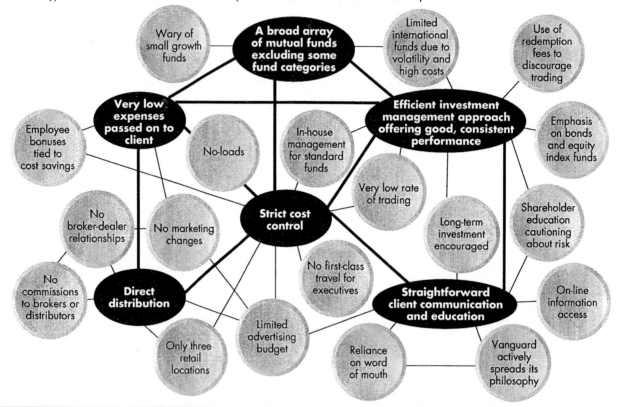

tency across nearly all activities, including product design that emphasizes ease of manufacturing, plants configured for low cost, aggressive purchasing to minimize material costs, and in-house parts production whenever the economics dictate.

Yet Bic goes beyond simple consistency because its activities are reinforcing. For example, the company uses point-of-sale displays and frequent packaging changes to stimulate impulse buying. To handle point-of-sale tasks, a company needs a large sales force. Bic's is the largest in its industry, and it handles point-of-sale activities better than its rivals do. Moreover, the combination of point-of-sale activity, heavy television advertising, and packaging changes yields far more impulse buying than any activity in isolation could.

Third-order fit goes beyond activity reinforcement to what I call *optimization of effort*. The Gap, a retailer of casual clothes, considers product availability in its stores a critical element of its strategy. The Gap could keep products either by holding store inventory or by restocking from warehouses. The Gap has optimized its effort across these activities by restocking its selection of basic clothing almost daily out of three warehouses, thereby minimizing the need to carry large in-store inventories. The emphasis is on restocking because the Gap's merchandising strategy sticks to basic items in relatively few colors. While comparable retailers achieve turns of three to four times per year, the Gap turns its inventory seven and a half times per year. Rapid restocking, moreover, reduces the cost of implementing

The competitive value of individual activities cannot be separated from the whole.

the Gap's short model cycle, which is six to eight weeks long.[3]

Coordination and information exchange across activities to eliminate redundancy and minimize wasted effort are the most basic types of effort optimization. But there are higher levels as well. Product design choices, for example, can eliminate the need for after-sale service or make it possible for customers to perform service activities themselves. Similarly, coordination with suppliers or distribution channels can eliminate the need for some in-house activities, such as end-user training.

In all three types of fit, the whole matters more than any individual part. Competitive advantage grows out of the *entire system* of activities. The fit among activities substantially reduces cost or increases differentiation. Beyond that, the competitive value of individual activities–or the associated skills, competencies, or resources – cannot be decoupled from the system or the strategy. Thus in competitive companies it can be misleading to explain success by specifying individual strengths, core competencies, or critical resources. The list of strengths cuts across many functions, and one strength blends into others. It is more useful to think in terms of themes that pervade many activities, such as low cost, a particular notion of customer service, or a particular conception of the value delivered. These themes are embodied in nests of tightly linked activities.

Fit and Sustainability

Strategic fit among many activities is fundamental not only to competitive advantage but also to the sustainability of that advantage. It is harder for a rival to match an array of interlocked activities than it is merely to imitate a particular sales-force approach, match a process technology, or replicate a set of product features. Positions built on systems of activities are far more sustainable than those built on individual activities.

Consider this simple exercise. The probability that competitors can match any activity is often

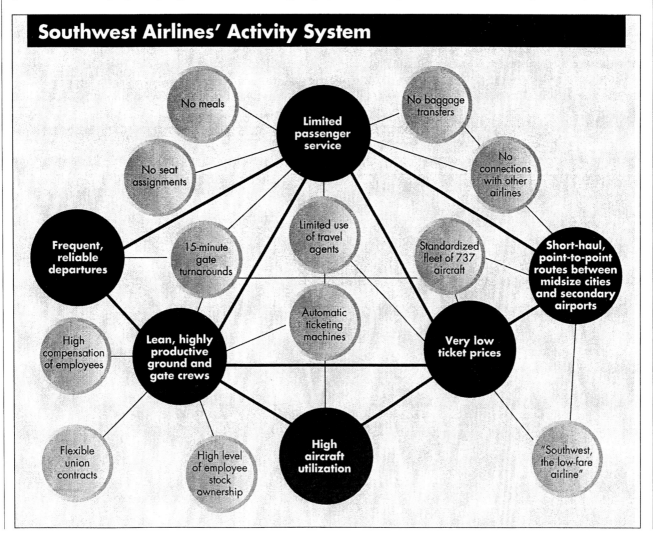

Southwest Airlines' Activity System

less than one. The probabilities then quickly compound to make matching the entire system highly unlikely (.9×.9= .81; .9×.9×.9×.9= .66, and so on). Existing companies that try to reposition or straddle will be forced to reconfigure many activities.

Strategic positions should have a horizon of a decade or more, not of a single planning cycle.

And even new entrants, though they do not confront the trade-offs facing established rivals, still face formidable barriers to imitation.

The more a company's positioning rests on activity systems with second- and third-order fit, the more sustainable its advantage will be. Such systems, by their very nature, are usually difficult to untangle from outside the company and therefore hard to imitate. And even if rivals can identify the relevant interconnections, they will have difficulty replicating them. Achieving fit is difficult because it requires the integration of decisions and actions across many independent subunits.

A competitor seeking to match an activity system gains little by imitating only some activities and not matching the whole. Performance does not improve; it can decline. Recall Continental Lite's disastrous attempt to imitate Southwest.

Finally, fit among a company's activities creates pressures and incentives to improve operational effectiveness, which makes imitation even harder. Fit means that poor performance in one activity will degrade the performance in others, so that weaknesses are exposed and more prone to get attention. Conversely, improvements in one activity will pay dividends in others. Companies with strong fit among their activities are rarely inviting targets. Their superiority in strategy and in execution only compounds their advantages and raises the hurdle for imitators.

When activities complement one another, rivals will get little benefit from imitation unless they successfully match the whole system. Such situations tend to promote winner-take-all competition. The company that builds the best activity system – Toys R Us, for instance – wins, while rivals with similar strategies – Child World and Lionel Leisure – fall behind. Thus finding a new strategic position is often preferable to being the second or third imitator of an occupied position.

The most viable positions are those whose activity systems are incompatible because of trade-offs. Strategic positioning sets the trade-off rules that define how individual activities will be configured and integrated. Seeing strategy in terms of activity systems only makes it clearer why organizational structure, systems, and processes need to be strategy-specific. Tailoring organization to strategy, in turn, makes complementarities more achievable and contributes to sustainability.

One implication is that strategic positions should have a horizon of a decade or more, not of a single planning cycle. Continuity fosters improvements in individual activities and the fit across activities, allowing an organization to build unique capabilities and skills tailored to its strategy. Continuity also reinforces a company's identity.

Conversely, frequent shifts in positioning are costly. Not only must a company reconfigure individual activities, but it must also realign entire sys-

Alternative Views of Strategy

The Implicit Strategy Model of the Past Decade

☐ One ideal competitive position in the industry
☐ Benchmarking of all activities and achieving best practice
☐ Aggressive outsourcing and partnering to gain efficiencies
☐ Advantages rest on a few key success factors, critical resources, core competencies
☐ Flexibility and rapid responses to all competitive and market changes

Sustainable Competitive Advantage

☐ Unique competitive position for the company
☐ Activities tailored to strategy
☐ Clear trade-offs and choices vis-à-vis competitors
☐ Competitive advantage arises from fit across activities
☐ Sustainability comes from the activity system, not the parts
☐ Operational effectiveness a given

14

tems. Some activities may never catch up to the vacillating strategy. The inevitable result of frequent shifts in strategy, or of failure to choose a distinct position in the first place, is "me-too" or hedged activity configurations, inconsistencies across functions, and organizational dissonance.

What is strategy? We can now complete the answer to this question. Strategy is creating fit among a company's activities. The success of a strategy depends on doing many things well—not just a few—and integrating among them. If there is no fit among activities, there is no distinctive strategy and little sustainability. Management reverts to the simpler task of overseeing independent functions, and operational effectiveness determines an organization's relative performance.

V. Rediscovering Strategy

The Failure to Choose

Why do so many companies fail to have a strategy? Why do managers avoid making strategic choices? Or, having made them in the past, why do managers so often let strategies decay and blur?

Commonly, the threats to strategy are seen to emanate from outside a company because of changes in technology or the behavior of competitors. Although external changes can be the problem, the greater threat to strategy often comes from within. A sound strategy is undermined by a misguided view of competition, by organizational failures, and, especially, by the desire to grow.

Managers have become confused about the necessity of making choices. When many companies operate far from the productivity frontier, trade-offs appear unnecessary. It can seem that a well-run company should be able to beat its ineffective rivals on all dimensions simultaneously. Taught by popular management thinkers that they do not have to make trade-offs, managers have acquired a macho sense that to do so is a sign of weakness.

Unnerved by forecasts of hypercompetition, managers increase its likelihood by imitating everything about their competitors. Exhorted to think in terms of revolution, managers chase every new technology for its own sake.

The pursuit of operational effectiveness is seductive because it is concrete and actionable. Over the past decade, managers have been under increasing pressure to deliver tangible, measurable performance improvements. Programs in operational effectiveness produce reassuring progress, although superior profitability may remain elusive. Business publications and consultants flood the market with information about what other companies are doing, reinforcing the best-practice mentality. Caught up in the race for operational effectiveness, many managers simply do not understand the need to have a strategy.

Companies avoid or blur strategic choices for other reasons as well. Conventional wisdom within an industry is often strong, homogenizing competition. Some managers mistake "customer focus" to mean they must serve all customer needs or respond to every request from distribution channels. Others cite the desire to preserve flexibility.

Organizational realities also work against strategy. Trade-offs are frightening, and making no choice is sometimes preferred to risking blame for a bad choice. Companies imitate one another in a type of herd behavior, each assuming rivals know something they do not. Newly empowered employees, who are urged to seek every possible source of improvement, often lack a vision of the whole and the perspective to recognize trade-offs. The failure to choose sometimes comes down to the reluctance to disappoint valued managers or employees.

The Growth Trap

Among all other influences, the desire to grow has perhaps the most perverse effect on strategy. Trade-offs and limits appear to constrain growth. Serving one group of customers and excluding others, for instance, places a real or imagined limit on revenue growth. Broadly targeted strategies emphasizing low price result in lost sales with customers sensitive to features or service. Differentiators lose sales to price-sensitive customers.

Managers are constantly tempted to take incremental steps that surpass those limits but blur a company's strategic position. Eventually, pressures to grow or apparent saturation of the target market lead managers to broaden the position by extending product lines, adding new features, imitating competitors' popular services, matching processes, and even making acquisitions. For years, Maytag Corporation's success was based on its focus on reliable, durable washers and dryers, later extended to include dishwashers. However, conventional wis-

Reconnecting with Strategy

Most companies owe their initial success to a unique strategic position involving clear trade-offs. Activities once were aligned with that position. The passage of time and the pressures of growth, however, led to compromises that were, at first, almost imperceptible. Through a succession of incremental changes that each seemed sensible at the time, many established companies have compromised their way to homogeneity with their rivals.

The issue here is not with the companies whose historical position is no longer viable; their challenge is to start over, just as a new entrant would. At issue is a far more common phenomenon: the established company achieving mediocre returns and lacking a clear strategy. Through incremental additions of product varieties, incremental efforts to serve new customer groups, and emulation of rivals' activities, the existing company loses its clear competitive position. Typically, the company has matched many of its competitors' offerings and practices and attempts to sell to most customer groups.

A number of approaches can help a company reconnect with strategy. The first is a careful look at what it already does. Within most well-established companies is a core of uniqueness. It is identified by answering questions such as the following:

☐ Which of our product or service varieties are the most distinctive?

☐ Which of our product or service varieties are the most profitable?
☐ Which of our customers are the most satisfied?
☐ Which customers, channels, or purchase occasions are the most profitable?
☐ Which of the activities in our value chain are the most different and effective?

Around this core of uniqueness are encrustations added incrementally over time. Like barnacles, they must be removed to reveal the underlying strategic positioning. A small percentage of varieties or customers may well account for most of a company's sales and especially its profits. The challenge, then, is to refocus on the unique core and realign the company's activities with it. Customers and product varieties at the periphery can be sold or allowed through inattention or price increases to fade away.

A company's history can also be instructive. What was the vision of the founder? What were the products and customers that made the company? Looking backward, one can reexamine the original strategy to see if it is still valid. Can the historical positioning be implemented in a modern way, one consistent with today's technologies and practices? This sort of thinking may lead to a commitment to renew the strategy and may challenge the organization to recover its distinctiveness. Such a challenge can be galvanizing and can instill the confidence to make the needed trade-offs.

dom emerging within the industry supported the notion of selling a full line of products. Concerned with slow industry growth and competition from broad-line appliance makers, Maytag was pressured by dealers and encouraged by customers to extend its line. Maytag expanded into refrigerators and cooking products under the Maytag brand and acquired other brands – Jenn-Air, Hardwick Stove, Hoover, Admiral, and Magic Chef – with disparate positions. Maytag has grown substantially from $684 million in 1985 to a peak of $3.4 billion in 1994, but return on sales has declined from 8% to 12% in the 1970s and 1980s to an average of less than 1% between 1989 and 1995. Cost cutting will improve this performance, but laundry and dishwasher products still anchor Maytag's profitability.

Neutrogena may have fallen into the same trap. In the early 1990s, its U.S. distribution broadened to include mass merchandisers such as Wal-Mart Stores. Under the Neutrogena name, the company expanded into a wide variety of products – eye-makeup remover and shampoo, for example – in which it was not unique and which diluted its image, and it began turning to price promotions.

Compromises and inconsistencies in the pursuit of growth will erode the competitive advantage a company had with its original varieties or target customers. Attempts to compete in several ways at once create confusion and undermine organizational motivation and focus. Profits fall, but more revenue is seen as the answer. Managers are unable to make choices, so the company embarks on a new round of broadening and compromises. Often, rivals continue to match each other until desperation breaks the cycle, resulting in a merger or downsizing to the original positioning.

Profitable Growth

Many companies, after a decade of restructuring and cost-cutting, are turning their attention to growth. Too often, efforts to grow blur uniqueness, create compromises, reduce fit, and ultimately undermine competitive advantage. In fact, the growth imperative is hazardous to strategy.

What approaches to growth preserve and reinforce strategy? Broadly, the prescription is to concentrate on deepening a strategic position rather than broadening and compromising it. One approach is to look for extensions of the strategy that leverage the existing activity system by offering features or services that rivals would find impossible or costly to match on a stand-alone basis. In other words, managers can ask themselves which activities, features, or forms of competition are feasible or less costly to them because of complementary activities that their company performs.

Deepening a position involves making the company's activities more distinctive, strengthening fit, and communicating the strategy better to those customers who should value it. But many companies succumb to the temptation to chase "easy" growth by adding hot features, products, or services without screening them or adapting them to their strategy. Or they target new customers or markets in which the company has little special to offer. A company can often grow faster – and far more profitably – by better penetrating needs and varieties where it is distinctive than by slugging it out in potentially higher growth arenas in which the company lacks uniqueness. Carmike, now the largest theater chain in the United States, owes its rapid growth to its disciplined concentration on small markets. The company quickly sells any big-city theaters that come to it as part of an acquisition.

Globalization often allows growth that is consistent with strategy, opening up larger markets for a focused strategy. Unlike broadening domestically,

separate units with different strategic positions. On the other, it has created an umbrella appliance company for all its brands to gain critical mass. With shared design, manufacturing, distribution, and customer service, it will be hard to avoid homogenization. If a given business unit attempts to compete with different positions for different products or customers, avoiding compromise is nearly impossible.

The Role of Leadership

The challenge of developing or reestablishing a clear strategy is often primarily an organizational one and depends on leadership. With so many forces at work against making choices and trade-offs in organizations, a clear intellectual framework to guide strategy is a necessary counterweight. Moreover, strong leaders willing to make choices are essential.

In many companies, leadership has degenerated into orchestrating operational improvements and making deals. But the leader's role is broader and far more important. General management is more than the stewardship of individual functions. Its core is strategy: defining and communicating the company's unique position, making trade-offs, and forging fit among activities. The leader must provide the discipline to decide which industry changes and customer needs the company will respond to, while avoiding organizational distractions and maintaining the company's distinctiveness. Managers at lower levels lack the perspective and the confidence to maintain a strategy. There will be constant pressures to compromise, relax trade-offs, and emulate rivals. One of the leader's jobs is to teach others in the organization about strategy – and to say no.

Strategy renders choices about what not to do as important as choices about what to do. Indeed, setting limits is another function of leadership. Deciding which target group of customers, varieties, and needs the company should serve is fundamental to developing a strategy. But so is deciding not to serve other customers or needs and not to offer certain features or services. Thus strategy requires constant discipline and clear communication. Indeed, one of the most important functions of an explicit, communicated strategy is to guide employees in making choices that arise because of trade-offs in their individual activities and in day-to-day decisions.

> At general management's core is strategy: defining a company's position, making trade-offs, and forging fit among activities.

expanding globally is likely to leverage and reinforce a company's unique position and identity.

Companies seeking growth through broadening within their industry can best contain the risks to strategy by creating stand-alone units, each with its own brand name and tailored activities. Maytag has clearly struggled with this issue. On the one hand, it has organized its premium and value brands into

Emerging Industries and Technologies

Developing a strategy in a newly emerging industry or in a business undergoing revolutionary technological changes is a daunting proposition. In such cases, managers face a high level of uncertainty about the needs of customers, the products and services that will prove to be the most desired, and the best configuration of activities and technologies to deliver them. Because of all this uncertainty, imitation and hedging are rampant: unable to risk being wrong or left behind, companies match all features, offer all new services, and explore all technologies.

During such periods in an industry's development, its basic productivity frontier is being established or reestablished. Explosive growth can make such times profitable for many companies, but profits will be temporary because imitation and strategic convergence will ultimately destroy industry profitability. The companies that are enduringly successful will be those that begin as early as possible to define and embody in their activities a unique competitive position. A period of imitation may be inevitable in emerging industries, but that period reflects the level of uncertainty rather than a desired state of affairs.

In high-tech industries, this imitation phase often continues much longer than it should. Enraptured by technological change itself, companies pack more features – most of which are never used – into their products while slashing prices across the board. Rarely are trade-offs even considered. The drive for growth to satisfy market pressures leads companies into every product area. Although a few companies with fundamental advantages prosper, the majority are doomed to a rat race no one can win.

Ironically, the popular business press, focused on hot, emerging industries, is prone to presenting these special cases as proof that we have entered a new era of competition in which none of the old rules are valid. In fact, the opposite is true.

Improving operational effectiveness is a necessary part of management, but it is *not* strategy. In confusing the two, managers have unintentionally backed into a way of thinking about competition that is driving many industries toward competitive convergence, which is in no one's best interest and is not inevitable.

Managers must clearly distinguish operational effectiveness from strategy. Both are essential, but the two agendas are different.

The operational agenda involves continual improvement everywhere there are no trade-offs. Failure to do this creates vulnerability even for companies with a good strategy. The operational agenda is the proper place for constant change, flexibility, and relentless efforts to achieve best practice. In contrast, the strategic agenda is the right place for defining a unique position, making clear trade-offs, and tightening fit. It involves the continual search for ways to reinforce and extend the company's position. The strategic agenda demands discipline and continuity; its enemies are distraction and compromise.

Strategic continuity does not imply a static view of competition. A company must continually improve its operational effectiveness and actively try to shift the productivity frontier; at the same time, there needs to be ongoing effort to extend its uniqueness while strengthening the fit among its activities. Strategic continuity, in fact, should make an organization's continual improvement more effective.

A company may have to change its strategy if there are major structural changes in its industry. In fact, new strategic positions often arise because of industry changes, and new entrants unencumbered by history often can exploit them more easily. However, a company's choice of a new position must be driven by the ability to find new trade-offs and leverage a new system of complementary activities into a sustainable advantage.

1. I first described the concept of activities and its use in understanding competitive advantage in *Competitive Advantage* (New York: The Free Press, 1985). The ideas in this article build on and extend that thinking.

2. Paul Milgrom and John Roberts have begun to explore the economics of systems of complementary functions, activities, and functions. Their focus is on the emergence of "modern manufacturing" as a new set of complementary activities, on the tendency of companies to react to external changes with coherent bundles of internal responses, and on the need for central coordination – a strategy – to align functional managers. In the latter case, they model what has long been a bedrock principle of strategy. See Paul Milgrom and John Roberts, "The Economics of Modern Manufacturing: Technology, Strategy, and Organization," *American Economic Review* 80 (1990): 511-528; Paul Milgrom, Yingyi Qian, and John Roberts, "Complementarities, Momentum, and Evolution of Modern Manufacturing," *American Economic Review* 81 (1991) 84-88; and Paul Milgrom and John Roberts, "Complementarities and Fit: Strategy, Structure, and Organizational Changes in Manufacturing," *Journal of Accounting and Economics*, vol. 19 (March-May 1995): 179-208.

3. Material on retail strategies is drawn in part from Jan Rivkin, "The Rise of Retail Category Killers," unpublished working paper, January 1995. Nicolaj Siggelkow prepared the case study on the Gap.

Reprint 96608   To place an order, call 1-800-545-7685.

9-711-462
REV: MAY 26, 2011

DAVID B. YOFFIE
RENEE KIM

Cola Wars Continue: Coke and Pepsi in 2010

Authorized for use only in educational programs at McMaster University until Jun 07, 2017.
Use outside these parameters is a copyright violation.

For more than a century, Coke and Pepsi vied for "throat share" of the world's beverage market. The most intense battles in the so-called cola wars were fought over the $74 billion carbonated soft drink (CSD) industry in the United States.[1] In a "carefully waged competitive struggle" that lasted from 1975 through the mid-1990s, both Coke and Pepsi achieved average annual revenue growth of around 10%, as both U.S. and worldwide CSD consumption rose steadily year after year.[2] According to Roger Enrico, former CEO of Pepsi:

> The warfare must be perceived as a continuing battle without blood. Without Coke, Pepsi would have a tough time being an original and lively competitor. The more successful they are, the sharper we have to be. If the Coca-Cola company didn't exist, we'd pray for someone to invent them. And on the other side of the fence, I'm sure the folks at Coke would say that nothing contributes as much to the present-day success of the Coca-Cola company than . . . Pepsi.[3]

That relationship began to fray in the early 2000s, however, as U.S. per-capita CSD consumption started to decline. By 2009, the average American drank 46 gallons of CSDs per year, the lowest CSD consumption level since 1989.[4] At the same time, the two companies experienced their own distinct ups and downs; Coke suffered several operational setbacks while Pepsi charted a new, aggressive course in alternative beverages and snack acquisitions.

As the cola wars continued into the 21st century, Coke and Pepsi faced new challenges: Could they boost flagging domestic CSD sales? How could they compete in the growing non-CSD category that demanded different bottling, pricing, and brand strategies? What had to be done to ensure sustainable growth and profitability?

Economics of the U.S. CSD Industry

Americans consumed 23 gallons of CSDs annually in 1970, and consumption grew by an average of 3% per year over the next three decades (see **Exhibit 1**). Fueling this growth were the increasing availability of CSDs and the introduction of diet and flavored varieties. Declining real (inflation-adjusted) prices that made CSDs more affordable played a significant role as well.[5] There were many

---

Professor David B. Yoffie and Research Associate Michael Slind prepared the original version of this case, "Cola Wars Continue: Coke and Pepsi in 2006," HBS No. 706-447. This version was prepared by Professor David B. Yoffie and Research Associate Renee Kim. This case was developed from published sources. HBS cases are developed solely as the basis for class discussion. Cases are not intended to serve as endorsements, sources of primary data, or illustrations of effective or ineffective management.

Copyright © 2010, 2011 President and Fellows of Harvard College. To order copies or request permission to reproduce materials, call 1-800-545-7685, write Harvard Business School Publishing, Boston, MA 02163, or go to www.hbsp.harvard.edu/educators. This publication may not be digitized, photocopied, or otherwise reproduced, posted, or transmitted, without the permission of Harvard Business School.

alternatives to CSDs, including beer, milk, coffee, bottled water, juices, tea, powdered drinks, wine, sports drinks, distilled spirits, and tap water. Yet Americans drank more soda than any other beverage. Within the CSD category, the cola segment maintained its dominance, although its market share dropped from 71% in 1990 to 55% in 2009.[6] Non-cola CSDs included lemon/lime, citrus, pepper-type, orange, root beer, and other flavors. CSDs consisted of a flavor base (called "concentrate"), a sweetener, and carbonated water. The production and distribution of CSDs involved four major participants: concentrate producers, bottlers, retail channels, and suppliers.[7]

Concentrate Producers

The concentrate producer blended raw material ingredients, packaged the mixture in plastic canisters, and shipped those containers to the bottler. To make concentrate for diet CSDs, concentrate makers often added artificial sweetener; with regular CSDs, bottlers added sugar or high-fructose corn syrup themselves. The concentrate manufacturing process involved relatively little capital investment in machinery, overhead, or labor. A typical concentrate manufacturing plant, which could cover a geographic area as large as the United States, cost between $50 million to $100 million to build.[8]

A concentrate producer's most significant costs were for advertising, promotion, market research, and bottler support. Using innovative and sophisticated campaigns, they invested heavily in their trademarks over time. While concentrate producers implemented and financed marketing programs jointly with bottlers, they usually took the lead in developing those programs, particularly when it came to product development, market research, and advertising. They also took charge of negotiating "customer development agreements" (CDAs) with nationwide retailers such as Wal-Mart. Under a CDA, Coke or Pepsi offered funds for marketing and other purposes in exchange for shelf space. With smaller regional accounts, bottlers assumed a key role in developing such relationships, and paid an agreed-upon percentage—typically 50% or more—of promotional and advertising costs. Concentrate producers employed a large staff of people who worked with bottlers by supporting sales efforts, setting standards, and suggesting operational improvements. They also negotiated directly with their bottlers' major suppliers (especially sweetener and packaging makers) to achieve reliable supply, fast delivery, and low prices.[9]

Once a fragmented business that featured hundreds of local manufacturers, the U.S. soft drink industry had changed dramatically over time. Among national concentrate producers, Coke and Pepsi claimed a combined 72% of the U.S. CSD market's sales volume in 2009, followed by Dr Pepper Snapple Group (DPS) and Cott Corporation (see **Exhibits 2, 3a** and **3b**). In addition, there were private-label manufacturers and several dozen other national and regional producers.

Bottlers

Bottlers purchased concentrate, added carbonated water and high-fructose corn syrup, bottled or canned the resulting CSD product, and delivered it to customer accounts. Coke and Pepsi bottlers offered "direct store door" (DSD) delivery, an arrangement whereby route delivery salespeople managed the CSD brand in stores by securing shelf space, stacking CSD products, positioning the brand's trademarked label, and setting up point-of-purchase or end-of-aisle displays. (Smaller national brands, such as Shasta and Faygo, distributed through food store warehouses.) Cooperative merchandising agreements, in which retailers agreed to specific promotional activity and discount levels in exchange for a payment from a bottler, were another key ingredient of soft drink sales.

The bottling process was capital-intensive and involved high-speed production lines that were interchangeable only for products of similar type and packages of similar size. Bottling and canning lines cost from $4 million to $10 million each, depending on volume and package type. But the cost of a large plant with multiple lines and automated warehousing could reach hundreds of millions of dollars. In 2010, DPS completed construction of a production facility in California with a capacity of 40 million cases at an estimated cost of $120 million.[10] While a handful of such plants could theoretically provide enough capacity to serve the entire United States, Coke and Pepsi each had around 100 plants for nationwide distribution.[11] For bottlers, their main costs components were concentrate and syrup. Other significant expenses included packaging, labor, and overhead.[12] Bottlers also invested capital in trucks and distribution networks. For CSDs, bottlers' gross profits routinely exceeded 40% but operating margins were usually around 8%, about a third of concentrate producers' operating margins (see **Exhibit 4**).

The number of U.S. soft drink bottlers had fallen steadily, from more than 2,000 in 1970 to fewer than 300 in 2009.[13] Coke was the first concentrate producer to build a nationwide franchised bottling network, and Pepsi and DPS followed suit. The typical franchised bottler owned a manufacturing and sales operation in an exclusive geographic territory, with rights granted in perpetuity by the franchiser. In the case of Coke, territorial rights did not extend to national fountain accounts, which the company handled directly. The original Coca-Cola franchise agreement, written in 1899, was a fixed-price contract that did not provide for renegotiation, even if ingredient costs changed. After considerable negotiation, often accompanied by bitter legal disputes, Coca-Cola amended the contract in 1921, 1978, and 1987. By 2009, 92% of Coke's U.S. concentrate sales for bottled and canned beverages was covered by its 1987 Master Bottler Contract, which granted Coke the right to determine concentrate price and other terms of sale.[14] Under this contract, Coke had no legal obligation to assist bottlers with advertising or marketing. Nonetheless, to ensure quality and to match Pepsi, Coke made huge investments to support its bottling network. In 2009, for example, Coke contributed $540 million in marketing support payments to its top bottler.[15]

The 1987 contract did not give complete pricing control to Coke, but rather used a formula that established a maximum price and adjusted prices quarterly according to changes in sweetener pricing. This contract differed from Pepsi's Master Bottling Agreement with its top bottler. That agreement granted the bottler perpetual rights to distribute Pepsi's CSD products but required it to purchase raw materials from Pepsi at prices, and on terms and conditions, determined by Pepsi. Pepsi negotiated concentrate prices with its bottling association, and normally based price increases on the consumer price index (CPI). Over the last two decades, however, concentrate makers regularly raised concentrate prices, often by more than the increase in inflation (see **Exhibit 5**).

Franchise agreements with both Coke and Pepsi allowed bottlers to handle the non-cola brands of other concentrate producers. Bottlers could choose whether to market new beverages introduced by a concentrate producer. However, concentrate producers worked hard to "encourage" bottlers to carry their product offerings. Bottlers could not carry directly competing brands, however. For example, a Coke bottler could not sell Royal Crown Cola, yet it could distribute 7UP if it did not carry Sprite. Franchised bottlers could decide whether to participate in test marketing efforts, local advertising campaigns and promotions, and new package introductions (although they could only use packages authorized by their franchiser). Bottlers also had the final say in decisions about retail pricing.

In 1971, the Federal Trade Commission initiated action against eight major concentrate makers, charging that the granting of exclusive territories to bottlers prevented intrabrand competition (that is, two or more bottlers competing in the same area with the same beverage). The concentrate makers argued that interbrand competition was strong enough to warrant continuation of the existing territorial agreements. In 1980, after years of litigation, Congress enacted the Soft Drink Interbrand Competition Act, which preserved the right of concentrate makers to grant exclusive territories.

Retail Channels

In 2009, the distribution of CSDs in the United States took place through supermarkets (29.1%), fountain outlets (23.1%), vending machines (12.5%), mass merchandisers (16.7%), convenience stores and gas stations (10.8%), and other outlets (7.8%). Small grocery stores and drug chains made up most of the latter category.[16] Costs and profitability in each channel varied by delivery method and frequency, drop size, advertising, and marketing (see **Exhibit 6**).

CSDs accounted for $12 billion, or 4% of total store sales in the U.S., and were also a big traffic draw for supermarkets.[17] Bottlers fought for shelf space to ensure visibility for their products, and they looked for new ways to drive impulse purchases, such as placing coolers at checkout counters. An ever-expanding array of products and packages created intense competition for shelf space.

The mass merchandiser category included discount retailers, such as Wal-Mart and Target. These companies formed an increasingly important channel. Although they sold Coke and Pepsi products, they (along with some drug chains) could also have their own private-label CSD, or sell a generic label such as President's Choice. Private-label CSDs were usually delivered to a retailer's warehouse, while branded CSDs were delivered directly to stores. With the warehouse delivery method, the retailer was responsible for storage, transportation, merchandising, and stocking the shelves, thereby incurring additional costs.

Historically, Pepsi had focused on sales through retail outlets, while Coke commanded the lead in fountain sales. (The term "fountain," which originally referred to drug store soda fountains, covered restaurants, cafeterias, and any other outlet that served soft drinks by the glass using fountain-type dispensers.) Competition for national fountain accounts was intense, especially in the 1990s. In 1999, for example, Burger King franchises were believed to pay about $6.20 per gallon for Coke syrup, but they received a substantial rebate on each gallon; one large Midwestern franchise owner said that his annual rebate ran $1.45 per gallon, or about 23%.[18] Local fountain accounts, which bottlers handled in most cases, were considerably more profitable than national accounts. To support the fountain channel, Coke and Pepsi invested in the development of service dispensers and other equipment, and provided fountain customers with point-of-sale advertising and other in-store promotional material.

After Pepsi entered the fast-food restaurant business by acquiring Pizza Hut (1978), Taco Bell (1986), and Kentucky Fried Chicken (1986), Coca-Cola persuaded competing chains such as Wendy's and Burger King to switch to Coke. In 1997, PepsiCo spun off its restaurant business under the name Tricon, but fountain "pouring rights" remained split along largely pre-Tricon lines.[19] In 2009, Pepsi supplied all Taco Bell and KFC restaurants and the great majority of Pizza Hut restaurants, and Coke retained deals with Burger King and McDonald's (the largest national account in terms of sales). Competition remained vigorous: In 2004, Coke won the Subway account away from Pepsi, while Pepsi grabbed the Quiznos account from Coke. (Subway was the largest account as measured by number of outlets.) In April 2009, DPS secured rights for Dr Pepper at all U.S. McDonald's restaurants.[20] Yet Coke continued to lead the channel with a 69% share of national pouring rights, against Pepsi's 20% and DPS' 11%.[21]

Coke and DPS had long retained control of national fountain accounts, negotiating pouring-rights contracts that in some cases (as with big restaurant chains) covered the entire United States or even the world. Local bottlers or the franchisors' fountain divisions serviced these accounts. (In such cases, bottlers received a fee for delivering syrup and maintaining machines.) Historically, PepsiCo had ceded fountain rights to local Pepsi bottlers. But in the late 1990s, Pepsi began a successful campaign to gain from its bottlers the right to sell fountain syrup via restaurant commissary companies.[22]

In the vending channel, bottlers took charge of buying, installing, and servicing machines, and for negotiating contracts with property owners, who typically received a sales commission in exchange for accommodating those machines. But concentrate makers offered bottlers financial incentives to encourage investment in machines, and also played a large role in the development of vending technology. Coke and Pepsi were by far the largest suppliers of CSDs to this channel.

Suppliers to Concentrate Producers and Bottlers

Concentrate producers required few inputs: the concentrate for most regular colas consisted of caramel coloring, phosphoric or citric acid, natural flavors, and caffeine.[23] Bottlers purchased two major inputs: packaging (including cans, plastic bottles, and glass bottles), and sweeteners (including high-fructose corn syrup and sugar, as well as artificial sweeteners such as aspartame). The majority of U.S. CSDs were packaged in metal cans (56%), with plastic bottles (42%) and glass bottles (2%) accounting for the remainder.[24] Cans were an attractive packaging material because they were easily handled and displayed, weighed little, and were durable and recyclable. Plastic packaging, introduced in 1978, allowed for larger and more varied bottle sizes. Single-serve 20-oz PET bottles, introduced in 1993, steadily gained popularity; in 2009, they represented 35% of CSD volume (and 52% of CSD revenues) in convenience stores.[25]

The concentrate producers' strategy toward can manufacturers was typical of their supplier relationships. Coke and Pepsi negotiated on behalf of their bottling networks, and were among the metal can industry's largest customers. In the 1960s and 1970s, both companies took control of a portion of their own can production, but by 1990 they had largely exited that business. Thereafter, they sought instead to establish stable long-term relationships with suppliers. In 2009, major can producers included Ball, Rexam (through its American National Can subsidiary), and Crown Cork & Seal.[26] Metal cans were essentially a commodity, and often two or three can manufacturers competed for a single contract.

The Evolution of the U.S. Soft Drink Industry[27]

Early History

Coca-Cola was formulated in 1886 by John Pemberton, a pharmacist in Atlanta, Georgia, who sold it at drug store soda fountains as a "potion for mental and physical disorders." In 1891, Asa Candler acquired the formula, established a sales force, and began brand advertising of Coca-Cola. The formula for Coca-Cola syrup, known as "Merchandise 7X," remained a well-protected secret that the company kept under guard in an Atlanta bank vault. Candler granted Coca-Cola's first bottling franchise in 1899 for a nominal one dollar, believing that the future of the drink rested with soda fountains. The company's bottling network grew quickly, however, reaching 370 franchisees by 1910.

In its early years, imitations and counterfeit versions of Coke plagued the company, which aggressively fought trademark infringements in court. In 1916 alone, courts barred 153 imitations of Coca-Cola, including the brands Coca-Kola, Koca-Nola, and Cold-Cola. Coke introduced and patented a 6.5-oz bottle whose unique "skirt" design subsequently became an American icon.

Candler sold the company to a group of investors in 1919, and it went public that year. Four years later, Robert Woodruff began his long tenure as leader of the company. Woodruff pushed franchise bottlers to place the beverage "in arm's reach of desire," by any and all means. During the 1920s and 1930s, Coke pioneered open-top coolers for use in grocery stores and other channels, developed automatic fountain dispensers, and introduced vending machines. Woodruff also initiated "lifestyle" advertising for Coca-Cola, emphasizing the role that Coke played in a consumer's life.

Woodruff developed Coke's international business as well. During World War II, at the request of General Eisenhower, Woodruff promised that "every man in uniform gets a bottle of Coca-Cola for five cents wherever he is and whatever it costs the company." Beginning in 1942, Coke won exemptions from wartime sugar rationing for production of beverages that it sold to the military or to retailers that served soldiers. Coca-Cola bottling plants followed the movement of American troops, and during the war the U.S. government set up 64 such plants overseas—a development that contributed to Coke's dominant postwar market shares in most European and Asian countries.

Pepsi-Cola was invented in 1893 in New Bern, North Carolina, by pharmacist Caleb Bradham. Like Coke, Pepsi adopted a franchise bottling system, and by 1910 it had built a network of 270 bottlers. Pepsi struggled, however; it declared bankruptcy in 1923 and again in 1932. But business began to pick up when, during the Great Depression, Pepsi lowered the price of its 12-oz bottle to a nickel—the same price that Coke charged for a 6.5-oz bottle. In the years that followed, Pepsi built a marketing strategy around the theme of its famous radio jingle: "Twice as much for a nickel, too."

In 1938, Coke filed suit against Pepsi, claiming that the Pepsi-Cola brand was an infringement on the Coca-Cola trademark. A 1941 court ruling in Pepsi's favor ended a series of suits and countersuits between the two companies. During this period, as Pepsi sought to expand its bottling network, it had to rely on small local bottlers that competed with wealthy, established Coke franchisees.[28] Still, the company began to gain market share, surpassing Royal Crown and Dr Pepper in the 1940s to become the second-largest-selling CSD brand. In 1950, Coke's share of the U.S. market was 47% and Pepsi's was 10%; hundreds of regional CSD companies, which offered a wide assortment of flavors, made up the rest of the market.[29]

The Cola Wars Begin

In 1950, Alfred Steele, a former Coke marketing executive, became CEO of Pepsi. Steele made "Beat Coke" his motto and encouraged bottlers to focus on take-home sales through supermarkets. To target family consumption, for example, the company introduced a 26-oz bottle. Pepsi's growth began to follow the postwar growth in the number of supermarkets and convenience stores in the United States: There were about 10,000 supermarkets in 1945; 15,000 in 1955; and 32,000 in 1962, at the peak of this growth curve.

Under the leadership of CEO Donald Kendall, Pepsi in 1963 launched its "Pepsi Generation" marketing campaign, which targeted the young and "young at heart." The campaign helped Pepsi narrow Coke's lead to a 2-to-1 margin. At the same time, Pepsi worked with its bottlers to modernize plants and to improve store delivery services. By 1970, Pepsi bottlers were generally larger than their Coke counterparts. Coke's network remained fragmented, with more than 800 independent franchised bottlers (most of which served U.S. cities of 50,000 or less).[30] Throughout this period, Pepsi sold concentrate to its bottlers at a price that was about 20% lower than what Coke charged. In the early 1970s, Pepsi increased its concentrate prices to equal those of Coke. To overcome bottler opposition, Pepsi promised to spend this extra income on advertising and promotion.

Coke and Pepsi began to experiment with new cola and non-cola flavors, and with new packaging options, in the 1960s. Previously, the two companies had sold only their flagship cola brands. Coke launched Fanta (1960), Sprite (1961), and the low-calorie cola Tab (1963). Pepsi countered with Teem (1960), Mountain Dew (1964), and Diet Pepsi (1964). Both companies introduced non-returnable glass bottles and 12-oz metal cans in various configurations. They also diversified into non-CSD industries.

Coke purchased Minute Maid (fruit juice), Duncan Foods (coffee, tea, hot chocolate), and Belmont Springs Water. In 1965, Pepsi merged with snack-food giant Frito-Lay to form PepsiCo, hoping to achieve synergies based on similar customer targets, delivery systems, and marketing orientations.

In the late 1950s, Coca-Cola began to use advertising messages that implicitly recognized the existence of competitors: "American's Preferred Taste" (1955), "No Wonder Coke Refreshes Best" (1960). In meetings with Coca-Cola bottlers, however, executives discussed only the growth of their own brand and never referred to its closest competitor by name. During the 1960s, Coke focused primarily on overseas markets, apparently basing its strategy on the assumption that domestic CSD consumption was approaching a saturation point. Pepsi, meanwhile, battled Coke aggressively in the United States, and doubled its U.S. share between 1950 and 1970.

The Pepsi Challenge

In 1974, Pepsi launched the "Pepsi Challenge" in Dallas, Texas. Coke was the dominant brand in that city, and Pepsi ran a distant third behind Dr Pepper. In blind taste tests conducted by Pepsi's small local bottler, the company tried to demonstrate that consumers actually preferred Pepsi to Coke. After its sales shot up in Dallas, Pepsi rolled out the campaign nationwide.

Coke countered with rebates, retail price cuts, and a series of advertisements that questioned the tests' validity. In particular, it employed retail price discounts in markets where a company-owned Coke bottler competed against an independent Pepsi bottler. Nonetheless, the Pepsi Challenge successfully eroded Coke's market share. In 1979, Pepsi passed Coke in food store sales for the first time, opening up a 1.4 share-point lead. In a sign of the times, Coca-Cola president Brian Dyson inadvertently uttered the name Pepsi at a 1979 bottlers' conference.

During this period, Coke renegotiated its franchise bottling contract to obtain greater flexibility in pricing concentrate and syrups. Its bottlers approved a new contract in 1978, but only after Coke agreed to link concentrate price changes to the CPI, to adjust the price to reflect any cost savings associated with ingredient changes, and to supply unsweetened concentrate to bottlers that preferred to buy their own sweetener on the open market.[31] This arrangement brought Coke in line with Pepsi, which traditionally had sold unsweetened concentrate to its bottlers. Immediately after securing approval of the new agreement, Coke announced a significant concentrate price increase. Pepsi followed with a 15% price increase of its own.

Cola Wars Heat Up

In 1980, Roberto Goizueta was named CEO of Coca-Cola, and Don Keough became its president. That year, Coke switched from using sugar to using high-fructose corn syrup, a lower-priced alternative. Pepsi emulated that move three years later. Coke also intensified its marketing effort, more than doubling its advertising spending between 1981 and 1984. In response, Pepsi doubled its advertising expenditures over the same period. Meanwhile, Goizueta sold off most of the non-CSD businesses that he had inherited, including wine, coffee, tea, and industrial water treatment, while retaining Minute Maid.

Diet Coke, introduced in 1982, was the first extension of the "Coke" brand name. Many Coke managers, deeming the "Mother Coke" brand sacred, had opposed the move. So had company lawyers, who worried about copyright issues. Nonetheless, Diet Coke was a huge success. Praised as the "most successful consumer product launch of the Eighties," it became within a few years not only the most popular diet soft drink in the United States, but also the nation's third-largest-selling CSD.

In April 1985, Coke announced that it had changed the 99-year-old Coca-Cola formula. Explaining this radical break with tradition, Goizueta cited a sharp depreciation in the value of the Coca-Cola trademark. "The product and the brand," he said, "had a declining share in a shrinking segment of the market."[32] On the day of Coke's announcement, Pepsi declared a holiday for its employees, claiming that the new Coke mimicked Pepsi in taste. The reformulation prompted an outcry from Coke's most loyal customers, and bottlers joined the clamor. Three months later, the company brought back the original formula under the name Coca-Cola Classic, while retaining the new formula as its flagship brand under the name New Coke. Six months later, Coke announced that it would henceforth treat Coca-Cola Classic (the original formula) as its flagship brand.

New CSD brands proliferated in the 1980s. Coke introduced 11 new products, including Caffeine-Free Coke (1983) and Cherry Coke (1985). Pepsi introduced 13 products, including Lemon-Lime Slice (1984) and Caffeine-Free Pepsi-Cola (1987). The number of packaging types and sizes also increased dramatically, and the battle for shelf space in supermarkets and other stores became fierce. By the late 1980s, Coke and Pepsi each offered more than 10 major brands and 17 or more container types.[33] The struggle for market share intensified, and retail price discounting became the norm. Consumers grew accustomed to such discounts.

Throughout the 1980s, the growth of Coke and Pepsi put a squeeze on smaller concentrate producers. As their shelf space declined, small brands were shuffled from one owner to another. Over a five-year span, Dr Pepper was sold (all or in part) several times, Canada Dry twice, Sunkist once, and A&W Brands once. Philip Morris acquired Seven-Up in 1978 for a big premium, racked up huge losses in the early 1980s, and then left the CSD business in 1985. In the 1990s, through a series of strategic acquisitions, Cadbury Schweppes emerged as the third-largest concentrate producer—the main (albeit distant) competitor of the two CSD giants. It bought the Dr Pepper/Seven-Up Companies in 1995, and continued to add such well-known brands as Orangina (2001) and Nantucket Nectars (2002) to its portfolio. Then in 2008, Cadbury's beverage business was spun off into an independent company, Dr Pepper Snapple Group.

Bottler Consolidation and Spin-Off

Relations between Coke and its franchised bottlers had been strained since the contract renegotiation of 1978. Coke struggled to persuade bottlers to cooperate in marketing and promotion programs, to upgrade plant and equipment, and to support new product launches.[34] The cola wars had particularly weakened small, independent bottlers. Pressures to spend more on advertising, product and packaging proliferation, widespread retail price discounting—together, these factors resulted in higher capital requirements and lower profit margins. Many family-owned bottlers no longer had the resources needed to remain competitive.

At a July 1980 dinner with Coke's 15 largest domestic bottlers, Goizueta announced a plan to refranchise bottling operations. Coke began buying up poorly managed bottlers, infusing them with capital, and quickly reselling them to better-performing bottlers. Refranchising allowed Coke's larger bottlers to expand outside their traditionally exclusive geographic territories. When two of its largest bottling companies came up for sale in 1985, Coke moved swiftly to buy them for $2.4 billion, preempting outside bidders. Together with other recently purchased bottlers, these acquisitions placed one-third of Coke's volume in company-owned operations. Meanwhile, Coke began to replace its 1978 franchise agreement with what became the 1987 Master Bottler Contract.

Coke's bottler acquisitions had increased its long-term debt to approximately $1 billion. In 1986, the company created an independent bottling subsidiary, Coca-Cola Enterprises (CCE), selling 51% of its shares to the public and retaining the rest. The minority equity position enabled Coke to separate its financial statements from those of CCE. As Coke's first "anchor bottler," CCE consolidated small territories into larger regions, renegotiated contracts with suppliers and retailers, merged redundant distribution and purchasing arrangements, and cut its work force by 20%. CCE also invested in building 50-million-case production lines that involved high levels of automation. Coke continued to acquire independent franchised bottlers and sell them to CCE. "We became an investment banking firm specializing in bottler deals," said Don Keough. [35] In 1997 alone, Coke put together more than $7 billion in such deals.[36] As of 2009, CCE was Coke's largest bottler. It handled about 75% of Coke's North American bottle and can volume, and logged annual sales of more than $21 billion.

In the late 1980s, Pepsi acquired MEI Bottling for $591 million, Grand Metropolitan's bottling operations for $705 million, and General Cinema's bottling operations for $1.8 billion. After operating the bottlers for a decade, Pepsi shifted course and adopted Coke's anchor bottler model. In April 1999, the Pepsi Bottling Group (PBG) went public, with Pepsi retaining a 35% equity stake in it. By 2009, PBG produced 56% of PepsiCo's total volume, while the total number of Pepsi bottlers had fallen from more than 400 in the mid-1980s to 106.[37]

Bottler consolidation made smaller concentrate producers increasingly dependent on the Pepsi and Coke bottling networks for distribution of their products. In response, DPS in 1998 bought and merged two large U.S. bottling companies to form its own bottler. In 2009, Coke had the most consolidated system, with its top 10 bottlers producing 94% of domestic volume. Pepsi's and DPS' top 10 bottlers produced 89% and 79% of the domestic volume of their respective franchisors.[38]

Adapting to the Times

Starting in the late 1990s, the soft drink industry encountered new challenges that suggested a possible long-term shift in the marketplace. Although Americans still drank more CSDs than any other beverage, U.S. consumption began to fizzle (see **Exhibit 1**). That stood in contrast to annual growth rates of 3% to 7% during the 1980s and early 1990s.[39]

This shift in consumption patterns evolved around the growing linkage between CSDs and health issues such as obesity and nutrition. New federal nutrition guidelines, issued in 2005, identified regular CSDs as the largest source of obesity-causing sugars in the American diet.[40] Schools throughout the nation banned the sale of soft drinks on their premises. Several states pushed for a "soda tax" on sugary drinks like sodas and energy beverages. A U.S. government study suggested that a 20% tax could cut the calorie intake from sugary drinks by up to 49 calories a day per person in the United States.[41] As of April 2010, 29 states already taxed sodas and around 12 more states were considering the measure.[42] In addition, a greater number of consumers started to perceive high-fructose corn syrup as unnatural and unhealthy. According to one market research study, 53% of Americans were concerned that the ingredient posed a health hazard in 2010, compared to 40% in 2004.[43] In fact, Coke's 2009 annual report identified obesity and health concerns as the number one risk factor to its business.[44]

In face of dwindling CSD sales (see **Exhibit 7**), Coke and Pepsi tried to stem the tide by enticing consumers with stepped-up innovation and marketing. In Coke's case, the company revealed a new Freestyle soda machine in 2009 which could create dozens of different kinds of custom beverages; restaurants had to pay a 30% premium for the Freestyle compared to a regular soda fountain.[45] Coke also placed a greater emphasis on promoting its brands, such as spending $230 million in advertising for its flagship Cola-Cola drink (see **Exhibit 8**). It also upped spending on sponsorships and global marketing, including $600 million for the World Cup in 2010.[46] Meanwhile, Pepsi redesigned its logo in 2008 with a three-year rebranding plan that could cost over $1 billion to rejuvenate its image. Pepsi

9

focused on promoting the company's overall portfolio as a snack and beverage company, such as through "The Power of One" concept. Market surveys on brand loyalty indicated that more consumers preferred Coke over Pepsi as their favorite CSD brand towards 2010, a slight setback for Pepsi after it had significantly narrowed the gap in the late 1990s.[47]

The Quest for Alternatives

Expanding the product mix offered another avenue for growth. Diet sodas, for example, rose to capture 30% of the CSD market in 2009 compared to 24% a decade ago.[48] Coca-Cola Zero became the most successful new CSD product launched in the second half of the decade. The beverage, which offered the "real Coca-Cola taste with zero calories", experienced consecutive double-digit growth since its introduction in 2005. It was primarily marketed to younger men around the world who shunned the "diet" label.

At the same time, both Coke and Pepsi intensified their efforts to use alternative sweeteners. Pepsi replaced high-fructose corn syrup with natural sugar for its brands, Pepsi Throwback and Mountain Dew Throwback. Another possible alternative was Stevia, an herb that could be used as a natural, zero-calorie sweetener. Coke and Pepsi both developed their own versions of a Stevia-based sweetener, which were approved to be used as a food additive by the U.S. Food and Drug Administration in 2008. New Stevia-based product releases followed, including Pepsi's reduced-calorie Trop 50 (orange juice), and Coke's Sprite Green, with plans to expand to more CSDs as well.

Despite some success with diet drinks, Coke and Pepsi realized that growth would involve "non-carbs"—a category that included juices and juice drinks, sports drinks, energy drinks, and tea-based drinks—and also on bottled water (see **Exhibit 9**). In 2009, while CSDs accounted for 63% of U.S. non-alcoholic refreshment beverage volume (down from 81% in 2000), the remaining volume was made up of bottled water at 20% (up from 7%) and non-carbs at 17% (up from 13%).[49]

Initially, Pepsi was more aggressive than Coke in shifting to non-CSDs. Declaring itself to be a "total beverage company," Pepsi developed a portfolio of non-CSD products that outsold Coke's rival product in several key categories, such as sports drink (Gatorade) and tea-based drinks (Lipton). Between 2004 and 2007, 77% of Pepsi's new products released in the U.S. market were non-carbs compared to Coke's 56%.[50] But starting in 2007, Coke aggressively expanded its non-carbs product portfolio through acquisitions. Most notable was its $4 billion purchase of Energy Brands, maker of the popular Vitaminwater drinks. The deal was the biggest acquisition Coke had ever made. Coke also entered the business of supplying coffee and tea to fountain/foodservice customers. By 2009, Pepsi had 43% of the U.S. non-carbs market share compared to Coke's 32%.[51]

In the $14 billion bottled-water category, both Pepsi (with Aquafina, 1998) and Coke (with Dasani, 1999) had introduced purified-water products that had surged to become leading beverage brands. Using their distribution prowess, they had outstripped competing brands, many of which sold spring water. However, the economic downturn in the late 2000s dampened future prospects for what had been the fastest growing beverage category between 2000 and 2007.[52] Price-sensitive consumers sought cheaper alternatives such as private label bottled-water or tap water, exhibiting little brand loyalty compared to CSDs. Environmentalists also became more vocal in their criticisms against the use of plastic bottles, known as PET, which had a recycling rate below 25%.[53] Bottled water started to generate negative operating profit margins. Coke also saw its market share in this category slip to 15% in 2009 (compared to 22% in 2004) while Pepsi's fell to 11% (compared to 14%).[54]

Internationalizing the Beverage Wars

As U.S. demand for CSDs softened, Coke and Pepsi also looked abroad for new growth. The United States remained the largest market, accounting for a third of global CSD consumption, followed by Mexico, Puerto Rico, and Argentina.[55] But improved access to markets in Asia and Eastern Europe stimulated new demand. In particular, China and India emerged as future battlegrounds with a large, growing middle class population. Each company planned to invest about $2 billion in China over the next few years to build up their market presence.

Coke flourished, and also relied upon, international markets far more than Pepsi. Through steady expansion, the Coca-Cola name had become synonymous with American culture. Served in more than 200 countries, Coke derived about 80% of its sales from international markets.[56] Pepsi, on the other hand, depended on the U.S. for roughly half of its total sales.[57] Earlier efforts to go after Coke in core international markets generated relatively little success. By the early 2000s, Pepsi chose to focus on emerging markets that were still up for grabs. Several of its top CSD markets were in Asia, Middle East, and Africa.

Since CSD consumption abroad was generally lower compared to the United States, Coke and Pepsi aggressively pursued non-carbs opportunities in global markets. For instance, juice was a popular category—its retail value in China was expected to grow 94% by 2012 compared to 30% for CSDs.[58] In Russia, Pepsi and PBC paid $1.4 billion for a 76% stake in Russia's largest juice producer, OAO Lebedyansky, in 2008. International operations, however, encountered several obstacles, including antitrust regulation, foreign exchange controls, advertising restrictions, and local competition. In one high-profile incident, the Chinese government rejected Coke's $2.4 billion bid to buy Huiyan Juice, a leading juice company in China. At the same time, overseas markets enabled Coke and Pepsi to broaden the scope of innovation. To tailor to local tastes, Coke offered Sprite Tea, which blended green tea with Sprite, while Pepsi experimented with beverages made out of Chinese herbs. New approaches to packaging abounded as well.[59] In China and India, use of small returnable glass bottles allowed Coke to reach poor, rural consumers at a very low price point, while boosting revenue-per-ounce.[60]

Evolving Structures and Strategies

Both at home and abroad, the growing popularity of alternative beverages brewed complications for CSD makers' traditional production and distribution practices. Concentrate companies became more directly involved in the manufacturing of several non-CSDs, ranging from Gatorade to Lipton Iced Tea. Such finished goods required a smaller but specialized production process that were challenging for bottlers to make with their existing infrastructure. As the popularity of non-carbs continued to grow, bottlers were frustrated that they were not fully participating in the new growth businesses. Coke and Pepsi sold the finished goods to their bottlers, who distributed them alongside their own bottled products at a percentage markup. In addition, Coke and Pepsi distributed some non-CSDs directly to the retailers' warehouses, bypassing bottlers.

Energy and sports drinks promised better margins than CSDs because they commanded premium prices and were usually chosen for immediate, single-serve consumption (see **Exhibit 10**). In convenience stores, energy drinks had an average case price of $34.32 compared to CSD's $8.99.[61] Yet volume for such products, while growing fast, remained small in comparison with CSD volume. This created issues with DSD, which worked best with high-volume, high consumer demand products.

All CSD companies faced the challenge of achieving pricing power in the take-home channels. In particular, the rapid growth of the mass-merchandisers, led by Wal-Mart, and various club stores posed a new threat to profitability for Coke, Pepsi, and their bottlers. Consolidation in the retail sector meant that the top ten customers represented as much as 40% of Coke's U.S. package volume.[62] In the case of Wal-Mart, it not only used its size to exert pricing pressure, it also insisted on negotiating marketing and shelving arrangements directly with concentrate makers. This left bottlers feeling vulnerable in their traditional practice of distributing products in their exclusive territories.

In addition, bottlers had to manage an ever-rising number of stock-keeping units (SKUs).[63] For instance, Pepsi wanted its bottlers to carry 47 different Gatorade SKUs in exchange for gaining distribution rights to smaller but more profitable channels like convenience and dollar stores.[64] Many non-CSDs sold in relatively low volume, leading to an increased use of "split pallets." By loading more than one product type on a pallet (the hard, wooden bed used to organize and transport merchandise), bottlers incurred higher distribution and sales costs. Some of Coke's biggest bottlers saw their cost of goods sold (including operating expenses) reach 90% of their sales, the highest level in more than two decades.[65]

Not surprisingly, bottlers complained over Coke's practice of charging a flat rate for its concentrate in the U.S. market. Coke's profits were tied to volume growth while bottlers' profits were driven by package types and where the drinks were sold.[66] Then in 2003, Coke and CCE moved toward "incidence pricing", an approach that Coke often used with its overseas bottlers, whereby Coke agreed to vary concentrate prices according to prices charged in different channels and for different packages. By 2009, around 90% of Coke's total volume was covered under incidence pricing agreements. Annual price negotiations were also replaced with multi-year concentrate-price agreements. With some bottlers, Coke pursued more 50-50 joint ventures. Motivating its independent bottlers became critical, especially for Coke, as they accounted for nearly 90% of Coke's worldwide sales volume.[67]

Bottler Consolidation, Again

In 2009, Pepsi announced that it would buy two of its biggest bottlers, PBG and PepsiAmericas, in a transaction worth $7.8 billion. The offer came just about ten years after Pepsi had spun off PBG into an independent company. The merger would consolidate more than 80% of Pepsi's North America beverage operations under one roof.[68] One analyst noted that the deal acknowledged the "changing realities of the North American beverage business."[69] Then Coke, which had been a loyal defender of the franchise bottling system, surprised the world with its decision to buy CCE's North American operations in February 2010. The deal brought back 90% of Coke's North America business under its control. In return, CCE bought Coke's own bottling operations in Norway and Sweden, and received the option to buy Coke's stake in its German bottling business at a later date.

Future of the Cola Wars?

Declining CSD sales, declining cola sales, and the rapid emergence of non-carbonated drinks appeared to be changing the game in the cola wars. By spending billions of dollars to bring bottling operations under Coke and Pepsi's direct control again, observers couldn't help but wonder: was this a fundamental shift in the cola wars or was this just one more round in a 100 year rivalry?

Exhibit 1   U.S. Beverage Industry Consumption Statistics

	1970	1975	1981	1985	1990	1995	2000	2005	2007	2008	2009
Historical Carbonated Soft Drink Consumption											
Cases[a] (millions)	3,090	3,780	5,180	6,500	7,780	9,000	9,950	10,220	9,920	9,620	9,420
Gallons/capita	22.7	26.3	34.2	40.3	46.9	50.9	53.0	51.9	49.3	47.4	46.0
As share of total beverage consumption	12.4%	14.4%	18.7%	22.1%	25.7%	27.9%	29.0%	28.3%	27.1%	26.0%	25.2%
U.S. Liquid Consumption Trends (gallons/capita)											
Carbonated soft drinks	22.7	26.3	34.2	40.3	46.9	50.9	53.0	51.7	49.3	47.4	46.0
Beer	22.8	21.8	20.6	24.0	24.0	21.9	21.8	21.4	22.0	21.7	21.0
Milk	18.5	21.6	24.3	25.0	24.2	22.8	21.3	20.3	21.7	21.4	21.5
Bottled water[b]	—	1.2	2.7	4.5	8.1	10.1	13.2	19.5	22.5	21.4	20.6
Coffee[c]	35.7	33.0	27.2	26.9	26.2	21.3	16.8	16.4	16.0	15.9	15.8
Juices	6.5	6.8	6.9	8.1	8.5	8.9	9.5	8.2	8.1	7.6	8.1
Tea[c]	5.2	7.3	7.3	7.3	7.0	6.8	7.0	7.0	7.1	7.3	7.3
Sports drinks[d]	—	—	—	—	—	1.3	2.2	4.2	4.9	4.6	4.0
Powdered drinks	—	4.8	6.0	6.2	5.4	4.5	3.0	2.6	2.2	2.3	2.4
Wine	1.3	1.7	2.1	2.4	2.0	1.8	1.9	2.2	2.5	2.6	2.6
Distilled spirits	1.8	2.0	2.0	1.8	1.5	1.2	1.2	1.4	1.4	1.4	1.4
Subtotal	114.5	126.5	133.3	146.5	153.8	151.5	150.9	155.2	155.9	152.7	150.7
Tap water/hybrids/all others	68.0	56.0	49.2	36.0	28.7	31.0	31.6	27.6	24.8	28.9	31.8
Total[e]	182.5	182.5	182.5	182.5	182.5	182.5	182.5	182.5	182.5	182.5	182.5

Source: Compiled from *Beverage Digest Fact Book 2001*, *The Maxwell Consumer Report*, Feb. 3, 1994; *Adams Liquor Handbook*, casewriter estimates; and *Beverage Digest Fact Book 2005*. Data for 1990 and afterward comes from *Beverage Digest Fact Book 2005* and *2010*, which reports that some of that data has been "restated compared to previous editions of the Fact Book."

[a] One case is equivalent to 192 oz.

[b] Bottled water includes all packages, single-serve as well as bulk.

[c] For 1985 and afterward, coffee and tea data are based on a three-year moving average.

[d] For pre-1992 data, sports drinks are included in "Tap water/hybrids/all others."

[e] This analysis assumes that each person consumes, on average, one half-gallon of liquid per day.

Exhibit 2   U.S. Soft Drink Market Share by Unit Case Volume (%)

	1970	1980	1985	1990	1995	2000	2005	2009E[a]
Coca-Cola Company								
Coca-Cola[b]	28.4	25.3	21.7	20.7	20.9	20.4	17.6	17.0
Diet Coke	—	—	6.8	9.3	8.8	8.7	9.8	9.9
Sprite and Diet Sprite	1.8	3.0	4.7	4.5	5.7	7.2	6.3	6.1
Caffeine Free Coke, Diet Coke	—	—	1.7	2.9	2.6	2.2	1.8	1.4
Fanta[c]	—	—	0.9	0.7	0.7	0.2	1.6	1.8
Barq's and Diet Barq's	—	—	—	—	0.2	1.2	1.1	1.1
Minute Maid brands	—	—	—	0.7	0.7	1.5	0.1	—
Tab	1.3	3.3	1.1	0.2	0.1	—	—	—
Others	3.2	4.3	2.6	2.8	3.3	4.2	4.9	4.6
Total	**34.7**	**35.9**	**39.5**	**41.1**	**42.3**	**44.1**	**43.1**	**41.9**
PepsiCo, Inc.								
Pepsi-Cola	17.0	20.4	19.3	17.6	15.0	13.6	11.2	9.9
Mountain Dew	0.9	3.3	3.1	3.9	5.7	7.2	6.5	6.7
Diet Pepsi	1.1	3.0	3.9	6.3	5.8	5.3	6.0	5.6
Sierra Mist	—	—	—	—	—	0.1	1.4	1.3
Diet Mountain Dew	—	—	—	0.5	0.7	0.9	1.4	1.9
Caffeine Free Pepsi, and Diet Pepsi	—	—	2.5	2.3	2.0	1.7	1.4	1.0
Mug Root Beer	—	—	—	0.3	0.3	0.8	0.7	0.7
Slice and Diet Slice	—	—	1.4	1.4	1.2	0.6	0.1	0.1
Others	0.8	1.1	0.1	0.1	0.2	1.2	2.7	2.7
Total	**19.8**	**27.8**	**30.3**	**32.4**	**30.9**	**31.4**	**31.4**	**29.9**
Dr Pepper Snapple Group[d]								
Dr Pepper (all brands)	3.8	6.0	4.5	5.2	6.8	7.5	7.6	8.3
7UP (all brands)	7.2	6.3	5.8	3.9	3.3	2.8	1.7	1.6
A&W brands	—	—	—	—	0.9	0.9	1.0	1.1
Sunkist	—	—	1.2	0.7	0.7	0.8	1.1	1.2
Canada Dry	—	—	1.5	1.2	1.0	0.9	0.8	1.0
Schweppes	—	—	0.5	0.6	0.5	0.4	0.4	0.5
Others	—	—	1.5	0.7	1.9	1.4	2.0	2.7
Total	**11.0**	**12.3**	**15.0**	**12.3**	**15.1**	**14.7**	**14.6**	**16.4**
Cott Corporation	—	—	—	—	2.7	3.3	5.4	4.9
Royal Crown Cos.	6.0	4.7	3.1	2.6	2.0	1.1	—	—
Other companies	28.5	19.3	12.1	11.6	7.0	5.4	5.5	6.9
Total case volume (in millions)	**3,670**	**5,180**	**6,385**	**7,780**	**8,970**	**9,950**	**10,224**	**9,416**

Source: Compiled from *Beverage Digest Fact Book 2001, 2005,* and *2010; The Maxwell Consumer Report,* February. 3, 1994; the Beverage Marketing Corporation, cited in *Beverage World,* March 1996 and March 1999.

[a] Expected market share. One unit case is equivalent to 192 oz.

[b] Between 1985 and 1995, market share includes Coca-Cola Classic. Coca-Cola drops the name "classic" in 2009.

[c] For the period before 1985, Fanta sales are included under "Others."

[d] For the years preceding 1988, Dr Pepper and 7UP brand shares refer to the shares of the respective independent companies, the Dr Pepper Company and the Seven-Up Company. Then, Cadbury Schweppes acquired A&W brands in 1993, Dr Pepper/Seven-Up Cos. brands in 1995, and Royal Crown brands in 2000. In 2008, Cadbury Schweppes' beverage brands came under the control of the Dr Pepper Snapple Group.

14

Exhibit 3a   Financial Data for Coca-Cola and PepsiCo ($ millions)

	1975	1980	1985	1990	1995	2000	2005	2007	2008	2009
Coca-Cola Company[a]										
Beverages, North America:										
Sales	—	1,486	1,865	2,461	5,513	7,870	6,676	7,836	8,280	8,271
Operating profits/sales	—	11.1%	11.6%	16.5%	15.5%	17.9%	23.3%	21.6%	19.1%	20.5%
Beverages, International:										
Sales	—	2,349	2,677	6,125	12,559	12,588	16,345	20,778	22,611	22,231
Operating profit/sales	—	21.0%	22.9%	29.4%	29.1%	27.1%	35.4%	33.2%	35.2%	34.6%
Consolidated:										
Sales	2,773	5,475	5,879	10,236	18,127	20,458	23,104	28,857	31,944	30,990
Net profit/sales	9.0%	7.7%	12.3%	13.5%	16.5%	10.6%	21.1%	20.7%	18.2%	22.0%
Net profit/equity	21.0%	20.0%	24.0%	36.0%	55.4%	23.4%	29.8%	27.5%	28.4%	27.5%
Long-term debt/assets	3.0%	10.0%	23.0%	8.0%	7.6%	4.0%	3.9%	7.6%	6.9%	10.4%
PepsiCo, Inc.[b]										
Beverages, North America:										
Sales	1,065	2,368	2,725	5,035	7,427	6,171	9,146	—	—	—
Operating profit/sales	10.4%	10.3%	10.4%	13.4%	16.7%	22.3%	22.3%	—	—	—
Beverages, International:										
Sales	—	—	—	1,489	3,040	1,981	—	—	—	—
Operating profit/sales	—	—	—	6.3%	3.9%	8.0%	—	—	—	—
PepsiCo Americas Beverages:										
Sales	—	—	—	—	—	—	—	11,090	10,937	10,116
Operating profit/sales	—	—	—	—	—	—	—	22.4%	18.5%	21.5%
Consolidated:										
Sales	2,709	5,975	7,585	17,515	19,067	20,438	32,562	39,474	43,251	43,232
Net profit/sales	4.6%	4.4%	5.6%	6.2%	7.5%	10.7%	12.5%	14.3%	11.9%	13.8%
Net profit/equity	18.0%	20.0%	30.0%	22.0%	19.4%	30.1%	28.6%	32.8%	42.5%	35.4%
Long-term debt/assets	35.0%	31.0%	36.0%	33.0%	35.9%	12.8%	7.3%	12.1%	21.8%	18.6%

Source: Company annual reports and Capital IQ database, accessed June 2010.

[a] Beverage sales consist mainly of concentrate sales. Coke's stake in CCE was accounted for by the equity method of accounting, with its share of CCE's net earnings included in its consolidated net income figure. In 1994, Coke began reporting U.S. data as part of a North American category that included Canada and Mexico.

[b] PepsiCo's sales figures included sales by company-owned bottlers. In 1998, PepsiCo began reporting U.S. data as part of a North American category that included Canada. As of 2000, data for "Beverages, North America" combined sales for what had been the Pepsi-Cola and Gatorade/Tropicana divisions. In 2003, PepsiCo ceased reporting its international beverage business separately from its international food business. In 2007, Pepsi merged its North America beverage sales with Latin America sales, and started to report their combined financial under PepsiCo Americas Beverages.

Exhibit 3b   Financial Data for Coca-Cola and PepsiCo's Largest Bottlers ($ millions)

	1975	1980	1985	1990	1995	2000	2005	2007	2008[a]	2009
Coca-Cola Enterprises[b] (CCE)										
Sales	—	—	—	3,933	6,773	14,750	18,743	20,936	21,807	21,645
Operating profit/sales	—	—	—	8.3%	6.9%	7.6%	7.6%	7.0%	-28.9%	7.1%
Net profit/sales	—	—	—	2.4%	1.2%	1.6%	2.7%	3.4%	-20.1%	3.4%
Net profit/equity	—	—	—	6.0%	5.7%	8.3%	14.0%	14.8%	NA	85.1%
Long-term debt/assets	—	—	—	39.0%	46.3%	46.7%	36.1%	30.7%	46.5%	48.1%
Pepsi Bottling Group (PBG)[c]										
Sales	—	—	—	—	—	7,982	11,885	13,591	13,796	13,219
Operating profit/sales	—	—	—	—	—	7.4%	8.6%	7.9%	4.7%	7.9%
Net profit/sales	—	—	—	—	—	2.9%	3.9%	3.9%	1.2%	4.6%
Net profit/equity	—	—	—	—	—	13.9%	22.8%	20.3%	12.1%	25.3%
Long-term debt/assets	—	—	—	—	—	42.3%	34.2%	36.4%	36.9%	40.5%

Source: Company annual reports.

[a] In 2008, CCE wrote off $7.6 billion to readjust the fair value of the company's intangible franchise assets and goodwill contracts, which resulted in a significant losses for the fiscal year. For more information, see "Notes to Consolidated Financial Statements" in CCE's 2008 annual report.

[b] Data represents CCE's consolidated financial data, as reported in CCE's annual reports, and does not reflect the combined financial data of the new CCE, following the sale of CCE's North America operations to Coke and CCE's purchase of Coke's bottling operations in Norway and Sweden. CCE's consolidated financial statements reflect wide fluctuations, affected by issues such as, but not limited to, debt write-offs, reassessments of franchise intangible assets to fair market value, and tax charges related to restructuring activities.

[c] PBG financial data for the pre-1999 period refer to the PepsiCo bottling operations that were combined and spun off to form PBG in 1998. From 1999, PepsiCo's share of PBG's net earnings was included in PepsiCo's consolidated net income figure. 2009's data does not reflect PepsiCo's purchase of PBG, as announced that year.

Exhibit 4   Comparative Costs of a Typical U.S. Concentrate Producer and Bottler, 2009

	Concentrate Producer		Bottler	
	Dollars per case[a]	Percent of net sales	Dollars per case[a]	Percent of net sales
Net sales	$0.98	100%	$4.63	100%
Cost of goods sold	$0.22	22%	$2.67	58%
Gross profit	$0.76	78%	$1.97	42%
Direct marketing expense	$0.21	21%	$0.45	10%
Selling & delivery expense	$0.00	0%	$0.85	18%
General & admin expense	$0.24	25%	$0.31	6%
Operating income	$0.30	32%	$0.36	8%

Sources: Compiled from estimates provided by beverage industry source, October 2010.

[a] One case is equivalent to 192 oz.

Exhibit 5   U.S. CSD Industry Pricing and Statistics, 1988-2009

	1988	1994	1998	2002	2006	2008	2009
Retail price per case, adjusted for inflation[a]	$10.79	$8.48	$7.63	$7.57	$7.47	$7.66	$7.98
Change in retail price[b]	—	-3.9%	-1.7%	-0.1%	-0.2%	0.4%	0.7%
Total Change 1988-2008:	**-1.4%**						
Concentrate price per case[c]	$0.79	$1.00	$1.14	$1.35	$1.50	$1.59	$1.65
Change in concentrate price	—	4.0%	3.3%	4.3%	2.7%	3.0%	3.8%
Total Change 1988-2009:	**3.6%**						
Volume (cases, in billions)	7.40	8.70	9.90	10.09	10.16	9.62	9.42
Change in volume	—	2.0%	3.3%	0.3%	0.2%	-2.7%	-2.1%
Total Change 1988-2009:	**1.2%**						
Consumption (gallons/capital)	40.30	50.00	54.00	52.60	51.10	47.40	46.00
Change in consumption	—	2.7%	1.9%	-0.4%	-0.7%	-3.7%	-3.0%
Total Change 1988-2009:	**0.6%**						
Consumer Price Index (2005=100)	60.57	75.91	83.48	92.11	103.22	110.23	109.88
Change in CPI	—	2.9%	2.4%	2.5%	2.9%	3.3%	-0.3%
Total Change 1988-2009:	**2.9%**						

Source: Compiled from *Beverage Digest Fact Book*, 2001, and every edition between 2006 and 2010.

[a] Refers to a 192-oz. case. Prices reflect inflation using the inflation calculator tool, U.S. Bureau of Labor Statistics website, http://data.bls.gov/cgi-bin/cpicalc.pl, accessed June 2010.

[b] All change figures are calculated using Compounded Annual Growth Rate (CAGR).

[c] For the purpose of this item only, concentrate price refers to a 288-oz. case. Concentrate price data for previous years appear in aggregated form in *Beverage Digest Fact Book* 2003, p. 64. After 2004, price is based on a weighted average of concentrate prices for the top 10 CSD brands, as released in *Beverage Digest Fact Book*, Appendix G, and based on the brands' market share for the given year. Concentrate prices were also affected by specific ingredients, such as corn and ethanol, which varied significantly from CPI in certain years.

Exhibit 6   U.S. Refreshment Beverages: Bottling Profitability per Channel, 2009

	Super-markets	Convenience retail	Super-centers[a]	Mass retailers[a]	Club stores[a]	Drug stores	Fountain, vending, and other	Total
Share of industry volume								
	37%	10%	11%	2%	7%	2%	31%	100%
Index of bottling profitability[b]								
Net price	1.00	2.24	1.13	1.10	0.93	1.23	2.09	NA
Variable profit	1.00	1.24	1.24	1.39	1.37	1.68	1.56	NA

Source: Compiled from estimates provided by beverage industry source, October 2010. All figures refer to the entire refreshment beverage industry.

[a] "Supercenters" include Wal-Mart Supercenter stories and similar outlets. "Mass Retailers" include standard Wal-Mart stores, Target stores, and the like. "Club Stores" include Sam's Club, Costco, and similar membership-based retailers.

[b] Using supermarket information as a baseline, these figures indicate variance by channel of both by-volume pricing and by-volume profit. The variable profit figures take into account cost of goods sold as well as delivery costs.

Exhibit 7   Non-Alcoholic Refreshment Beverage Megabrands, 2004 and 2009[a]

Brand (Owner)	Category	2009 Cases (mil)	2009 Share (%)	2004 Cases (mil)	2004 Share (%)	Annual Volume Change[b] 2004–09	Annual Change in Market Share[b] 2004–09
Coke (Coke)	CSD	2,913.1	19.6%	3,272.3	23.4%	-2.3%	-3.5%
Pepsi (Pepsi)	CSD	1,681.5	11.3%	2,098.4	15.0%	-4.3%	-5.5%
Mountain Dew (Pepsi)	CSD	900.1	6.1%	871.1	6.2%	0.7%	-0.3%
Dr Pepper (DPS)	CSD	784.0	5.3%	738.3	5.3%	1.2%	0.0%
Sprite (Coke)	CSD	573.0	3.9%	683.2	4.9%	-3.5%	-4.5%
Gatorade (Pepsi)	Non-Carb	553.7	3.7%	546.0	3.9%	0.3%	-1.0%
Aquafina (Pepsi)	Water	325.0	2.2%	251.0	1.8%	5.3%	4.1%
Dasani (Coke)	Water	289.7	1.9%	223.0	1.6%	5.4%	3.5%
Poland Spring (Nestlé Waters)	Water	280.1	1.9%	217.0	1.5%	5.2%	4.8%
7UP (DPS)	CSD	150.9	1.0%	186.7	1.3%	-4.2%	-5.1%
Minute Maid (Coke)	CSD/Non-Carb	95.5	0.6%	176.4	1.3%	-11.5%	-14.3%
Sierra Mist (Pepsi)	CSD	149.9	1.0%	166.9	1.2%	-2.1%	-3.6%
Lipton (Pepsi/Unilever)	Non-Carb	235.3	1.6%	164.0	1.2%	7.5%	5.9%
Crystal Geyser (CG Roxanne)	Water	223.7	1.5%	135.5	1.0%	10.5%	8.4%
Arrowhead (Nestlé Waters)	Water	156.4	1.1%	127.0	0.9%	4.3%	4.1%
PowerAde (Coke)	Non-Carb	177.6	1.2%	122.7	0.9%	7.7%	5.9%
Nestlé Pure Life (Nestlé Waters)	Water	469.4	3.2%	113.2	0.8%	32.9%	32.0%
Barq's (Coke)	CSD	103.7	0.7%	112.5	0.8%	-1.6%	-2.6%
Sunkist (DPS)	CSD	116.9	0.8%	105.2	0.8%	2.1%	0.0%

Source: Compiled from *Beverage Digest Fact Book 2005* and *2010;* and casewriter estimates.

[a] *Beverage Digest Fact Book* defines a "megabrand" as a "brand or trademark with total volume of more than 100 million 192-oz cases." A megabrand encompasses all varieties (Coke Classic, Diet Coke, Cherry Coke, and so on) of a given trademark ("Coke"). Only single-serve products are included here.

[b] All changes calculated using compounded annual growth rates.

Exhibit 8 Advertising Spending for Selected Refreshment Beverage Brands (in $ thousands)

	Market share[a]		Advertising spending[b]		Per 2009
	2009	2008	2009	2008	share point[c]
Coca-Cola	15.3%	15.2%	234,000	254,000	$15,294
Pepsi-Cola	8.8%	9.0%	136,000	145,000	$15,456
Mountain Dew	4.6%	4.5%	24,000	31,000	$5,217
Dr Pepper	4.1%	3.9%	76,000	64,000	$18,537
Gatorade	3.1%	3.6%	119,000	162,000	$38,387

Source: Created by casewriter based on "Special Report: 100 Leading National Advertisers," *Advertising Age*, June 21, 2010.

[a] Share of the total single-serve non-alcoholic beverage market. *Advertising Age's* market share data may slightly differ from *Beverage Digest's* data, seen in case Exhibit 2.

[b] Spending as measured across 19 national media channels using data tracked by Kantar Media and Kantar Media's Marx.

Exhibit 9 U.S. Non-CSDs Unit Case Volume (in millions)

	2002	2004	2006	2007	2008	2009
Packaged water	3,221.6	3,785.6	4,588.1	4,847.2	4,712.1	4,588.9
Juice & juice drinks	3,030.5	3,034.2	2,612.2	2,534.9	2,512.4	2,498.8
Sports drinks	488.1	620.5	912.3	950.4	856.9	843.3
Ready-to-drink tea	430.7	455.2	556.6	625.4	623.7	706.1
Energy drinks	28.9	63.7	135.3	177.0	217.3	218.0

Source: Compiled from estimates provided by beverage industry sources, September 2010. One case is equivalent to 192 oz.

Exhibit 10 Gross Profit Margins for Selected Beverages (%)

	Retail's gross margin	Brand's gross margin
Ready-to-drink coffee	35%	60%
Ready-to-drink tea	35%	60%
Energy	35%	70%
Sports	35%	65%
Juice	25%	35%
Water	35%	45%
CSD	30%	70%

Source: Compiled by casewriter using data from Marc Greenberg, "Coca-Cola Company Presentation" Deutsche Bank Securities Inc., April 12, 2010, p. 7.

Endnotes

[1] *Beverage Digest Fact Book 2010*, p. 15. *Beverage Digest's* definition includes energy drinks.

[2] See Exhibits 1, 3a, and 3b in this case.

[3] Roger Enrico, *The Other Guy Blinked and Other Dispatches from the Cola Wars* (New York: Bantam Books, 1988).

[4] *Beverage Digest Fact Book 2010*, p. 24.

[5] Robert Tollison et al., *Competition and Concentration* (Lexington Books, 1991), p. 11.

[6] *Beverage Digest Fact Book 2010*, p. 42.

[7] Unless otherwise noted, information on industry participants and structures comes from Michael E. Porter (with research associate Rebecca Wayland), "Coca-Cola versus Pepsi-Cola and the Soft Drink Industry," HBS No. 391-179 (Boston: Harvard Business School Publishing, 1994); Andrew J. Conway et al., "Global Soft Drink Bottling Review and Outlook: Consolidating the Way to a Stronger Bottling Network", Morgan Stanley Dean Witter, August 4, 1997; and from casewriter interviews with industry executives.

[8] Casewriter conversation with industry insider, October 2010.

[9] Ibid.

[10] "Dr Pepper Snapple Group Breaks Ground on $120 Million Production Facility in Southern California," Dr Pepper Snapple Group press release (Victorville, CA, October 22, 2008).

[11] Coca-Cola 2009 Annual Report (Atlanta, The Coca-Cola Company, 2010), and PepsiCo 2009 Annual Report (Purchase, PepsiCo, 2010).

[12] Bonnie Herzog and Daniel Bloomgarden, "Coca-Cola Enterprises", Salomon Smith Barney, February 19, 2003, pp. 31–32; Bonnie Herzog and Daniel Bloomgarden., "Pepsi Bottling Group", Salomon Smith Barney, February 24, 2003, pp. 26–27.

[13] Timothy Muris, David Scheffman, and Pablo Spiller, *Strategy, Structure, and Antitrust in the Carbonated Soft Drink Industry* (Quorum Books, 1993), p. 63; Beverage Digest Fact Book 2010, p. 73.

[14] Coca-Cola 2009 Annual Report, p. 7.

[15] Coca-Cola Enterprises 2009 Annual Report (Atlanta: Coca-Cola Enterprises, 2010), p. 50.

[16] *Beverage Digest Fact Book 2010*, p. 40.

[17] Casewriter conversation with industry observer, October 2010. Total store sales include those from supermarkets, mass merchandisers, and drug stores.

[18] Nikhil Deogun and Richard Gibson, "Coke Beats Out Pepsi for Contracts with Burger King, Domino's," *The Wall Street Journal*, April 15, 1999.

[19] "History" section of entry for PepsiCo, Hoover's Online, http://www.hoovers.com, accessed December 2005; *Beverage Digest Fact Book 2005*, p. 62.

[20] *Beverage Digest Fact Book 2010*, p.60.

[21] Ibid, p.59. Market shares do not include duel outlets, such as those where Coke's pouring rights overlap with Dr Pepper's. If such outlets were included, Pepsi and DPS' market share would be higher.

[22] Ibid, p. 63.

[23] Casewriter examination of ingredients lists for Coke Classic and Pepsi-Cola, November 2005.

[24] Casewriter conversation with industry analyst, January 2006.

[25] *Beverage Digest Fact Book 2010*, p. 69.

[26] Ibid, p. 70.

[27] Unless otherwise attributed, all historical information in this section comes from J.C. Louis and Harvey Yazijian, *The Cola Wars* (Everest House, 1980); Mark Pendergrast, *For God, Country, and Coca-Cola* (Charles Scribner's, 1993); and David Greising, *I'd Like the World to Buy a Coke* (John Wiley & Sons, 1997).

[28] Louis and Yazijian, *The Cola Wars*, p. 23.

[29] David B. Yoffie, *Judo Strategy* (Harvard Business School Press, 2001), Chapter 1.

[30] Pendergrast, p. 310.

[31] Ibid, p. 323.

[32] Timothy K. Smith and Laura Landro, "Coke's Future: Profoundly Changed, Coca-Cola Co. Strives to Keep on Bubbling," *The Wall Street Journal*, April 24, 1986.

[33] Muris, Scheffman, and Spiller, p. 73.

[34] Greising, p. 88.

[35] Ibid, p. 292.

[36] *Beverage Industry*, January 1999, p. 17.

[37] *Beverage Digest Fact Book 2010*, p. 73.

[38] Ibid, p. 74.

[39] *Beverage Digest Fact Book 1999*, p. 38.

[40] Rosie Mestel, "Soft Drink, Soda, Pop: Whatever You Call Them, These Sugar Drinks Are Getting Nutritional Heat," *The Evansville Courier*, September 26, 2005, p. D1; Scott Leith, "Obesity Weighs Heavily on Colas," *The Atlanta Journal-Constitution*, February 6, 2005, p. C1; Raja Mishra, "In Battle of Bulge, Soda Firms Defend Against Warning," *The Boston Globe*, November 28, 2004, p. A1.

[41] "Coke and Pepsi Are Vulnerable to Tax on Soda," Forbes.com, September 10, 2010, http://blogs.forbes.com/investor/2010/09/10/coke-and-pepsi-are-vulnerable-to-tax-on-soda/, accessed September 13, 2010.

[42] Tom Graves and Esther Y. Kwon, "Industry Surveys: Foods & Nonalcoholic Beverages," Standard & Poor's, June 10, 2010, p. 4.

[43] Melanie Warner, "For Corn Syrup, the Sweet Talk Gets Harder," *The New York Times*, May 1, 2010.

[44] The Coca-Cola Company 10K filing for fiscal year ending December 31, 2009, p. 14.

[45] Jeremiah McWilliams, "Coke Bets of Freestyle Growth," *The Atlanta Journal - Constitution*, August 1, 2010, via Factiva, accessed September 2010.

[46] Valerie Bauerlein and Robb M. Stewart, "Coke Pours the Pressure on in World Cup of Marketing," *The Wall Street Journal*, June 29, 2010.

[47] "A Growing World of Refreshment," Coca-Cola Investor Relations Overview, 2010, http://www.thecoca-colacompany.com/investors/pdfs/investor_relations_overview.pdf, accessed October 2010.

[48] *Beverage Digest Fact Book 2010*, p. 48.

[49] *Beverage Digest Fact Book 2001*, p. 11, *Beverage Digest Fact Book 2005*, p. 11, and *Beverage Digest Fact Book 2010*, p.11.

[50] Marc Greenberg, "Beverage Industry, A Cup Half-full: Gulping the US Profit Pool," Deutsche Bank, May 17, 2007, p. 22.

[51] *Beverage Digest Fact Book 2010*, p. 102.

[52] Ibid, p. 25.

[53] Bob Keefe, "Coke's Bottle Recipe Sweet: New Material Includes Sugarcane, Molasses," *The Atlanta Journal-Constitution*, May 14, 2009.

[54] *Beverage Digest Fact Book 2010*, p. 110.

[55] Ibid, p. 87.

[56] Christopher Williams, "Coke's Fortunes are Set to Pop," *Barron's*, August 17, 2009, via Factiva, accessed September 2010.

[57] Citigroup Global Markets Research, "PepsiCo", October 17, 2010.

[58] Sky Canaves, Geoffrey A. Fowler, and Betsy McKay, "Coke Bets $2.4 Billion on Chinese Juice Market," *The Wall Street Journal Asia*, September 4, 2008.

[59] Caroline Wilbert and Shelley Emling, "Obesity Weighs on Coke," *Atlanta Journal-Constitution*, October 27, 2005, p. A1.

[60] Leslie Chang, Chad Terhune, and Betsy McKay, "As Global Growth Ebbs, Coke Makes Rural Push into China and India," *The Asian Wall Street Journal*, August 11, 2004, p. A1.

[61] *Beverage Digest Fact Book 2010*, p. 46.

[62] "The Coca-Cola Company and Coca-Cola Enterprise Inc. Announce Strategic Advancement of Their Partnership in North America and Europe," Thomson StreetEvents Final Transcript, February 25, 2010.

[63] "CSDs Have Most—and Proliferating—SKU's, but Number Is Small Relative to Volume," *Beverage Digest*, November 22, 2002, http://www.beverage-digest.com/editorial/021122.php, accessed December 2005; casewriter communication with industry analyst, November 2005.

[64] *Beverage Digest Newsletter*, September 24, 2010, p. 3.

[65] *Beverage Digest Fact Book 2010*, p. 86.

[66] Chad Terhune, "Advertising: Coke Bottler in Mexico Threatens to Cut Marketing," *The Wall Street Journal*, November 1, 2005.

[67] Christopher Williams, "Coke's Fortunes are Set to Pop," *Barron's*, August 17, 2009, via Factiva, accessed September 2010.

[68] PepsiCo, "Q4 2009 PepsiCo Earnings Conference Call" transcript, February 11, 2010, p. 4.

[69] "Special Issue: PepsiCo Seeks to Buy Two Big Bottlers," *Beverage Digest*, April 20, 2009, vol. 54, no. 9.

40

9B11M015

ROGERS COMMUNICATIONS INC.[1]

Kevin Melhuish wrote this case under the supervision of Professor Ariff Kachra solely to provide material for class discussion. The authors do not intend to illustrate either effective or ineffective handling of a managerial situation. The authors may have disguised certain names and other identifying information to protect confidentiality.

> Always keep the number one in the market in your cross-hairs. Avoid getting distracted by targeting number four or five. There's a reason those companies are not number one. Always aim high and look for vulnerability in the market leader.[2]
>
> —Ted Rogers, Founder of Rogers Communications Inc.

Nadir Mohamed, president and chief executive officer (CEO) of Rogers Communications Inc. (Rogers) considered these words from the company's founder, Edward 'Ted' S. Rogers. It had been nearly two years since Mohamed had taken the reins of the company following Ted's death at the age of 75. During this interval, competition in the telecommunications industry in Canada had intensified and brought an assembly of changes. Innovation was at an all-time high, and the notoriously rapid pace of change in the industry was accelerating. Rogers was a force to be reckoned with in all areas of the telecommunications sector including wireless, television, Internet and landline telephone. Rogers had impressive 2009 results, growing profits by approximately 23 per cent from the previous year, but Mohamed still contemplated the future growth opportunities of the company that he now controlled. From his vantage point on the 10th floor of Rogers' corporate headquarters, Mohamed could see Ted's former office, which had since been converted into a boardroom. As he stared across the hall, Mohamed asked himself two pressing questions: What were Rogers' vulnerabilities, and what should be the strategic direction of the company moving forward?

THE TELECOMMUNICATIONS INDUSTRY

There was an intense race for market share in the telecommunications industry: consider that in 2009, Rogers incurred expenses of $433[3,4] to acquire each new customer. By comparison, Rogers' two biggest

---

[1] *This case has been written on the basis of published sources only. Consequently, the interpretation and perspectives presented in this case are not necessarily those of Rogers Communications Inc. or any of its employees.*
[2] *Ted Rogers and Robert Brehl, Relentless: The True Story of the Man Behind Rogers Communications, HarperCollins, Toronto, 2008, p. 115.*
[3] *All amounts are denominated in Canadian dollars unless otherwise indicated.*
[4] *Rogers Communications Inc. 2009 Annual Report.*

competitive threats, BCE (Bell) and Telus, had costs of acquisitions of $350[5] and $337,[6] respectively. To retain existing customers, Rogers offered discounts of five, 10 and 15 per cent, respectively, for those who bundled two (double play), three (triple play) or four (quadruple play) services together (see Exhibit 1). Bundling also helped to reduce churn, which was the percentage of customers who discontinued their services and often switched to a competitor over a given period of time. Historical churn rates in Canada had ranged from between 1.00 to 1.70 per cent.[7]

Wireless technologies, and more specifically mobile devices, were driving revenues in this capital intensive industry. Prior to the emergence of wireless, wireline technologies such as television, Internet and landline telephone services fuelled the industry's growth.

Wireless

Rogers, Bell and Telus were Canada's three national wireless carriers and collectively serviced approximately 95 per cent of the country's total subscribers. Rogers owned 37 per cent market share representing 8.5 million customers, and competed in the wireless marketplace under its Rogers Wireless, Fido and Chatr brands. Bell controlled 30 per cent market share, serving 6.8 million customers under its Bell Mobility, Virgin Mobile and Solo Mobile brands, while Telus claimed 28 per cent market share representing 6.5 million customers under its three brands: Telus Mobility, Koodo and Mike. Each flagship and discount brand offered similar voice and data plans that were competitively priced. Each carrier also had comparable relationships with major mobile device suppliers, and provided a portfolio of smart phones and talk-and-text cell phones that were available to their consumers and enterprise customers. For selected year-over-year wireless and wireline customer statistics across competitors, (see Exhibit 2: from 2006 to 2009 Rogers' and Telus' wireless subscriber base has grown by 8 and 9 per cent respectively. Bell's subscriber growth rate has been five per cent.

Wireless penetration in Canada, meaning the percentage of the population who owned a mobile device, was 69 per cent in 2009. Penetration in Canada was expected to grow by approximately four to five percentage points each year for the next several years. By comparison, the United States had a penetration rate of 93 per cent, while residents of the United Kingdom had more than one device apiece at 129 per cent penetration. Globally, the most significant growth for wireless was in the Asia-Pacific region: China and India both had relatively low levels of penetration at 46 per cent and 30 per cent, respectively.[8]

Mobile Devices

Rogers and Bell had undertaken similar strategies in recent years by pushing customers to adopt smart phones, while Telus had focused on price-sensitive customers that used talk-and-text devices. More than half of Canada's smart phone users were Rogers' subscribers, and 31 per cent of all Rogers Wireless customers were smart phone users in 2009, up from 19 per cent in 2008. Furthermore, Rogers activated approximately 1.5 million smart phones in 2009, of which 55 per cent were upgrades from existing customers while 45 per cent were from new subscribers.

---

[5] *BCE Inc. 2009 Annual Report.*
[6] *Telus Corporation 2009 Annual Report.*
[7] *Rogers, BCE and Telus Annual Reports.*
[8] *"Asia Pacific Mobile Observatory: The Parallel Development Paths of the Mobile Industry in Asia Pacific," GSM Association and A.T. Kearney, http://www.atkearney.com/images/global/pdf/GSMA_AsiaReport.pdf, accessed on June 27, 2010.*

Nokia, Samsung and LG had the most significant presence amongst mobile device manufacturers globally, and controlled approximately 28, 17 and seven per cent of total worldwide market share, respectively.[9] Apple and Research in Motion (RIM) were the fourth and fifth largest global suppliers, each owning approximately three per cent total worldwide market share. In Canada and the United States, however, RIM and Apple were the most prominent mobile device manufacturers with approximately 12 per cent market share each and used their own proprietary software on their devices. Conversely, Google's open-source software, Android, was the most widely adopted mobile operating system in North America, and more than one-quarter of all smart phones worldwide were Android devices. Samsung was the top Android seller worldwide, but other mobile device manufacturers including Motorola and HTC used Android software on select devices.

RIM's relationship with Rogers and Bell dated back to 2000, while Telus first partnered with the BlackBerry manufacturer in 2003. Initially targeted towards enterprise customers, RIM had begun to increase its presence within the consumer segment. In 2009, RIM provided services to approximately 25 million subscribers on more than 475 wireless carriers worldwide, and BlackBerry handheld sales accounted for 82 per cent of RIM's total revenues. Service contributed to 13 per cent of RIM's revenues, while other software accessories tallied the remaining five per cent of the company's top-line.[10] Geographically distributed, 63 per cent of RIM's revenues came from the United States, eight per cent from Canada, six per cent from the United Kingdom and 23 per cent from the rest of the world.[11]

Apple launched the iPhone in Canada in July 2008; Rogers remained the exclusive Canadian provider of the iPhone until November 2009, when Bell and Telus gained access to the device upon upgrading their wireless networks. Originally launched as a consumer product, Apple had seen its market share increase in the enterprise segment. In 2009, iPhone sales made up approximately 18 per cent of Apple's total revenues, while Macs (Apple's personal computer product) generated 38 per cent of the company's top-line; in addition, iPod and iTunes sales respectively contributed 22 per cent and 11 per cent of the company's total revenues.[12] Apple also launched the iPad, its tablet computer product in 2010. RIM's response to the iPad, the BlackBerry Playbook, was scheduled to be released in 2011.

The relationship between mobile device manufacturers, wireless carriers and consumers was interesting, especially given that consumers were demanding more sophisticated devices such as new BlackBerry and iPhone models that commanded high price points. As a stand-alone device, an iPhone cost between $650 and $750 depending on the model, yet consumers only paid between $150 and $250 for the newest device. The difference was made up by wireless carriers such as Rogers, Bell and Telus, who provided customers with an approximate subsidy of $500 in return for a long-term contract, with larger subsidies being granted for longer contracts.

Contracts were typically one to three years in length, and customers faced significant monetary penalties if they prematurely terminated their contracts. In addition, some manufacturers such as Apple not only benefitted from carrier-furnished subsidies, but they also imposed strict terms on these same carriers by limiting their ability to cut prices or significantly differentiate wireless subscription plans.

[9] Gartner Press Release, "Gartner Says Worldwide Mobile Phone Sales Grew 35 Percent in Third Quarter 2010; Smartphone Sales Increased 96 Percent," Gartner Press Release, Gartner, November 10, 2010, www.gartner.com/it/page.jsp?id=1466313, accessed on November 27, 2010.
[10] Research in Motion Limited 2009 Annual Report.
[11] Ibid.
[12] Apple Inc. 2009 Annual Report.

Cell Sites

Wireless networks operated on grids that divided geographical areas into regions known as cells, and each cell then connected to what was known as a cell site. Cell sites included a set of radio frequencies and wireless antennas that provided service to customers. In urban areas, antennas were commonly mounted on office buildings or multiple dwelling units such as apartment buildings. In rural areas, antennas were often attached to cell phone towers. In Canada, telecommunications companies owned their cell phone towers, whereas in the United States only the larger carriers owned their towers. The smaller carriers thus relied on tower providers that built towers and then leased out space. The implicit trade-off for incumbents was control and the expense of building the infrastructure, as costs were not distributed between multiple carriers.

Wireless Networks

Wireless networks were the core of the telecommunications industry because they determined the amount of geographic coverage and bandwidth that wireless carriers could provide. Rogers, Bell and Telus' networks included coverage of nearly all of Canada at 95, 93 and 93 per cent, respectively. Coverage could be expanded by increasing the density of cell sites, in addition to establishing roaming partnerships both domestically and internationally. Roaming partnerships allowed wireless customers to connect to a location away from their home network for an incremental fee while their home network was out of reach. Rogers had the most international roaming partnerships of all Canadian carriers.[13] While Rogers, Bell and Telus customers each had access to wireless networks, and thus the ability to use their mobile devices in more than 200 countries worldwide, Rogers had a distinct network advantage.

Wireless networks or platforms were based on standards of digital technology. Rogers operated on both the global system for mobile communication (GSM) and the high speed packet access (HSPA) wireless networks. Bell and Telus each operated on an HSPA platform, and partnered together in November 2009 to upgrade from less widely-adopted code division multiple access (CDMA) and evolution-data optimized (EVDO) platforms. Prior to upgrading, Bell and Telus customers did not have access to many advanced mobile devices because these networks were incapable of supporting such devices.

Despite the upgrade, GSM was the global standard for wireless services, and approximately 80 per cent of all mobile devices worldwide operated on GSM technology. Because Rogers had the only GSM network in Canada, the company earned roaming revenues from international customers using their mobile devices in Canada to which Bell and Telus did not have access: this was because customers travelling to Canada with GSM devices automatically roamed on the Rogers network. The strength of Rogers' network had granted it the ability to secure long-term contracts with frequent business travellers — a heavily-coveted customer subset because of their high levels of usage — because they still had access to their mobile devices outside of Canada due to Rogers' extensive roaming partnerships.

Wireless Data

In addition to coverage, bandwidth — meaning the amount of voice and data traffic that could be carried by a wireless network — also determined the quality and speed of service that telecommunications companies could provide. As customers increasingly demanded data-driven services on their mobile devices such as video streaming and Internet browsing capabilities, aggregate data traffic stood to surpass

---

[13] *GSM Coverage Maps – Canada, GSM World, www.mobileworldlive.com/maps/, accessed on July 12, 2010.*

aggregate voice traffic: this presented a double-edged sword for wireless carriers. While data was nearly twice as profitable as voice, it utilized more bandwidth and was therefore more costly for carriers to service its customers; for example, Apple's iPhone consumed five to seven times the bandwidth of a regular talk-and-text device.

Wireless carriers needed to find the adequate balance between migrating customers to data-driven devices such as smart phones, while also regularly investing in their networks to handle the additional capacity. The need to continually invest in growing network capacity presented significant capital expenditure requirements for carriers, given that Rogers, Bell and Telus each spent nearly $1 billion in 2009 to maintain and strengthen their respective wireless networks: This was particularly important because data, more so than voice services, represented an ongoing growth opportunity for the telecommunications industry in Canada.

Rogers, Bell and Telus each experienced significant wireless data revenue growth in 2009. Data traffic contributed to 20 per cent of Rogers Wireless' revenues, growing 33 per cent over the previous year. Similarly, data made up 18 per cent of both Bell Mobility and Telus Mobility's revenues, up 32 per cent and 26 per cent respectively from the previous year. Even with customers incrementally adopting data-driven devices, the key industry metric of average revenue per user (ARPU) for all three carriers declined in 2009: Rogers Wireless' ARPU fell from $64.34 in 2008 to $63.59 in 2009; Bell Mobility's ARPU dropped from $54.29 in 2008 to $51.70 in 2009; Telus Mobility's ARPU in 2009 was $58, down from $63 over the previous year. Prior to these declines, Rogers and Bell respectively experienced ARPU growth of approximately 15 per cent and six per cent between 2006 and 2008, while Telus' ARPU growth remained flat over the same tenure.[14]

Advanced Wireless Services Auction

Industry Canada released wireless spectrum for auction across the country in 2008. Spectrum allowed wireless carriers to transmit signals such as cell phone services over electromagnetic waves. Spectrum did not, however, automatically allow carriers to provide wireless services, as they first needed to build out wireless networks, and buying spectrum and building networks both required extensive cash flows.

Of the spectrum made available, Industry Canada set aside approximately 44 per cent for new entrants, which were defined as carriers with less than 10 per cent of the country's wireless revenue. Industry Canada mandated that new entrants would be allowed to share cell sites and roam on the networks of incumbent carriers for five years within their licensed territories and for 10 years nationally.[15] In return, incumbents were entitled to receive roaming revenues from the new entrants. Industry Canada, however, did not impose restrictions on re-selling the spectrum after it had already been auctioned off. In total, the auction concluded after 331 rounds of bidding with $4.25 billion in proceeds generated — more than three times the amount initially expected. The auction prompted existing players to expand and new competitors to enter the Canadian market, changing the competitive landscape. For a breakdown of the auction's winning bidders and a high-level summary of wireless competitors, see Exhibits 3 and 4.

---

[14] *Rogers, BCE and Telus Annual Reports.*
[15] *Rogers Communications Inc. 2008 Annual Report.*

Page 6   9B11M015

New Entrants to the Market

The new entrant first to market was WIND Mobile (WIND). WIND served its first wireless customer in Canada in 2009, while three other new entrants — Mobilicity, Public Mobile and Vidéotron — each launched their own wireless services throughout 2010. The other new entrant, Shaw, purchased spectrum as well, but intentionally lagged the market and planned to launch its wireless offering in 2011 to complete its quadruple play of service offerings.

WIND had intentions of eventually becoming Canada's fourth national wireless carrier to match the likes of Rogers, Bell and Telus. WIND offered unlimited voice and data plans, and unlike the industry's incumbents, did not require its customers to remain locked into a contract; as a result, wireless devices were more expensive to end-customers because they were not subsidized through a long-term commitment. The launch of WIND in Canada was initially delayed because of issues with its ownership structure. WIND's parent company Globalive was Canadian-owned, but Orascom Telecom Holding — an international wireless carrier with more than 80 million subscribers worldwide — owned a 65 per cent equity stake in the company; as such, WIND was initially barred from competing in Canada because they were non-compliant with foreign ownership restrictions as mandated by Canada's regulator, the Canadian Radio-television and Telecommunications Commission (CRTC).[16] Yet amid controversy and backlash from Rogers, Bell and Telus, the CRTC and Industry Canada later allowed WIND to launch its wireless offering.

Mobilicity and Vidéotron did not intend to compete on a national scale like WIND; instead, Mobilicity offered unlimited voice and data plans without the necessity of a contract in ten major Canadian cities, while Vidéotron offered similar wireless plans with no contractual obligation in its home province of Quebec. The other new entrant, Public Mobile, took a completely different approach to the market, as it did not offer data plans to customers; rather, Public Mobile targeted the nearly one-third of Canadians that did not own a mobile device, and provided customers with contract-free unlimited talk-and-text plans. After its first eight months of operation, WIND had secured over 100,000 wireless customers in Canada, while all other new entrants had yet to publicly announce their own interim subscriber counts.

WIRELINE

Rogers, Bell, Telus and Shaw were the four major wireline providers in Canada, and each offered its own triple play of television, Internet and landline telephone services. Rogers' wireline segment was concentrated geographically to serve Ontario and Atlantic Canada, while Bell offered wireline services nationally. Bell mainly competed with Rogers in Ontario, while its subsidiary, Bell Aliant, competed with Rogers' offerings in Atlantic Canada.

The major wireline service providers in British Columbia and Alberta were Telus and Shaw, although Shaw also competed with Rogers in Northern Ontario. Notable small regional players included Vidéotron, Manitoba Telecom Services (MTS) and SaskTel, all of which offered their own quadruple play of services in their respective provinces of Quebec, Manitoba and Saskatchewan. Eastlink also provided wireline services in Atlantic Canada, while Cogeco competed in regionalized areas of Ontario and Quebec.[17]

---

[16] *The purpose of the CRTC was to ensure that the country's telecommunications and broadcasting systems adequately served the Canadian public. The CRTC did not regulate wireless or wireline pricing or the quality and content of media properties; rather, the CRTC promoted natural competition to drive the market instead of government regulation.*
[17] *Rogers owned approximately 40 per cent of Cogeco's voting shares and 36 per cent of its equity.*

TELEVISION

Rogers and Shaw were first to market with television in Canada, debuting analog cable in 1967 and 1971, respectively. With superior audio and picture quality, as well as the ability to offer customers access to specialty channels and premium services such as high definition (HDTV) and video-on-demand (VOD), digital cable had since replaced analog as the standard; more so, Canadian signals were required to be converted from analog to digital in 2011 — a transition the United States previously completed in 2009.[18]

In 2009, 72 per cent of Rogers' television customers were digital cable subscribers, while Shaw lagged behind at 57 per cent digital penetration; the other respective 28 per cent and 43 per cent of Rogers and Shaw subscribers remained on analog rather than digital cable.[19,20] Alternatively, Bell (Bell TV, formerly Bell ExpressVu) and Shaw (Shaw Direct, formerly Star Choice) first began offering satellite services in 1997. Satellite was comparable to digital cable in its channel and quality offerings but did not support VOD capabilities. Internet protocol television (IPTV) on the other hand did support VOD and was similar to digital cable.

Bell launched its IPTV service in 2010, while Telus had offered IPTV services since 2005. Telus and Bell also had a partnership whereby Telus distributed Bell's satellite service in Western Canada under the Telus brand. IPTV's distinguishing difference was that its service was transferred through data packets over broadband Internet and fibre-optic cables. IPTV was a relatively new technology in Canada and a complete cross-country rollout was estimated to cost telecommunications companies multiple billions of dollars and take years to complete.

Shaw had the most significant presence in television between its cable and satellite offerings, controlling 28 per cent market share and serving nearly 3.2 million customers. Comparatively, Rogers claimed 20 per cent market share with approximately 2.3 million customers, while Bell owned 17 per cent of the market and had nearly two million television subscribers. Telus, the newest entrant, significantly lagged behind its competitors in television, serving approximately 170,000 customers and claiming one per cent market share (see Exhibit 5).[21] From 2006 to 2009 Shaw's and Rogers' Internet subscriber base has grown by 14 and 8 per cent respectively. Bell's and Telus' subscriber growth rate has been three per cent each (See Exhibit 2).

There were differences as to how customers gained access to television through their cable or satellite services, but the underlying fundamentals were the same. With cable, television signals were transmitted through fibre-optic cable wires and connected to hubs which then broadcasted television signals. Similarly, with satellite there were central broadcast centres that acted as hubs and transmitted signals to individual dishes that were then picked up by satellite receivers.

The processes involved with laying fibre-optic cable wires and setting up satellite hubs were capital intensive. In populous urban areas with limited underground structures, burying fibre-optic cables below street level could cost up to $500,000 per kilometre. By comparison, laying fibre-optics in rural areas cost approximately $20,000 per kilometre, while aerial cables cost about $10,000 per kilometre assuming existing support structures were already in place.

---

[18] Digital signals were more efficient than their analog counterparts, and because of this the conversion to digital freed up previously occupied airwaves. The newly-vacant airwaves would then be used for public safety services such as fire, police and emergency dispatch.
[19] Rogers Communications Inc. 2009 Annual Report.
[20] Shaw Communications Inc. 2009 Annual Report.
[21] Rogers, BCE, Telus and Shaw Annual Reports.

Customers typically pre-paid for their television services, which included their selected channel offerings, additional à la carte and premium services as well as their hardware rental — either a digital set-top box or satellite receiver — each month. Television hardware was a commodity. Rogers' and Telus' television hardware was supplied by Scientific Atlanta (a Cisco company) while Motorola supplied Bell and Shaw. Related to hardware, satellite installations tended to take longer than cable installations because satellite dishes were required to be physically mounted.

Telecommunications companies were required to purchase programming rights annually to broadcast individual networks. Historically, specialty channels were purchased for a fee-for-carriage, while over-the-air (OTA) channels were provided at no cost; for example, Rogers would need to pay NBC Universal, the owner of CNBC (a specialty channel) for the rights to broadcast its channel, but would receive CBC (an OTA channel) for free.

In 2009, public broadcasters (the providers of OTA channels) operated at a loss for the first time ever, while telecommunications companies continued to grow profits; in 2010, the CRTC ruled that because specialty channels were allowed to charge fees, broadcasters of OTA channels were entitled to the same rights too. Under the new policy, OTA networks could choose to negotiate compensation for their signals every three years, with the caveat being that broadcasters gave up regulatory protection that required telecommunications companies to carry conventional networks at a preferential point on the dial.[22]

Telecommunications companies, however, did not have any influence over the actual shows that were broadcast, unless they owned the particular channel or were able to secure preferential status. These programming costs had increased substantially in recent years, and fees from telecommunications companies to broadcasters for programming rights amounted to $2.5 billion in 2009. This was due in part to the growth of subscriptions and the willingness-to-pay of customers that wanted specialty and multicultural channels, two major sources of content and revenue.

Monthly television revenues had increased industry-wide over the 2000s. In 2005, cable and IPTV television services generated revenues of $42.77 per customer each month, while monthly revenues had increased to $52.75 in 2009, representing a compound annual growth rate (CAGR) of 5.4 per cent. Similarly, monthly satellite revenues had a CAGR of 8.2 per cent over the same tenure, rising from $48.15 per customer in 2005 to $66.08 in 2009.[23] By comparison, the consumer price index rose approximately nine per cent between 2005 and 2009.[24]

Media consumption habits in Canada were changing, as Canadians were watching less television than in previous years. In 2009, Canadians watched approximately 22 hours of television each week, down from 24 hours weekly in 2005, and incrementally spending more time online.[25] While television was a more mature industry than wireless, Rogers' television ARPU increased nearly seven per cent between 2008 and 2009, from $60.47 to $64.61. There were also areas for growth including premium services such as HDTV and VOD, which had yet to be adopted en masse in Canada. Rogers launched HDTV in 2001, while Bell and Shaw followed suit in 2002. In 2009, Rogers' HDTV penetration was 43 per cent, up from 27 per cent

[22] *To give an example, CBC was channel six on the dial in Toronto; if CBC chose to negotiate its compensation, the CRTC mandate suggested that CBC was no longer required to have preferential treatment and could be moved to a higher and less attractive position on the dial.*
[23] *Communications Monitoring Report, Canadian Radio-television and Telecommunications Commission, July 2010, www.crtc.gc.ca/eng/publications/reports/policymonitoring/2010/cmr2010.pdf, accessed on September 12, 2010.*
[24] *"Consumer Price Index, 1995 to Present," Bank of Canada, www.bankofcanada.ca/en/cpi.html, accessed on September 26, 2010.*
[25] *"The Global Media Intelligence Report: North America," eMarketer, September 2010, www.emarketer.com/Reports/All/Emarketer_2000722.aspx, accessed on October 25, 2010.*

in 2007 and 37 per cent in 2008. By comparison, Bell and Shaw both lagged behind Rogers at 40 per cent and 38 per cent HDTV penetration, respectively.

As for VOD, only 10 per cent of Canadians regularly watched paid VOD content in 2009,[26] even though Rogers and Shaw had offered VOD capabilities since 2002, while Telus first offered VOD services in 2006. Despite this low usage, trends were changing and Canadians were increasingly warming to VOD. Industry-wide VOD revenues were approximately $145 million in 2009, up from $2.9 million in 2003. Furthermore, the VOD market was likely to become increasingly lucrative for cable and IPTV providers given that the CRTC ruled in 2010 that advertising was permitted on the VOD platform, and that telecommunications companies were allowed to sell advertising specifically for their on-demand programming.

INTERNET

Internet penetration in Canada was 69 per cent in 2009 and was expected to rise by approximately one percentage point each year for the following several years. Seventy-three per cent of Internet services in Canada were broadband rather than dial-up, and by 2013, nearly 80 per cent of all Internet users in Canada were expected to be using broadband services.[27] Broadband provided faster speeds than dial-up, and the two most widespread broadband services in Canada were cable and Digital Subscriber Line (DSL) Internet.

Rogers and Shaw offered cable Internet services, while Bell and Telus provided customers with DSL Internet, both relatively priced. Rogers and Telus were first-movers in Canada, serving their first high-speed Internet customers in 1995, followed by Shaw in 1996 and Bell in 1997. Within broadband, Bell controlled the most market share at 21 per cent, serving upwards of two million customers. Shaw had 1.9 million broadband subscribers accounting for 19 per cent of the market, while Rogers and Telus trailed at 16 per cent and 12 per cent market share, respectively. Rogers and Telus served approximately 1.6 million and 1.2 million broadband Internet customers each. In 2009, Rogers' Internet ARPU was $40.20, up approximately six per cent from $37.82 in 2008.[28]

There were also a number of regional Internet providers in Canada, the most significant of which was Vidéotron. Serving nearly 1.2 million subscribers in Quebec, Vidéotron owned approximately 12 per cent market share. Cogeco, SaskTel and MTS each competed regionally in Ontario, Saskatchewan and Manitoba, but only claimed respectively five, two and two per cent of the Canadian broadband Internet market as a whole.

Telecommunications companies in Canada also offered portable Internet services whereby customers could access the Internet from anywhere. Customers bypassed the traditional modem connection, and instead used a USB key or portable router that provided download speeds of up to three megabytes per second. By comparison, Rogers' fastest non-portable Internet service offered download speeds of up to 50 megabytes per second. Yet even with its ease of access, portable Internet had yet to reach widespread adoption in Canada, with few customers choosing to have portable-only access.

Authorized for use only in educational programs at McMaster University until Jun 07, 2017.
Use outside these parameters is a copyright violation.

---

[26] Charles S. Golvin and Jacqueline Anderson, "The State of Consumers and Technology: Benchmark 2009, Canada," Forrester Research, December 23, 2009, www.forrester.com/rb/Research/state_of_consumers_and_ technology_benchmark_2009%2C/q/id/55020/t/2, accessed on October 10, 2010.

[27] Lisa E. Phillips, "Canada Online: Users and Usage," eMarketer, October 2009, www.emarketer.com/Reports/All/Emarketer_2000602.aspx, accessed on July 2, 2010.

[28] Rogers, BCE, Telus and Shaw Annual Reports.

As a country, Canada was a relatively connected population. Canadians were among the world's most frequent users of social networking sites, considering that 54 per cent of Internet users in Canada participated in social networking in 2009 —this figure was expected to rise to 68 per cent by 2014.[29] Moreover, online video streaming continued to permeate itself into the daily habits of Canadians, as 52 per cent of the population streamed video monthly in 2009, and online video was expected to have a CAGR of almost 65 per cent between 2009 and 2014.[30] Canada was also the first country outside the United States to gain access to Netflix, which offered paid on-demand video streaming over the Internet.

The most frequent Internet users in Canada were those under the age of 18, followed by customers between the ages of 35 and 44. Younger generations often used the Internet as a substitute for traditional television and telephone services, and also complemented much of their online behaviour with their mobile devices such as using smart phones for Internet browsing. Conversely, older generations' aggregate browsing tendencies tended to be more mutually exclusive from other forms of media, although patterns were shifting towards increased convergence.

As customers' media habits continued to migrate away from traditional mediums such as television and instead gravitated towards the Internet, service providers were continually required to upgrade their wireline network capacities to handle additional bandwidth demands. In particular, customers who participated in online activities that utilized heavy amounts of bandwidth, such as peer-to-peer file sharing, were more costly to telecommunications companies than low bandwidth users who strictly browsed websites and used email services.

Collectively, this evidence showcased an exploitable opportunity for telecommunications companies with robust wireless and wireline segments. Due to the ever-increasing convergence of wireless and wireline services, companies that effectively leveraged their quadruple play of services were likely to capture improved bottom-line performance when these services were implemented effectively.

LANDLINE TELEPHONE

There were two types of landline telephone services in Canada: switched-circuit and voice over Internet protocol (VoIP). VoIP offered comparable local and long-distance services to switched-circuit, and converted voices into digital units that were reassembled into an analog signal. VoIP represented significant savings for telecommunications companies given that the incremental costs of supporting VoIP calls were negligible because the voice data was supported on existing IP networks via fibre-optic cables and existing telephone lines. There was, however, a significant capital expenditure required to initially rollout VoIP services; nevertheless, it represented an important reduction in barriers to entry and led to an emergence of new entrants, and specifically new VoIP entrants.

All competitors offered comparable voice quality and similar services such as voicemail and 911 functionality. Bell first began leasing telephones to customers shortly after its initial invention in 1880, and historically had a stranglehold on landline services in Canada. Rogers first entered the landline segment in 1989, but exited in 1995 after losing $500 million throughout its time in market; however, 10 years later Rogers decided to re-enter the landline telephone market. Telus first offered VoIP landline services in 1999 after merging with BC Tel, while Shaw served its first VoIP landline customer in 2005. Rogers, Telus and

[29] Mike Froggatt, "Canada Social Media Marketing," *eMarketer*, November 2010, www.emarketer.com/Reports/All/Emarketer_2000734.aspx, accessed on December 20, 2010.
[30] Mike Froggatt, "Canada Advertising and the Online Consumer," eMarketer, October 2010, www.emarketer.com/Reports/All/Emarketer_2000733.aspx, accessed on December 20, 2010.

Shaw each offered VoIP landline services to customers, while Bell remained on switched-circuit. To compete with Bell, many VoIP providers such as Rogers had lowered prices by up to 25 per cent.

Due to the new entrants, Bell's market share had consistently been eroded year-over-year; nevertheless, Bell remained the dominant landline player, controlling 37 per cent market share and serving nearly 6.9 million customers. Telus had over four million landline subscribers, owning 22 per cent market share, while Rogers and Shaw significantly lagged behind their competitors with five and four per cent market share, respectively, representing less than one million landline customers each. Smaller VoIP competitors included Primus and Vonage, both of which had less than one per cent market share apiece even after operating in Canada since 1997 and 2004, respectively.

The future of landline telephone services in Canada was unclear given the emergence of technologies such as Skype and customers' continuing willingness to substitute their traditional landlines with mobile devices. In fact, the number of wireless-only households in Canada was approximately 10 per cent in 2009, up from nearly five per cent in 2005. Landline penetration in Canada was 56 per cent in 2009, and was expected to trend downward to 44 per cent by 2014.[31] Lastly, unlike the company's television and Internet ARPUs, Rogers' landline telephone ARPU declined almost 12 per cent between 2008 and 2009, from $50.99 to $45.62, respectively.

MEDIA

Rogers, Bell and Shaw each had a significant media presence in Canada, but the opposite was true for Telus. Rogers owned the five CityTV networks across Canada, the OMNI television stations, Rogers Sportsnet and The Shopping Channel, as well as 54 radio stations including 680 News, the Fan 590 and CHFI. They were also Canada's largest magazine publisher, as they published more than 70 consumer magazines and professional publications including Maclean's and Chatelaine. Rogers had a presence in sports entertainment and owned the Toronto Blue Jays baseball team as well as their home stadium, the Rogers Centre. Rogers also had a partnership with the Buffalo Bills to host a regular season National Football League game at the Rogers Centre every year until 2012, and owned the naming rights to Rogers Arena, the home arena of the National Hockey League's (NHL) Vancouver Canucks.

Shaw's media assets included voting control of Corus Entertainment, which owned over 50 radio stations, multiple specialty television channels and Nelvana Limited — a production and distribution company of animated children's programs. Shaw also owned an 80 per cent voting interest and 20 per cent equity interest in Canwest, which owned the Global television network and a national newspaper, The National Post. Comparatively, Bell owned the CTV television network and its accompanying specialty channels including TSN and Business News Network. Bell also owned the naming rights of the Bell Centre — the home arena of the NHL's Montreal Canadiens — as well as a minority ownership stake in the hockey team. Bell was the lead sponsor of the Toronto International Film Festival and owned 15 per cent of the national newspaper, The Globe and Mail.

Of particular importance to the sustainability of media was the ability for telecommunications companies to source content for their mediums: these mediums included television channels, radio stations and newspapers. Because Rogers owned CityTV, for example, they were responsible for filling its scheduling blocks with programming; therefore, CityTV developed some of its programming in-house, but also purchased individual shows which it then had the rights to broadcast. This same practice occurred for radio

---

[31] *"Canada Telecommunications Report Q4 2010," Business Monitor International,* October 1, 2010, *store.businessmonitor.com/telecommunications/canada_telecommunications_report, accessed on November 24, 2010.*

stations, but to a lesser extent because more programming was developed in-house for radio in comparison to television.

The future of media within the telecommunications industry was unpredictable given the volatility of the sector: publishers had struggled to adapt their business model to the growing popularity of the Internet, printing and distribution expenses continued to rise and advertisers were slowly reallocating larger portions of their budgets away from most traditional mediums. In 2009, advertising spending amounted to approximately $11.1 billion in Canada, and was expected to rise to $11.9 billion in 2011.[32] Internet advertising was expected to grow nearly 15 per cent in 2011, while television and magazine advertising were expected to increase by a more conservative three per cent and two per cent, respectively.[33] In addition, mobile advertising spending in Canada, such as advertising on wireless devices, was expected to more than double between 2009 and 2011.[34]

Media did not provide the same percentage of revenues as wireless or wireline segments for the telecommunications companies in Canada; however, it appeared as though the industry was betting on increased convergence between media, wireless and wireline services, and that new forms of distributing content would emerge in the near future.

RETAIL

Retail locations of Canada's telecommunications companies allowed customers to purchase wireless and wireline services, test new products, receive technical help and pick up or exchange hardware. Rogers' distribution network included over 3,600 independent dealer and retail locations across the country, as well as the near 450 company-owned Rogers Wireless, Fido and Rogers Plus (formerly Rogers Video) stores. Comparatively, Bell had over 2,000 stores and authorized dealers to serve customers, including a partnership with entertainment retailer HMV. Bell also owned The Source and its network of 750 retail locations primarily in malls throughout Canada. Telus and Shaw had smaller distribution networks than Rogers and Bell, although both had company-owned and independent retail locations. Telus also owned the imaging and digital photo retailer Black's and its 113 stores nationwide.

The new wireless entrants also formed retailing alliances of their own: WIND had a partnership with the video rental chain Blockbuster, in addition to its own company-owned stores, while Public Mobile had a retailing agreement with the newspaper and magazine vendor Gateway Newstands. WIND mobile devices were sold in 33 Blockbuster stores across the country, while there were 152 Gateway Newstands outlets in Toronto that sold Public Mobile devices. The other pair of new entrants, Mobilicity and Vidéotron, had over 200 retail outlets apiece where customers could purchase their devices. Lastly, all competitors had online retail presences where customers could purchase each company's services.

ROGERS COMMUNICATIONS INC.

Rogers Communications Inc. (RCI) was the holding company for the organization's three wholly-owned business units: Rogers Wireless, Rogers Cable and Rogers Media. The publicly-traded company was rooted in family tradition and had a rich history of entrepreneurship. The company's founder, Edward

---

[32] Mike Froggatt, "Canada Advertising and the Online Consumer," eMarketer, October 2010, www.emarketer.com/Reports/All/Emarketer_2000733.aspx, accessed on December 20, 2010.
[33] Ibid.
[34] "The Global Media Intelligence Report: North America," eMarketer, September 2010, www.emarketer.com/Reports/All/Emarketer_2000722.aspx, accessed on October 25, 2010.

'Ted' S. Rogers, grew up as an underdog: a sickly child, Ted tragically lost his father to a ruptured aneurysm when he was only five years old, igniting the emotional drive that would motivate him to establish the Rogers empire that he built from the ground up.

Often described by co-workers and the press as a controlling risk-taker and micromanager, Ted was known for making tough decisions. He wagered the company more than once, bringing Rogers near bankruptcy on multiple occasions throughout its history. Ted's exterior may have been gentle, but his management style was often demanding and uncompromising; he was regarded as a true visionary, as evidenced by the successful bets he made on radio, television, Internet and wireless before they reached widespread popularity (see Exhibit 6). Headstrong in operations and strategy, Ted's renowned work ethic and ability to get executives to piece together his own innovative ideas made him into an icon and one of Canada's most respected entrepreneurs. Throughout his career, his business card always read "Ted Rogers, Senior Salesperson," showcasing his tenacity and passion for the art of making deals.

In 2009, RCI earned approximately $11.7 billion in revenues while generating approximately $1.5 billion in profits between its three business units. For a historical perspective of Rogers' profitability and balance sheet performance, see Exhibits 7 and 8. In addition, see Exhibit 9 for a breakdown of each business unit's year-over-year revenue composition, Exhibit 10 for a comparison of profitability across the industry's four major competitors (Rogers, Bell, Telus and Shaw) and Exhibit 11 for selected competitive financial statistics.

ROGERS' CAPABILITIES

Leadership

Often pegged by analysts as Ted's likely successor, Nadir Mohamed assumed his role of president and CEO of RCI after previous stints as CEO of Rogers Wireless, as well as chief operating officer of the communications division of RCI. An experienced telecommunications executive, Mohamed left Telus to begin his tenure at Rogers in 2000. Carved from a different mould, Mohamed was not the risk-taker that Ted was, but rather a modest consensus-builder with a reputation for facilitating incremental change with a keen eye for the bottom line.

Ted was the majority shareholder when he led Rogers. Prior to his death, Ted controlled RCI through his ownership of voting shares of a private holding company. Under his estate arrangements, the voting shares of that company, and consequently voting control of RCI, passed to the Rogers Control Trust. The Rogers Control Trust owned approximately 91 per cent of the outstanding RCI class A shares — the only class of issued shares carrying the right to vote in all circumstances — and approximately 7.5 per cent of the RCI class B shares.

The chair of the trust was Ted's son, Edward, while Ted's daughter Melinda was the vice-chair. Both Edward and Melinda were senior executives at Rogers and were also members of the company's board of directors. Many members of the Rogers board of directors also had long-standing personal and professional relationships with the Rogers family. The Rogers Control Trust had a 13-member advisory committee that included seven members of the Rogers family, including Ted's widow Loretta, and all four of the Rogers children, in addition to Alan Horn (Rogers' chairman) and Philip Lind (Rogers' vice-chairman) amongst others.

Organizational Structure

Rogers employed more than 28,000 people, and with customer expectations increasing across Canada, Mohamed opted to restructure the company after taking over for Ted. Under Ted, there were separate CEOs and executive teams for Rogers Wireless, Rogers Cable and Rogers Media, as well as an additional hierarchy at the holding company level. Moving away from separate executive teams for each business unit, Mohamed established three business groups dedicated to communications services, network organization and emerging business and corporate development.

The communications services group was dedicated to the integration of Rogers' wireless and wireline segments; the network organization group was responsible for driving future innovation, improving time to market and controlling the technological aspects of the company; the emerging business and corporate development group was accountable for overseeing major strategic initiatives including mergers and acquisitions. Upon restructuring, the members of Ted's original senior leadership team remained in place. The former CEOs of Rogers Wireless and Rogers Cable respectively assumed roles as the leaders of the communications services and emerging business and corporate development groups, while the company's former chief technology officer was appointed as head of the network organization group.

Technology

Rogers' networks were amongst the most advanced in the world because of early adoption and regular investments in new technologies each year. The next generation of wireless technology in development was known as Long Term Evolution (LTE). LTE was a fourth generation or 4G technology that was designed to provide voice and data transfer speeds faster than previous technologies: these previous technologies were GSM, which was second generation or 2G technology, and HSPA, which was third generation or 3G technology. Rogers' wireless network offered an efficient path to the future, given that it was fully backwards compatible with LTE, but Bell and Telus were also well positioned to adopt LTE with their upgraded networks.

With regards to wireline technology, all of Rogers' services such as television, Internet and landline telephone were provided on the same wireline cable network across Canada. This singular network presented a significant cost advantage for Rogers over its competitors; for example, consider that Bell used multiple wireline networks because it offered satellite television, IPTV, DSL Internet and switched-circuit landline telephone services.

All of Canada's telecommunications companies had a commitment to improve their technology capabilities each year, assuming capital expenditures as a proxy. In 2009, Rogers spent approximately $1.9 billion in capital expenditures across its wireless and wireline services, marking a three per cent decline from 2008. By comparison, Bell, Telus and Shaw spent approximately $2.8 billion, $2.1 billion and $776 million respectively in capital expenditures in 2009, with Bell and Telus reducing their spending by four per cent and 23 per cent respectively over the previous year; Shaw increased spending by seven per cent (see Exhibit 12).[35]

---

[35] *Rogers, BCE, Telus and Shaw Annual Reports.*

Customer Service

The backbone of Rogers' customer service initiatives was its call centres, all of which were located throughout five provinces in Canada. Bell and Telus, on the other hand, had call centres located throughout North America and also outsourced customer service initiatives internationally. Rogers' call centre employees were known as customer service consultants (CSCs), and were available by telephone or online 24 hours a day all 7 days of the week. They collectively handled more than 30 million calls and 300,000 email requests each year. This was significant because the average service call within the industry cost telecommunications companies between $5-12 to handle, while a lengthy, complicated call could cost up to $30. CSCs received extensive training to resolve customer concerns and adhered to documented policies and processes for forwarding complaints up the hierarchy with the goal of resolving each customer's issue. To improve customer service, CSCs also conducted monthly surveys with customers to gauge satisfaction with their service delivery and relationship with the company as a whole.

Given the technological intricacies involved with many of its products and services, Rogers had a fleet of more than 2,100 vehicles (compared to Bell's 2,000) to serve its customers' technical needs. When mobile devices required service, Rogers used its network of branded retailers to advise its customers; moreover, any wireline product that proved unsatisfactory was guaranteed to be replaced within three business days. Rogers only sold wireless devices that passed its comprehensive engineering certification process that included up to 1,000 checkpoints to ensure quality, performance and reliability.

Rogers also had a dedicated team to engage with customers looking for help in online forums and blogs: the most significant of these efforts that was unique to Rogers was RedBoard, the company's official blog. RedBoard provided customers with access to news and updates from Rogers, and also provided a medium to engage in reciprocal online dialogue with the company. Additional customer service initiatives included the Office of the Ombudsman, which provided customers with a neutral mediator concerning unresolved complaints, and the Rogers Customer Commitment that helped customers understand what they could expect from Rogers as their service provider. Even with these practices in place and Rogers' churn figures outperforming its competitors, the company's customer service initiatives lagged behind Bell and Telus. According to J.D. Power and Associates, Rogers Wireless and Fido respectively scored 613 and 655 based on a 1,000-point scale on overall wireless customer service ratings. By comparison, two of Bell's brands, Bell Mobility and Virgin Mobile, scored 610 and 758, respectively. A pair of Telus brands on the other hand, Telus Mobility and Koodo, respectively achieved grades of 649 and 755.[36]

These results indicated that Canadians were not satisfied with the customer service they received from these telecommunications companies. The crux of these issues revolved around miscommunication: many customers complained about the inconsistent customer service experience between the physical in-store, call centre and online customer service offerings at their disposal.

Branding

Rogers had nationally-recognized and highly-respected brands that stood strongly in Canada for innovation, entrepreneurial spirit, choice and value. From its most recent valuation of Canadian brands, Interbrand valued Rogers' brand to be worth approximately $2.3 billion, up 33 per cent from its 2008

[36] "Customer Loyalty and Advocacy for Wireless Phone Providers in Canada Declines Notably Amid Rapidly Evolving Technology and a Changing Competitive Landscape," J.D. Power and Associates, October 27, 2009, http://businesscenter.jdpower.com/JDPAContent/CorpComm/News/content/Releases/pdf/2009242-cwcs.pdf, accessed on June 29, 2010.

estimate:[37] this placed Rogers as the eighth-most valuable Canadian brand, and second-most valuable telecommunications brand in Canada behind Bell, which ranked seventh overall.

Rogers, Bell and Telus each ranked within the top 10 largest advertisers in Canada by total advertising dollars spent.[38] Rogers had adopted similar branding efforts year-over-year, while Telus had remained true to its heritage and opted to continue its animal-themed branding initiatives. Conversely, Bell launched a new corporate brand in 2008, including a new logo and tagline.

THE FUTURE

As the telecommunications industry continued to change, Mohamed considered many alternatives at his disposal. Customer behaviours were continually evolving, technologies were increasingly converging and the intersection between content and distribution was ever-present. Without embracing these changes, the company risked losing market share to more adaptive rivals. Rogers planned to sustain growth by continuing to bundle its quadruple play of wireless and wireline services, but the future strategic direction of the company was open to debate. Competitive rivalry was at unparalleled levels, and Rogers had to continue to find the proper balance between innovation and integration of its services. As Ted always said, the best was yet to come, and Mohamed was confident of that guarantee. In the meantime, he needed to determine where it was imperative for Rogers to be leading instead of lagging, and then allocate resources accordingly to follow through on that plan.

---

[37] "Best Canadian Brands 2010," _Interbrand_, May 2010, www.interbrand.com/Libraries/Branding_Studies/Best_Canadian_Brands_2010.sflb.ashx, accessed on July 8, 2010.
[38] _Nielsen Advertising Expenditures_, The Nielsen Company, December 2010.

Exhibit 1

REPRESENTATIVE ROGERS BUNDLES

The boxes below indicate various Rogers' service offerings along with their respective pricing a la carte. Bundles are not strictly limited to these offerings, but rather can be used as a sample to build representative bundles and showcase the available discounts.

Bundle Two Services: Save 5% (Double Play)
Bundle Three Services: Save 10% (Triple Play)
Bundle Four Services: Save 15% (Quadruple Play)

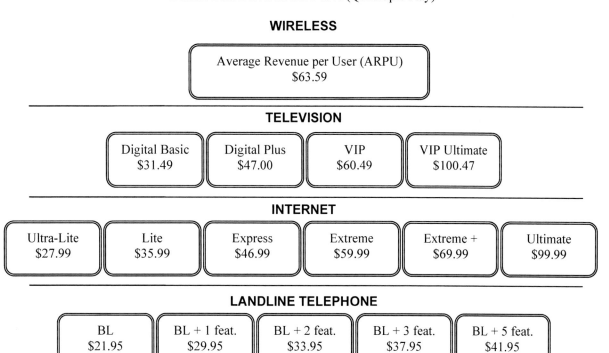

WIRELESS

Average Revenue per User (ARPU)
$63.59

TELEVISION

| Digital Basic $31.49 | Digital Plus $47.00 | VIP $60.49 | VIP Ultimate $100.47 |

INTERNET

| Ultra-Lite $27.99 | Lite $35.99 | Express $46.99 | Extreme $59.99 | Extreme + $69.99 | Ultimate $99.99 |

LANDLINE TELEPHONE

| BL $21.95 | BL + 1 feat. $29.95 | BL + 2 feat. $33.95 | BL + 3 feat. $37.95 | BL + 5 feat. $41.95 |

Note: BL denotes Basic Line.

Exhibit 2

CUSTOMER STATISTICS BY COMPANY

	Rogers				Bell			
	2006	2007	2008	2009	2006	2007	2008	2009
Wireless								
Subscribers	6,778,000	7,338,000	7,942,000	8,494,000	5,954,000	6,216,000	6,497,000	6,833,000
Average Revenue per User (ARPU)	$ 56.13	$ 61.20	$ 64.34	$ 63.59	$ 51.18	$ 53.92	$ 54.29	$ 51.70
Churn (average per month)	1.32%	1.15%	1.10%	1.06%	1.50%	1.70%	1.60%	1.70%
Cost of Acquisition ($/subscriber)	$ 399	$ 401	$ 459	$ 433	$ 420	$ 404	$ 395	$ 350
Wireline								
Television Subscribers	2,277,000	2,295,000	2,320,000	2,296,000	1,820,000	1,822,000	1,852,000	1,949,000
Internet Subscribers	1,297,000	1,451,000	1,571,000	1,619,000	1,877,000	2,004,000	2,054,000	2,057,000
Landline Telephone Subscribers	366,000	656,000	840,000	937,000	8,439,000	7,745,000	7,309,000	6,862,000

	Telus				Shaw			
	2006	2007	2008	2009	2006	2007	2008	2009
Wireless								
Subscribers	5,056,000	5,568,000	6,129,000	6,524,000		N/A		
Average Revenue per User (ARPU)	$ 63.00	$ 64.00	$ 63.00	$ 58.00		Shaw will begin offering		
Churn (average per month)	1.33%	1.45%	1.57%	1.58%		wireless services in 2011		
Cost of Acquisition ($/subscriber)	$ 412	$ 395	$ 351	$ 337				
Wireline								
Television Subscribers	Unreported	35,000	78,000	170,000	3,075,528	3,118,739	3,152,961	3,190,841
Internet Subscribers	1,111,000	1,175,000	1,220,000	1,215,000	1,317,455	1,637,603	1,783,367	1,914,021
Landline Telephone Subscribers	4,548,000	4,404,000	4,246,000	4,048,000	212,707	385,357	611,931	829,717

Source: Rogers, BCE, Telus and Shaw Annual Reports.

Exhibit 3

SUMMARY OF ADVANCED WIRELESS SERVICES AUCTION

	Total Amount of Winning Bids	Total Number of Winning Bids	Total Population Covered by Bids	Primary Geographic Focus
Rogers	$ 999,367,000	59	30,007,094	Expansion of Rogers' existing nationwide network
Telus	$ 879,889,000	59	30,007,094	Expansion of Telus' existing nationwide network
Bell	$ 740,928,000	54	27,245,106	Expansion of Bell's existing nationwide network
Vidéotron	$ 554,549,000	17	14,687,045	Regional spectrum in Quebec and parts of Ontario
WIND Mobile	$ 442,099,000	30	23,265,134	Spectrum in most regions nationwide, but excluding most of Quebec
Mobilicity	$ 243,159,000	10	16,121,864	Spectrum in most major Canadian cities outside of Saskatchewan, Manitoba, Quebec and Atlantic Canada
Shaw	$ 189,519,000	18	9,351,375	Regional spectrum in Western Canada and Northern Ontario
SaskTel	$ 65,690,000	3	975,717	Expansion of SaskTel's existing regional network in Saskatchewan
Public Mobile	$ 52,385,077	4	17,675,254	Spectrum in Southern and Eastern Ontario and Southern and Eastern Quebec
MTS	$ 40,773,750	3	1,118,283	Expansion of MTS' existing regional network in Manitoba
Eastlink	$ 25,628,000	19	4,886,983	Regional spectrum in Atlantic Canada, Southwestern Ontario and Grande Prairie, Alberta
Novus Wireless Inc.	$ 17,900,000	2	6,887,060	Regional spectrum in British Columbia and Alberta
Others	$ 2,823,500	4	1,043,232	Blue Canada Wireless, Celluworld and Rich Telecom bought regional spectrum in each of its local markets

Source: Industry Canada

Exhibit 4

COMPETITIVE SUMMARY OF THE CANADIAN WIRELESS LANDSCAPE

	Primary Geographic Focus	Bundle Options	Discount Brand	Contract Required	Voice Plans	Data Plans	Unlimited Voice and Data Plans
Rogers							
Rogers Wireless	Nationwide	Quadruple play	No	Yes	Yes	Yes	No
Fido	Nationwide	Quadruple play	No	Yes	Yes	Yes	No
Chatr	Nationwide	Quadruple play	Yes	No	Yes	No	No
Bell							
Bell Mobility	Nationwide	Quadruple play	No	Yes	Yes	Yes	No
Virgin Mobile	Nationwide	Quadruple play	No	Yes	Yes	Yes	No
Solo Mobile	Nationwide	Quadruple play	Yes	No	Yes	No	No
Telus							
Telus Mobility	Nationwide	Quadruple play	No	Yes	Yes	Yes	No
Koodo	Nationwide	Quadruple play	Yes	No	Yes	No	No
Mike	Nationwide	Quadruple play	No	Yes	Yes	No	No
WIND Mobile	Nationwide (eventually)	Single play	No	No	Yes	Yes	Yes
Shaw	Western Canada	Quadruple play	N/A	N/A	N/A	N/A	N/A
Vidéotron	Quebec	Quadruple play	No	No	Yes	Yes	Yes
Mobilicity	Ten major Canadian cities	Single play	Yes	No	Yes	Yes	Yes
Public Mobile	Ontario	Single play	Yes	No	Yes	No	No
SaskTel	Saskatchewan	Quadruple play	No	Yes	Yes	Yes	Yes
MTS	Manitoba	Quadruple play	No	Yes	Yes	Yes	No

Note: Shaw has N/A across multiple categories because they had not launched their wireless offering; contract and plan details were yet to be made public.
Source: Rogers, BCE, Telus, WIND Mobile, Shaw, Vidéotron, Mobilicity, Public Mobile, SaskTel, and MTS Corporate Websites

Exhibit 5

**COMPETITIVE SUMMARY OF THE CANADIAN TELEVISION LANDSCAPE
SELECTED COMPETITORS**

	First Year of Service	Technology	Market Share	HDTV	VOD
Rogers	1967 - Cable	Analog cable Digital cable	20%	Yes	Yes
Bell	1997 - Satellite 2010 - IPTV	Satellite IPTV	17%	Yes	No
Telus	2005 - IPTV	Satellite (partnership with Bell) IPTV	1%	Yes	Yes
Shaw	1971 - Cable 1997 - Satellite	Analog cable Digital cable Satellite	28%	Yes	Yes (cable only)

Exhibit 6

HISTORY OF ROGERS COMMUNICATIONS INC.

1960	Ted Rogers purchased Canada's first FM radio station, CHFI
1967	Ted Rogers formed Rogers Cable TV Limited and began offering analog cable television services
1969	Rogers Community Television premiered
1979	Rogers became the largest cable company in Canada through its acquisition of Canadian Cablesystems
1979	Rogers became a public company
1981	Rogers began cable operations in the United States
1985	Cantel, the predecessor to Rogers Wireless, launched Canada's first cellular service
1986	The holding company, Rogers Communications Inc., was formed
1988	Rogers Video (later renamed Rogers Plus) was created
1989	Rogers sold its cable assets in the United States and ceased American operations
1989	Rogers launched landline telephone services after buying 40 per cent of CNCP Communications (later renamed Unitel)
1994	Rogers acquired Maclean Hunter, at the time the largest takeover in Canadian history
1995	Rogers sold its stake in Unitel and temporarily exited the landline telephone segment
1995	Rogers became the first cable company in North America to launch high-speed Internet access
1996	Cantel was rebranded as Cantel AT&T, marking the first time in history that AT&T had shared its brand
1999	Rogers launched its digital cable television offering
1999	AT&T and British Telecom combined to purchase 33% of Cantel AT&T
2000	Rogers acquired the Toronto Blue Jays
2001	AT&T bought out British Telecom's ownership stake in Cantel AT&T
2002	Rogers launched its GSM wireless network
2004	Rogers acquired the Skydome (later renamed Rogers Centre)
2004	Rogers bought out AT&T's ownership stake and then purchased Microcell to become Canada's largest wireless carrier
2005	Rogers reentered the landline telephone market after acquiring Call-Net Enterprises
2007	Rogers acquired the five CityTV television stations across Canada
2007	Rogers achieved investment grade status on its debt for the first time in the company's history
2008	Rogers purchased nearly $1 billion of wireless spectrum during Industry Canada's advanced wireless services auction
2008	The company's founder, Ted Rogers, died at the age of 75
2009	Nadir Mohamed assumed the role of president and CEO of Rogers Communications Inc.

Exhibit 7

ROGERS COMMUNICATIONS INC.
CONSOLIDATED STATEMENTS OF INCOME
(IN MILLIONS OF DOLLARS, EXCEPT PER SHARE AMOUNTS)

	2005	2006	2007	2008	2009
Revenues:					
Rogers Wireless	$ 3,860	$ 4,580	$ 5,503	$ 6,335	$ 6,654
Rogers Cable	2,492	3,201	3,558	3,809	3,948
Rogers Media	1,097	1,210	1,317	1,496	1,407
Corporate and Eliminations	(115)	(153)	(255)	(305)	(278)
	$ 7,334	$ 8,838	$ 10,123	$ 11,335	$ 11,731
Operating Expenses:					
Cost of Sales	$ 940	$ 956	$ 961	$ 1,303	$ 1,380
Sales and Marketing	1,122	1,226	1,322	1,334	1,207
Operating, General and Administrative	3,062	3,763	4,251	4,569	4,681
Depreciation and Amortization	1,489	1,584	1,603	1,760	1,730
Other	66	18	490	345	165
	$ 6,679	$ 7,547	$ 8,627	$ 9,311	$ 9,163
Operating Income	655	1,291	1,496	2,024	2,568
Interest on Long-Term Debt	699	620	579	575	647
Other Expenses (Income)	(1)	(7)	31	23	(59)
Income before Income Taxes	(43)	678	886	1,426	1,980
Income Taxes	2	56	249	424	502
Net Income (loss)	(45)	622	637	1,002	1,478
Adjusted Net Income (loss)	$ 47	$ 684	$ 1,066	$ 1,260	$ 1,556
Adjusted Net Income (loss) per share	$ 0.08	$ 1.08	$ 1.67	$ 1.98	$ 2.51

Source: Rogers Annual Reports.

Exhibit 8

ROGERS COMMUNICATIONS INC.
CONSOLIDATED BALANCE SHEETS
(IN MILLIONS OF DOLLARS)

	2005	2006	2007	2008	2009
Assets:					
Current Assets	$ 1,289	$ 1,734	$ 2,143	$ 2,296	$ 2,255
Property, Plant and Equipment	6,152	6,732	7,289	7,898	8,197
Goodwill	3,036	2,779	3,027	3,024	3,018
Intangible Assets	2,627	2,152	2,086	2,761	2,643
Investments	138	139	485	343	547
Other Long-Term Assets	592	569	295	760	358
	$ 13,834	$ 14,105	$ 15,325	$ 17,082	$ 17,018
Liabilities and Shareholders' Equity:					
Current Liabilities	$ 1,992	$ 2,470	$ 2,742	$ 2,716	$ 2,748
Long-Term Debt	7,453	6,537	6,032	8,506	8,463
Derivative Instruments	787	769	1,609	616	1,004
Other Long-Term Liabilities	74	129	214	184	133
Future Income Tax	-	-	104	344	397
Shareholders' Equity	3,528	4,200	4,624	4,716	4,273
	$ 13,834	$ 14,105	$ 15,325	$ 17,082	$ 17,018

Source: Rogers Annual Reports.

Exhibit 9

**ROGERS COMMUNICATIONS INC.
YEAR-OVER-YEAR REVENUE BREAKDOWNS
(TOTALS IN MILLIONS OF DOLLARS)**

	2005	2006	2007	2008	2009
Rogers Communications Inc. (RCI)					
Rogers Wireless	53%	52%	54%	56%	57%
Rogers Cable	34%	36%	35%	34%	34%
Rogers Media	15%	14%	13%	13%	12%
	$ 7,334	$ 8,838	$ 10,123	$ 11,335	$ 11,731
Rogers Wireless					
Postpaid Voice	86%	84%	76%	73%	70%
Wireless Data	8%	11%	13%	15%	20%
Prepaid Voice	6%	5%	5%	4%	4%
Equipment Services	-	-	6%	8%	6%
	$ 3,860	$ 4,580	$ 5,503	$ 6,335	$ 6,654
Rogers Cable					
Television	45%	44%	43%	44%	45%
Broadband Internet	15%	16%	17%	18%	20%
Landline Telephone	11%	11%	13%	13%	13%
Business Solutions	19%	19%	16%	14%	12%
Retail	11%	10%	11%	11%	10%
	$ 2,492	$ 3,201	$ 3,558	$ 3,809	$ 3,948
Rogers Media					
Television	42%	43%	43%	48%	51%
Publishing	25%	24%	23%	20%	19%
Radio	19%	19%	20%	18%	16%
Sports Entertainment	15%	14%	14%	14%	14%
	$ 1,097	$ 1,210	$ 1,317	$ 1,496	$ 1,407

Note: Percentages may not add to 100 per cent in some instances due to rounding discrepancies.

Source: Rogers Annual Reports.

Exhibit 10

COMPARATIVE STATEMENTS OF INCOME BY COMPANY (FY 2009)
(IN MILLIONS OF DOLLARS, EXCEPT PER SHARE AMOUNTS)

	Rogers		Bell		Telus		Shaw	
Revenues by Segment:								
Wireless	$	6,654	$	4,558	$	4,735	$	-
Wireline		3,948		13,840		5,152		3,391
Media		1,407		-		-		-
Other		(278)		(663)		(281)		-
	$	11,731	$	17,735	$	9,606	$	3,391
Operating Expenses:								
Cost of Sales	$	1,380	$	4,525				
Sales and Marketing		1,207		6,121	$	5,925	$	1,852
Operating, General and Administrative		4,681						
Depreciation and Amortization		1,730		3,371		1,722		584
Other		165		527		190		-
	$	9,163	$	14,544	$	7,837	$	2,436
Operating Income		2,568		3,191		1,769		955
Interest on Long-Term Debt		647		723		433		237
Other Expenses (Income)		(59)		18		32		(8)
Income before Income Taxes		1,980		2,450		1,304		726
Income Taxes		502		368		203		191
After Tax Expenses		-		452		99		-
Net Income (loss)		1,478		1,630		1,002		535
Adjusted Net Income (loss)	$	1,556	$	1,630	$	1,002	$	535
Adjusted Net Income (loss) per share	$	2.51	$	2.50	$	3.14	$	1.25

Note: (1) Bell did not separate its sales and marketing or operating, general and administrative expenses. Therefore, the figures were combined above, representing $6,121 million.

(2) Telus did not separate its cost of sales, sales and marketing, or operating, general and administrative expenses. Therefore, the figures were combined above, representing $5,925 million.

(3) Shaw did not separate its cost of sales, sales and marketing, or operating, general and administrative expenses. Therefore, the figures are combined above, representing $1,852 million.

Source: Rogers, BCE, Telus and Shaw Annual Reports.

Exhibit 11

FINANCIAL STATISTICS (FY 2009, EXCEPT MARKET CAPITALIZATION)

	Market Capitalization ($ billions)[1]	Share Price ($) High	Share Price ($) Low	Outstanding Shares (in thousands)	P/E Ratio	Adjusted Net Income ($ millions)	EPS ($)	Debt to Equity	Cash ($ millions)	Total Assets ($ millions)
Rogers	21.74	40.50	27.72	592,410	14.6	1,556	2.51	1.98	383	17,018
Bell	25.04	27.68	18.45	767,200	13.1	1,630	2.50	0.64	687	38,050
Telus	14.08	37.50	29.12	318,000	14.1	1,002	3.14	0.80	41	19,219
Shaw	9.68	20.94	13.40	430,237	18.0	535	1.25	1.07	254	8,938
Vidéotron	2.22	29.34	14.81	64,300	8.0	278	4.32	3.26	300	8,353
MTS	1.78	37.32	30.62	64,668	17.5	102	1.57	0.79	110	2,896
Cogeco	0.88	29.47	19.32	16,757	23.9	37	2.20	3.00	39	2,705

[1] Toronto Stock Exchange, Google Finance, www.finance.google.com, accessed September 3, 2010.

Note: (1) Vidéotron is a subsidiary of Quebecor Inc., and thus the above Vidéotron financial statistics are in fact Quebecor Inc. statistics.
   (2) SaskTel and Eastlink are not public companies; therefore, comparable financial statistics were not available.

Source: Rogers, BCE, Telus, Shaw, Quebecor, MTS, and Cogeco Annual Reports, Standard & Poor's and Google Finance.

Exhibit 12

CAPITAL EXPENDITURES BY COMPANY (FY 2005-2009)
(IN MILLIONS OF DOLLARS)

	2005	2006	2007	2008	2009
Rogers	$ 1,355	$ 1,712	$ 1,796	$ 2,021	$ 1,955
Bell	3,357	3,121	3,140	2,986	2,854
Telus	1,319	1,618	1,770	2,741	2,103
Shaw	437	558	640	726	776

Source: Rogers, BCE, Telus and Shaw Annual Reports.

9-713-478

FEBRUARY 5, 2013

JAN W. RIVKIN

STEFAN H. THOMKE

DANIELA BEYERSDORFER

LEGO (A): The Crisis

In late 2004, Jørgen Vig Knudstorp faced the toughest challenge of his young career. A mere thirty-six years old, Knudstorp had recently been named CEO of the LEGO Group – a long successful toymaker with a world-renowned brand, but a company suddenly on the brink of financial collapse (**Exhibit 1**). If Knudstorp failed to make the right decisions, and fast, the LEGO Group would likely slip from the hands of its founding family and be swallowed up by one of the giant conglomerates that increasingly dominated the toy industry.

Hard decisions faced Knudstorp at every turn. Should the LEGO Group fall back to the plastic-brick product lines that defined its past, or should it continue into the new product lines that many considered its future? Within the plastic-brick arena, should the company continue to make most of its own products, or should it shift to a contract manufacturer? Why was the Group running out of some products and awash in inventory of others? Why had complexity and costs risen so dramatically and made so many products unprofitable? Indeed, why was Knudstorp struggling to figure out which products were truly unprofitable and which made money?

The Toy Industry

As Knudstorp reflected on the LEGO Group's crisis, he considered the evolution of the global toy market. The industry booked wholesale revenues of $61 billion in 2004. The retail market for toys grew at a steady pace of about 4% per year, but demand for specific fad toys could surge or collapse rapidly.

Industry observers noted a few important trends. First, fad toys seemed to be rising and product life cycles declining, perhaps not surprising for an industry, as one journalist put it, "subject to the whims of [kids] who can't decide which shoe to put on which foot."[1] Second, in many parts of the world, children had more after-school activities and less unscheduled time to play than in the past. Third, for kids over three years old, demand had shifted toward technology, either in a toy itself or in the form of toys coming with access codes to online worlds.[2] As children gave up traditional toys earlier for videogames and online activities, childhood became shorter and adolescence longer. Parents were often torn between buying the toys their kids wanted and those they considered good for their children.

Professors Jan W. Rivkin and Stefan H. Thomke and Europe Research Center Assistant Director Daniela Beyersdorfer prepared this case. HBS cases are developed solely as the basis for class discussion. Cases are not intended to serve as endorsements, sources of primary data, or illustrations of effective or ineffective management.

Thousands of toymakers served the world market, but increasingly, a handful led the industry. Mattel, the world's leading toymaker by revenue ($5.1 billion in 2004), featured brands like Fisher-Price, Barbie, Hot Wheels, and American Girl dolls.[3] Hasbro, the second largest player ($3.0 billion), housed brands such as Transformers, Monopoly, GI Joe, Play-Doh, and Playskool. To win consumer attention, retail shelf space, and sales, toymakers introduced new products, cut their wholesale prices, sponsored cooperative ads and promotions with retailers, provided in-store support, and advertised to consumers. The impact of new product introductions was muted by rapid imitation and limited protection of intellectual property. To boost brand presence among consumers, toymakers often licensed characters from media companies. Mattel, for example, was the "favored creator of toys based on Disney and Pixar characters."[4]

Toymakers increasingly manufactured in Asia, where labor was inexpensive and subcontractors stood ready to produce goods on their behalf. The majority of toys sold in the U.S., for instance, were manufactured in China by outside contractors, while global players such as Hasbro specialized in new product development, sales, and marketing.

Toymakers went to market via diverse retail channels, including independent toy specialists, chain stores, discount stores, department stores, and online stores. In choosing among toys to stock their shelves, retailers focused on profit per square foot and consequently considered margin, turn, and product space requirements. In a highly seasonal business in which consumers bought a large fraction of their toys during the holiday season, retail purchasing occurred mainly in the second half of the year.[5] Retail competition had heated up in recent years. In the United States, for instance, pressure from the likes of Wal-Mart and Target had driven Toys R Us, the nation's largest toy chain, to hire investment bankers to review its "strategic alternatives" in 2004.

Building the LEGO Group (1916-1992)

To the toy market, the LEGO Group brought a heritage that reached back to 1916, when Ole Kirk Kristiansen, a humble carpenter, bought a wood workshop in the rural Danish village of Billund and began to build houses and furniture for farmers. In 1932, he added wooden toys to his production and chose the name LEGO, formed from the Danish words "LEg GOdt" ("play well"). Only later did he learn that in Latin "lego" meant "I assemble." Aiming for quality, he wrote on his wall, "Only the best is good enough."

Ole's son Godtfred started working in the business in 1932 at age 12. In 1947, the firm became the first in Denmark to buy a plastic injection-molding machine. By 1949, its portfolio had grown to 200 plastic and wooden toys, including the automatic binding brick, a forerunner of the modern LEGO brick. In 1954, during a ferry ride to England, a purchasing agent complained to Godtfred that toy departments were a mess: toys lacked a systematic organization. The comments moved Godtfred to consider a "LEGO system of play." Such a system began to form in 1958, when the company changed the design of its bricks to match its current form. When a fire destroyed the LEGO Group's wooden warehouse in 1960, Godtfred discontinued wooden toy production. Knudstorp reflected:

> Godtfred Kirk Christiansen bet the whole farm on one-third of his business, plastic toys, and not just any toy – the brick. Godtfred Kirk Christiansen felt he had stumbled onto something unique with this brick. You can build anything out of it. It doesn't fall apart when you throw it around. And you can add to this system forever as it allows you to create a new toy every day, make endless variations, thereby inspiring and challenging a child's imagination and creativity. Godtfred Kirk Christiansen realized that in this system, the value of play expands exponentially the more elements you have.

In 1963, Godtfred laid out ten principles of "good play" that defined LEGO product characteristics (**Exhibit 2**). By 1967, the company produced LEGO bricks in 218 distinct shapes. In 1977, Godtfred's son Kjeld Kirk Kristiansen joined the company's management. Born in the same year as the brick, Kjeld felt, in Knudstorp's words, that "the LEGO brick is more than a toy. He knows what the brick can be and what it can do for humanity."

From early on, a strong culture of creativity at the LEGO Group favored the steady introduction of new products and themes based on the brick system. The high quality of bricks and the standardized spacing between studs ensured that all elements made after 1958 were compatible with one another, resulting in enormous opportunities for creativity. The Group expanded its audience in 1968 with larger "DUPLO" bricks for children under five and, in 1977, with the LEGO Technic line for teens. By 1980, about 70% of Western European families with children under 14 owned LEGO bricks.

By that time, a three-phase production process lay at the heart of Group operations. First, in the molding phase, injection-molding machines produced plastic elements in massive numbers. Because it took a molding tolerance of 0.002 millimeters to make bricks clutch each other right, Godtfred focused on developing industrial excellence and cutting-edge capabilities in material science and production technology. Second, in the decoration phase, specialized parts were painted. Third, in the packaging phase, the many small elements that made up a product were placed in a box along with an instruction manual.

Godtfred controlled the company's operations closely, and no new product, brick, or color was introduced without his approval. Until the early 1980s, LEGO bricks came in five base colors: black, white, red, blue, and yellow. Kjeld felt that the company's sustained growth required new bricks, but it took him 10 to 15 years to convince his father to add the color green. Kjeld also added new themes, began to collaborate with the MIT Media Lab on robots in the mid-1980s, expanded into Eastern Europe and Asia, and maintained a strong position in America and a leading one in Western Europe.

The LEGO Group enjoyed steady organic growth and profitability. By 1992, it was a top 10 global toy manufacturer, and according to *Advertising Age,* accounted for about 80% of the construction toy market (which accounted for a few percent of the total toy market). With its products so popular among consumers, LEGO Group management came to see retailers as "a necessary evil." Christian Iversen, Executive VP of LEGO Corporate Center, recalled:

> We were used to stable growth and expansion, driven by our growing pipeline. This was further fueled when the Berlin Wall came down, with millions of young Eastern Europeans eager to get their hands on Western products. If anything, the LEGO Group worked hard to *control* sales growth. The head of production, a strong person on Kjeld's team, watched production costs and capacity closely. When I joined in 1993, the first meeting I attended was about how to shelve several product introductions so that projected growth would fall to the target range of 8-10%. We had such a grip on the market and unmet demand that we could gradually add new products and more or less decide five years out what and how much we wanted to sell.

The Growth Period That Wasn't (1993-1998)

In the early 1990s, several shifts in the toy market caught the LEGO Group's management by surprise. Knudstorp explained:

> Birth rates in our core markets—Western Europe and North America—declined, as did household spending on toys. Between 1993 and 2003, the total profit pool in the industry

decreased by 50%. Traditional mom & pop stores started to disappear. Retail channels consolidated, and mass discounters featured toys more aggressively. Mattel, Hasbro, and others pushed manufacturing to the Far East. Finally, market research suggested that children had less time for unstructured play, had shorter attention spans, and looked more for instant gratification as well as fashionable and electronic products. These changes did not play to our strengths.

In 1993, Kjeld Kirk Kristiansen suffered a severe illness and left the company for a year. Upon his return, he built a five-person management team to help him run the company. Increasingly, Kjeld pushed responsibility to frontline managers so they could be more responsive to market dynamics. The head of production was dismissed. Growth became the new focus. Fueling the drive to grow was a desire to leverage the LEGO Group's position among the world's top-10 brands for families with children. Iversen said:

> The other companies on that list, such as Disney and Nike, were much larger than us. We concluded that our brand must have huge untapped potential. This potential seemed to lie outside our core play systems, so we stretched our brand and explored opportunities in new areas. We experimented with new ways to push out more products, without necessarily having an eye on their margin. The businesses were encouraged to make their own decisions. Suddenly you couldn't speak to an important retail customer without offering an account-specific product. We also did studies on how to grow in untapped markets like Southern Europe and concluded that we needed products tailored to those markets.

The Group branched out beyond the brick. Inspired by the success of its family leisure park in small Billund, it opened LEGOLAND Windsor (U.K.) in 1996. The same year, the company launched www.lego.com and began to develop videogame software related to its products. LEGO Media was set up in London to develop media products linked to LEGO play themes (e.g. movies, television programs, or books). The company introduced children's wear in 1993, watches in 1996, and LEGO® MINDSTORMS robotic bricks in 1998. Knudstorp reflected on the company's strategy during these years: "All of these efforts to push our boundaries felt natural in our Disney-like brand stretch strategy. There seemed to be potential everywhere." Expansions tended to be done in-house, not through partners. Mike Moynihan, VP of marketing, explained: "The mentality was that only we sufficiently knew our brand, and the expression of it could therefore not be outsourced."

In its brick-based product lines, the Group launched a host of new themes and products. Designers created LEGO products with more complex and chunkier pieces for some sets, so that children could build objects faster and arrive sooner at the playing part of the experience. The number of distinct components rose. In cases where brick shapes were more pre-defined, such as the lower and upper side of a car, they were harder to combine with other pieces.

Despite management's efforts and significant investments to grow the top line, sales stagnated. In 1998, the LEGO Group faced the first financial loss in its history.

The Fix that Wasn't (1999-2004)

To restore profitability and growth, Kjeld brought in a new CFO, Poul Plougmann, who soon became COO and took over day-to-day management. Ploughman's experience with turnarounds at Danish companies led the press to announce the arrival of "Mr. Fix-it." A restructuring program was launched to cut costs by DKK 1 billion (about US$140 million) and lay off up to 1,000 employees (more than 10% of total staff). Of the 100 top executives, more than 60 were asked to leave.

4

Ploughman's "Fitness Program" included measures to streamline production, reduce organizational layers, and increase responsibility and customer focus, all to build a simpler, more responsive, global business system. When management announced these drastic measures, employees stood up and applauded.

Change To develop stronger leaders who could take the group into new areas, Ploughman moved managers around rapidly. People stayed in one position for 6-12 months before rotating or being replaced by someone who could do a better job. General leadership experience was valued more than direct experience with LEGO toys.

Design responsibilities were shifted from small, rural Billund to global product development concept centers in creative locales such as Milan, London, and San Francisco. Production was streamlined and geared to match forecasts. Several tool-making factories were sold, and certain manufacturing processes that were difficult to automate were transferred from the LEGO Group's main factory in Billund to a new plant in the Czech Republic. In sales, senior management consolidated 25 country-level sales companies into five regional entities. The incentives of salespeople were tied, in part, to whether their actual sales exceeded their forecasts. Back-office functions were globalized.

Management decided in 1999 to sell directly to consumers through two initiatives: an online shop and LEGO-owned retail stores in Europe and the United States. Iversen recalled that "this was both about meeting the consumer in the right places, online and in our own stores, and about building the brand. Another reason was that we found ourselves increasingly working with discounters that were squeezing us on their shelves. This made it impossible to display the wealth of our brand."

The Group's product line continued to evolve. Among the most prominent product launches in 1999 was the brick-based LEGO Star Wars™ theme. While the LEGO Group had developed many play themes over the years, LEGO Star Wars was the first in-licensed brand. The decision had not been an easy one. Long-time employees bristled at the idea of placing the word "War" on a LEGO box and putting laser guns in the hands of LEGO minifigures, who traditionally carried nothing more lethal than a pirate's sword. The financial potential of the partnership was also difficult to assess. Iversen recalled that "these debates about the danger of eroding our brand heated up when we launched LEGO Star Wars. But we saw it as an opportunity to be more 'in tune' and add storytelling to building." More licensed products followed, including "Winnie the Pooh and Friends" in 1999 and "Harry Potter" in 2001.

In 2002, the company repositioned the preschool line, LEGO DUPLO, under a new brand name. Mads Nipper, Executive VP of Markets & Products, explained: "We tried to tap into mothers' emphasis on child development and make the product more learning-focused." The expansion of theme parks continued with the opening of LEGOLAND California in 1999 and LEGOLAND Germany in 2002. Projects like videogames continued to flourish, but some lifestyle initiatives, such as wristwatches and publishing, were cut back after 2000.

Consequences   Knudstorp recalled the ensuing difficulties in operations:

> When I was brought in as a consultant in 2001 to analyze the supply chain, I realized nobody had kept an eye on complexity. Product developers argued that the number of distinct shapes did not matter, as the marginal cost of an extra mold was so low. And management did not see the impact of this on design, manufacturing, servicing of retailers, forecasting, and managing inventory. You could be out of stock for a product just because you miss one of its 675 pieces, which you did not make when you got the forecast wrong. The total number of

components was not visible, but in 2004 we discovered that it had more than doubled since 1993. We had 3,560 different shapes, 157 colors, and 10,900 elements in our assortment. Each shape required a mold, and a mold cost €50,000 on average, or up to €300,000 for complicated ones.

Exhibit 3 shows the number of distinct LEGO components over time. Bali Padda, Executive VP of Global Supply Chain, also recalled the company's operations situation:

> When I joined in 2002, there was a lack of discipline, of accountability, and a costing system that I could not figure out. I couldn't understand how net production prices were determined or which products were profitable. It took me six months to get a sense of our fill rate to customers [the proportion of demand delivered without delay from stock on hand]. I found out it was anywhere between 5% and 70%, and my colleagues told me not to worry. My inventory costs were exploding, we had a lot of write-offs and obsolescence, and I couldn't explain anything! We started to control costs, for example by ordering fewer molds, but sometimes we could not meet demand anymore. Balancing supply and demand was further complicated by individuals directly calling their friends in manufacturing and asking them to produce more of this or that.

The LEGO Group's major customers were frustrated by stock-outs and slow-moving inventory. The typical retailer devoted nine linear feet to LEGO products in 2004, earned a 19% gross margin on LEGO sales, and saw LEGO inventory turn over two times a year. Chain-wide, Wal-Mart, Target, and Toys R Us reported gross margins of 22.9%, 33.6%, and 32.4%, respectively, in 2004. Their inventory turns across all products were 7.5x, 6.0x, and 2.1x, respectively. Padda recalled, "When I met the Wal-Mart buyer for the first time in 2004, he asked me: 'Can you please tell me why I shouldn't put dog food on the shelves [instead of LEGO products]?'"

Among the Group's new products, the LEGO Star Wars line thrived, rising to become 35% of total revenue. The repositioning of LEGO DUPLO proved less successful. Nipper recalled, "Many consumers found the new products did not live up to our promise and missed the LEGO DUPLO brand. A German retailer bluntly asked me, 'Have you absolutely lost your mind?' This was only one of several innovation and marketing approaches at the time that customers did not understand." Increasingly, senior leaders noticed that managers were attributing poor results to factors beyond their control; weak sales, for instance, might be blamed on nice weather, which discouraged consumers from buying indoor toys.

The company's results were characterized by large profit swings. The Group saw 28% top-line growth and a return to profitability in 1999, a sales downturn and a loss in 2000, and a decent profit in 2001. Revenue grew in 2002, stimulated by new product launches, a new Star Wars film, growth in core products, and a strong U.S. dollar, but profit fell.

By 2003, it became clear that the new growth strategy wasn't working. Sales plunged by 29% to DKK 6.8 billion, and the company lost DKK 935 million. Management acknowledged that the substantial investment in expanding the product portfolio and consequent cost increases had not produced the desired results. Worse yet, some new products had cannibalized core products and eroded earnings. In a year without Star Wars or Harry Potter movie launches, the unsatisfactory sales of products with movie tie-ins accounted for more than 50% of the overall sales decrease. Iversen summarized the situation: "We were pregnant with many initiatives and their costs, and the market environment turned against us." In December 2003, Kjeld Kristiansen asked Plougmann and four of his 14-person management team to leave the company. When 2004 brought another loss and pushed the LEGO Group to the brink of bankruptcy, Kristiansen invested in the company, retired as CEO, and handed the position to Knudstorp.

A Newcomer and a Company on the Brink

The appointment of then 35-year old Jørgen Knudstorp as the LEGO Group's first outside CEO surprised industry observers. Born a short distance from Billund, Knudstorp had earned a PhD in Business Economics at the University of Aarhus, Denmark and had started his career as a consultant at McKinsey & Company before joining the LEGO Group as Director of Strategic Development in 2001. Iversen recalled that "the reaction in the Danish corporate community was: 'How can they put a 'rookie' in charge when they are struggling to survive?' But Kjeld had gotten to know Jørgen, had come to trust his views, and liked his values."

Knudstorp and his management team knew that saving the company would be no easy task. Iverson described an early, sobering meeting with the Group's board:

> Jørgen bluntly told the board that if they wanted the business to survive in the long run, this could not be a quick fix. He said that if he was a financial investor, he would advise them to sell. But if they did not want to sell, they needed to believe that the LEGO family firm could do it right. They needed to allow us to deliver long term and not quarter by quarter, and they would have to sacrifice some of the 'sacred cows.'

Among the sacred cows that might be sacrificed was the Group's approach of making its own products. Knudstorp wondered whether he should outsource manufacturing to a third party:

> We had lost our edge in manufacturing and supply chain management in the 1990s when many competitors like Hasbro started outsourcing things, and our costs were out of control.… It should be easy to find professional manufacturers able to operate the factories better than we could.

Beyond manufacturing and supply chain management, all aspects of the company's strategy were on the table for discussion, including its product line, its approach to consumers and retailers, and its processes for innovation and planning, To get his bearings among the many decisions, Knudstorp began to look for LEGO's "core." Doing so was difficult, however, as financial pressure mounted:

> I had the banks breathing down my neck and asking for immediate repayment of all outstanding debt. We quickly needed to close or sell items to generate cash. My CFO listened to my theory about the 'core' and said, 'I don't get all you're saying, but what I take away is that a core is something which makes a superior return. But if you take this to the extreme, since our business is almost destroyed, there is no meaningful core in that sense.'

7

Exhibit 1 LEGO Group Selected Financials, 1995–2004

(in DKK million)	1995	1996	1997	1998	1999	2000	2001	2002	2003	2004
Income Statement										
Revenues	6,844	7,534	7,616	7,680	9,808	9,467	9,000	9,601	6,792	6,315
Expenses	N/A	N/A	N/A	N/A	(8,615)	(10,145)	(8,142)	(8,795)	(7,902)	(6,252)
Operating profit before special items	N/A	N/A	N/A	N/A	N/A	N/A	858	806	(1,110)	63
Special items*	N/A	N/A	N/A	N/A	(555)	(191)	(122)	0	(455)	(1,225)
Financial income and expenses	N/A	N/A	N/A	N/A	(122)	(201)	(215)	(189)	67	(75)
Profit before income tax	676	699	171	(282)	516	(1,070)	521	617	(1,498)	(1,237)
Net profit for the year	431	470	62	(194)	274	(831)	366	326	(935)	(1,931)
Balance Sheet										
Total Assets	9,535	10,061	9,767	11,250	12,694	12,280	14,093	12,560	10,049	8,089
Equity	5,961	5,913	5,437	5,841	6,970	6,266	6,225	6,478	4,892	2,948
Liabilities and Provisioning	3,574	4,148	4,330	5,409	5,714	6,014	7,868	6,082	5,157	5,141
Cash Flow Statement										
Cash flows from operating activities	N/A	N/A	N/A	N/A	N/A	N/A	1,227	1,853	944	774
Investments in property, plant, and equipment	748	1,490	745	1,397	968	1,156	1,478	1,264	709	457
Cash flows from financing activities	N/A	N/A	N/A	N/A	N/A	N/A	870	(1,003)	(560)	(29)
Total cash flows	N/A	N/A	N/A	N/A	N/A	N/A	771	(290)	(215)	538
Employees										
Average number (full time)	8,535	8,178	8,668	8,670	7,821	7,669	7,658	8,316	8,298	7,345
Financial Ratios (in %)										
Gross margin	N/A	N/A	N/A	N/A	N/A	N/A	65.4	70.0	61.3	57.7
Operating margin (ROS)	N/A	N/A	N/A	N/A	N/A	N/A	8.2	8.4	(23.0)	(18.4)
Net profit margin	6.3	6.2	0.8	(2.5)	2.8	(8.8)	4.1	3.4	(13.8)	(30.6)
Return on equity (ROE)	7.2	7.9	1.1	(3.3)	3.9	(13.3)	5.9	5.0	(19.1)	(65.5)
Return on invested capital (ROIC)**	N/A	N/A	N/A	N/A	N/A	N/A	9.1	8.2	(12.8)	1.2
Equity ratio	62.5	58.8	55.7	51.9	54.9	51.0	44.2	51.6	48.7	36.4
Exchange rate										
Dollars per DKK (end of year)	0.180	0.168	0.146	0.156	0.135	0.126	0.119	0.141	0.169	0.183

Source: LEGO Group, Annual Reports 2005, 2000, 1999.

Notes: * The Special items category included different items in different years; it may therefore not be fully comparable.
     ** ROIC = EBITA before special items / average invested capital.

Exhibit 2   The Ten Product Characteristics Defined by Godtfred Kirk Christiansen in 1963

1. Unlimited play potential
2. For girls and for boys
3. Fun for every age
4. Year-round play
5. Healthy, quiet play
6. Long hours of play
7. Development, imagination, creativity
8. The more LEGO, the greater the value
9. Extra sets available
10. Quality in every detail

Source: LEGO Group website, http://aboutus.lego.com/en-us/group/future.aspx, accessed May 2011.

Exhibit 3   Number of Distinct LEGO Components (Shapes, Colors, Decorations), 1980-2005E

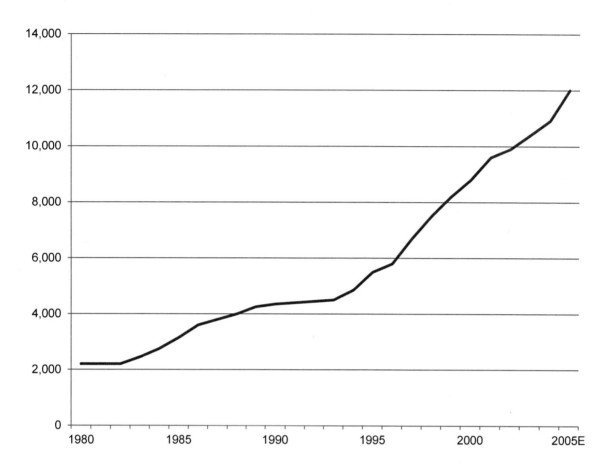

Source: LEGO Group.

Endnotes

[1] "Building profits child's play for Lego," *The Economist*, May 7, 2011. Accessed via Factiva, May 2011.

[2] Philp, Matt. "Toy Story," *Dominion Post*, April 2, 2011. Accessed via Factiva, May 2011.

[3] Santoli, Michael. "Play Time for Mattel," *Barron's Online*, December 13, 2010. Accessed via Factiva, May 2011.

[4] Santoli, Michael. "Play Time for Mattel," *Barron's Online*, December 13, 2010. Accessed via Factiva, May 2011.

[5] Mattel Annual Report 2010.

Husky Injection Molding Systems

From his second-story office, Robert Schad looked out over the production bays below where new Husky plastic injection molding machines were going through their paces. Since founding Husky in 1953, Schad had built the Canadian company into one of the world's premier manufacturers of plastic injection molding equipment. Customers used Husky equipment to make plastic products ranging from soft drink bottles and yogurt cups to automotive components and computer housings. Husky was known for building the highest-performance machines in the business…and charging a hefty premium for them.

In the early 1990s, Husky had enjoyed explosive growth and profitability. Revenue had grown from $250 million in 1992 to more than $600 million in 1995, net income had quadrupled, and the company registered a return on equity approaching 40%.[1] Then suddenly, in late 1995, everything seemed to fall apart. Competitors entered Husky's most lucrative markets with equipment sold at very low prices. At the same time, a shortage developed for certain of the resins used to make plastic products, and machine demand plummeted. The resulting excess capacity triggered a market share battle among machine competitors. It looked like 1996 was going to be a tough year financially.

Schad and the rest of Husky's management team struggled with how to respond. Some members of the team argued that the company had to stand and defend its traditional markets, while others favored fighting fire with fire and expanding into competitors' markets. Some advocated slashing expenditures aggressively, while others argued that generous funding of engineering, development, and service was money well spent. And all of the managers looked to Schad—at 67, still the driving force in the company and deeply involved in day-to-day operating decisions—for clear direction.

The Market for Injection Molding Equipment[2]

The market for plastic injection molding equipment and related services, in which Husky participated, was part of the larger, roughly trillion-dollar global plastics sector. Three types of players comprised the plastics sector: processors, resin makers, and equipment manufacturers. (See **Figure 1**.) *Processors* manufactured thousands upon thousands of plastic items and sold them to downstream manufacturers, retailers, and end-consumers. Common plastic products included automobile dash boards and bumpers, food packaging, synthetic fibers, catheters and syringes,

---

Assistant Professor Jan Rivkin prepared this case as the basis for class discussion rather than to illustrate either effective or ineffective handling of an administrative situation.

electrical connectors, trash barrels, toys, piping, and computer keyboards. Processors ranged from Plastipak, which made soda bottles and other containers, to Motorola, which produced cellular telephones, to General Motors, which made plastic automotive parts.

Figure 1   The Plastics Sector

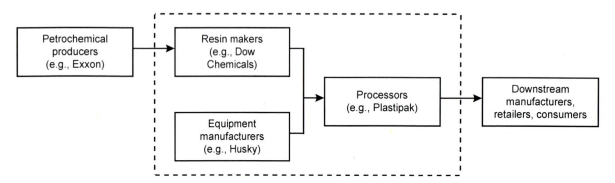

To make this diverse array of products, processors bought resins and capital equipment. Sold as tiny pellets, often by the tankerful, resin was the raw material that was melted down and reshaped into plastic products. *Resin makers* such as BASF, Dow Chemicals, and Du Pont produced plastic resin from petrochemicals. Resin came in various chemical forms, with polyethylene, polypropylene, polyethylene terephthalate (PET), and polyvinyl chloride (PVC) among the most common. *Equipment manufacturers,* including Husky and many others, made the machinery that converted resin into products.

Because of its favorable performance characteristics and its low cost, plastic was displacing glass, metal, wood, and paper in numerous applications. From 1982 to 1996, the global volume of plastic resin consumed grew at an average clip of 6% per year. Growth was expected to continue at a comparable rate, especially as plastic became more heavily used in countries that traditionally employed little. Per capita consumption exceeded 80 kilograms per year in North America and Western Europe while in other areas, annual consumption per person was less than 15 kilograms.

Processors used a variety of techniques, including extrusion, blow molding, and injection molding, to form products from resin. Most products were clearly best produced by one of these techniques. In the extrusion process, plastic resin was melted and fed through a die to produce a thin shape such as a film, sheet, or tube. Blow molding involved blowing hot resin into a mold to make a hollow shape such as a container.

Injection molding. Many of the most complicated plastic shapes required injection molding, the process for which Husky made equipment. A basic injection molding system consisted of two components: a mold and a machine. (See **Figures 2** and **3**). The mold included two pieces of machined metal with cavities between the pieces in the shape of the desired plastic parts. One half of the mold (the "hot half") rested in the stationary platen of the machine, and the other (the "cold half") was attached to the moving platen. While a clamp on the machine held the halves of the mold together under high pressure, a barrel on the machine melted the resin and a piston injected the molten resin into the mold cavity. Seconds later, when the resin was cooled and the plastic parts solidified, the clamp opened and released the parts. A set of controls synchronized the system's actions.

2

Figure 2   Injection Molding System

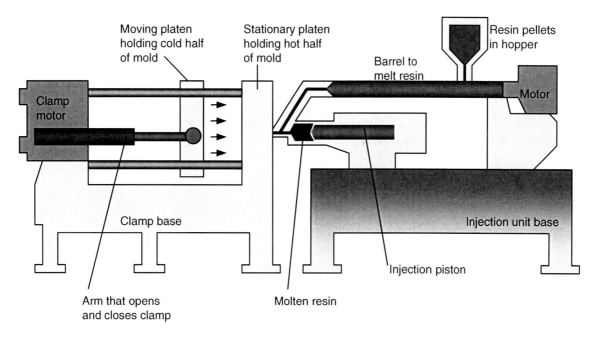

Figure 3   An Injection Mold

Source: Husky

Advanced injection molding systems incorporated other pieces of equipment. Robotic devices removed cooled products from the mold. Highly engineered "hot runners," built into molds themselves, heated the often intricate distribution channels between the pump and the mold cavity, making sure that the resin waiting in the channels remained molten while the part in the cavity solidified. Hot runners improved the quality of parts and reduced resin waste.

The force which the machine clamp could exert on a mold affected the type of product which a machine-mold combination could manufacture. Consequently, injection molding machines were sometimes categorized by the force they could exert. Small, 60-tonne machines made simple products such as electronic components, syringes, and computer keyboard keys.[1] Large, 4,000-tonne machines were employed to produce big items such as car bumpers or to make multiple items in a single mold. Still on the drawing boards were 8,000-tonne machines which could mold entire plastic car bodies in a single piece. Prices ranged from $20,000 for small, standard machines to as much as $6,000,000 for massive, customized equipment.

Processors spent $19.0 billion on injection molding equipment and services in 1995. **Exhibit 1** shows one breakdown of the market by end application. **Exhibit 2** divides the market by the type of equipment or service purchased.

Use and purchase of injection molding systems. For many processors, injection molding systems lay at the heart of their manufacturing operations. Both machines and molds were potentially large capital expenditures, and accordingly, processors utilized the equipment heavily. Machines and molds were typically expected to run two or three shifts a day, 365 days per year. Processors' production managers monitored the quality of a system's output carefully. If a system produced defective output, resin was wasted. Moreover, defects caused problems downstream for the processor or the processor's customers. Processors' engineers also maintained their injection molding systems carefully. The breakdown of a system could bring a large portion of a processor's operations to a halt.

Processors purchased new injection molding equipment when demand for their own products increased or when their old systems became outdated. The purchase of a system was often a complex process, lasting several months and involving many individuals. In choosing among equipment vendors, engineers, operations managers, purchasing personnel, and senior managers all played a role, and these individuals sometimes had different priorities. An operations manager, for instance, might worry about how a machine would fit onto a crowded factory floor. Purchasing personnel might focus on the up-front capital cost of the equipment, while a senior manager might pay special attention to operating costs. These different points of view were related; in calculating operating costs, for instance, a senior manager might take account of crowding on the factory floor by including some cost per square foot of equipment. (An annual cost of $20 - $100 per square foot was typical.)

Exhibit 3 shows the structure of the costs that a processor would incur to make a typical injection-molded plastic item. Virtually all of these costs could be influenced by which vendor and which system a processor chose. Accordingly, sophisticated customers often made extensive calculations when comparing vendors or systems. An equipment vendor's reputation and its history with a particular customer played significant roles in the purchase decision, as did the vendor's record on after-sales service and maintenance. On balance, customers who bought many systems seemed to prefer to buy from just one or a small handful of vendors.

A processor generally bought machines and molds separately, from different equipment makers. Because processors occasionally changed the shapes of the items they manufactured, molds tended to have shorter lives than machines. Over the course of a machine's life, a processor might purchase two to four or even more molds per machine. It was also common for processors to

---

[1] A "tonne" is a metric ton, equal to 1,000 kilograms or 2,200 pounds.

refurbish old molds, for instance to make them use less resin or to modify the part made with the mold.

For some customers, the item produced by the injection molding system was their major product, and the system was their primary capital expenditure. For example, virtually all of the capital equipment bought by Plastipak, a $425 million maker of soda bottles and other containers, was related to plastics processing. Other purchasers considered such systems a smaller part of their operations. For instance, Chrysler spent a tiny fraction of its 1995 capital budget of $4.1 billion on injection molding equipment.

Production. Injection molding machines were typically produced in very different ways and in very different settings than related molds. Machines were usually made in dedicated factories by companies that had invested heavily in specialized tooling and skills. Smaller machines were built-for-stock on assembly lines while the largest, most sophisticated machines were made to order and assembled in job-shop settings. Machine makers commonly produced many of their components in-house. Most raw inputs, such as steel, could be obtained at competitive prices, but some (e.g., hydraulic systems and electronic controls) were supplied by only a few companies worldwide. The unit costs of machine makers tended to fall until a company achieved an annual output of 500 machines or more.

Many types of *molds* could be made efficiently with standard machine tools. Only skilled craftsmen could make intricate molds, and mold production was commonly treated as a black art best taught through apprenticeship.

Sales and service. Most makers of injection molding machines sold their equipment in multiple countries, but focused their efforts on one or two regions of the globe. Machine makers typically deployed company-employed sales people in selected regions only and used independent sales representatives, or agents, to sell elsewhere. (See the bottom row of **Exhibit 4.**) Paid on commission, an independent agent would usually represent several manufacturers and carry a range of products. An agent might, for instance, sell blow-molding and extrusion equipment as well as injection molding equipment. The most skilled agents served as technical consultants and system integrators for the processors.

Machine makers deployed highly trained service technicians that were, in contrast to sales people, almost exclusively company employees. Technicians responded when a customer reported a problem with a machine. Since a machine breakdown could halt a processor's operations, customers cared a great deal about speedy service. This was especially true when a processor's own engineers could not repair a machine. At most machine makers, the service and sales organizations reported separately to top managers.

Mold makers handled sales and service quite differently than did machine producers. Small mold makers had no formal sales force and obtained business mainly by word of mouth in a locale. Even relatively large mold makers had only a few sales representatives. Similarly, most mold makers had no dedicated service organization. Processors maintained their own molds or relied on ordinary, local machine shops for service.

Technology. Although the basic science of injection molding was well developed, equipment makers continued to make significant technological strides. Ongoing technical efforts made molding systems faster, more efficient, and more reliable. Specialized machines were developed to produce certain products very efficiently. New machinery was being designed to open new markets; plastic beer bottles and all-plastic automobiles were, according to some, within the reach of the industry. Other efforts attempted to produce thinner plastic items or to use more recycled plastic.

Progress in the production of soda bottles was typical. (As discussed below, Husky played a prominent role in this particular market.) Most soda bottles were produced from polyethylene terephthalate (PET) by a two-step process. In the first step, a "preform" was made in an injection molding system. As shown in **Figure 4**, a preform looked like a plastic test tube with screw threads on the top. In the second step, a blow-molding process heated and stretched the preform into the shape of a bottle. In principle, preforms could be produced on any generic injection molding machine. In practice, however, equipment vendors had developed specialized machines tailored to the special operational needs of preform production. In 1977, injection molding machines could make eight preforms at a time and 820 preforms per hour. By 1995, state-of-the-art, specialized machines could make 96 at a time and 19,000 per hour.

Figure 4   PET preforms and bottles

Source: Husky

Not all customers used such high-speed, specialized machines. Processors who made smaller volumes of soda bottles sometimes used a "single-stage" system, which produced a bottle from resin in one step. Roughly 20% of PET soda bottles were produced with single-stage systems. This portion was shifting as soda bottle processors consolidated globally and attained the volumes to justify the greater investment in faster two-stage systems. Single-stage systems were gaining popularity, however, among makers of specialized containers such as mayonnaise and pickle jars, which were not produced in volumes as great as soda bottles.

Equipment makers, as well as resin makers and processors, devoted considerable effort to promoting the recycling of plastics. Some industry observers argued that the industry's long-term growth depended on extensive recycling, and recycling had become common in many developed countries. PET bottles were among the most commonly recycled plastic items. In 1995, over 1.2 billion pounds of PET bottles, representing a quarter of all such bottles, were recycled in the United States.[3] Recycled PET was traded as a commodity in a well-established market.

Competitors. For the most part, injection molding machines were made by different companies than were molds. In the machine market, an estimated 80 companies had accounted for 80% of global sales in the mid-1970s. By the mid-1990s, that number had dwindled to 15. As **Exhibit 4** shows, remaining machine makers differed in the range of products they offered, application markets they served, and regions they covered. Production of *molds* remained fragmented in 1995, with over 10,000 mold makers competing worldwide in 1995. Many mold makers were small, owner-operated machine shops. (Individual competitors are described below.)

Husky[4]

Born in southwestern Germany, Robert Schad emigrated to Canada in 1951 with just $25 and a character reference from Albert Einstein, a family friend, in his pocket. An engineer by training, he soon set up a machine shop to build snowmobiles. The "Huskymobile" flopped, and Schad turned to performing machining jobs for other companies. An opportunity soon arose to bid on a contract to make injection molds. Largely unfamiliar with such molds, Schad submitted a bid 50% lower than competitors, won the contract, and lost money on it. By the late 1950s, Schad and Husky had established a reputation as a high-quality maker of plastic molds, especially "thinwall" molds used to make vending cups and other containers.

In 1961, Husky introduced its first injection molding machine: a specialized, high-speed system for making thinwall containers. Sales of the initial machine were slow, nearly sending Husky into bankruptcy. The speed and quality of subsequent models excited customers, however, and sales took off. As requests for the machine came in from around the globe, Husky expanded to Europe in the mid-1960s and established a joint venture in Japan in 1971. Unlike rivals, the company offered a fully integrated system of thinwall mold, machine, and product-handling equipment.

A series of events in 1973-74 pushed Husky, once again, to the brink of bankruptcy. A global oil shortage sent the cost of resin soaring. Production of plastic products fell and, with it, demand for plastic production equipment. At the same time, large rivals introduced "multi-cavity" machines in the thinwall segment, which could produce several containers at a time. Already stretched by recent expansion, Husky had little money to develop similar machines. Schad recalled:[5]

> We were on our way to bankruptcy. In fact, the bank asked us to go into receivership. Every penny we could scrape together, we used to keep R&D going.... Because of our capability to make thinwall molds, Owens-Illinois, a major container maker, asked us to work with them on PET packaging. It was PET that saved us.

A new line of molding systems, tailored for the production of PET bottle preforms, pulled Husky out of its crisis by the end of the 1970s. Husky introduced machines and molds to make PET preforms just as soft drink makers began to shift rapidly to plastic bottles. With a quick series of product innovations, Husky established itself as the leading firm in the preform niche. By 1995, the company estimated that 60% of the world's preforms were manufactured on Husky systems. Profits from this area allowed the company to expand into other product lines and additional countries during the 1980s and early 1990s. (See **Exhibit 5** for historical financial data.)

Products. By the 1990s, Husky offered products for a series of particular applications: PET preforms, thinwall containers, and certain end-uses in the closure, automotive, and technical markets for customers who were particularly attuned to service or who wanted an especially rugged machine. Husky provided a comprehensive and integrated product line for the end uses it served. For PET preforms, for instance, it made specialized machines, molds, hot runners, and robots.

Machines. Industry experts generally divided the market for injection molding machines into three classes: small-tonnage machines with clamping forces below 150 tonnes, medium-tonnage machines (150 – 900 tonnes), and large-tonnage machines (more than 1,000 tonnes). The bulk of Husky's sales were in the medium-tonnage class, most dedicated to the PET preform and thinwall applications. The company held small shares in the rest of the medium- and large-tonnage markets, where it made customized machines for particularly demanding applications. It had virtually no sales in the small-tonnage segment. (See **Exhibit 2**.)

Molds. Husky participated selectively in the market for molds, making only the molds for PET preforms, thinwall and other containers, and closures such as bottle tops. For other applications, Husky had formed alliances with a set of mold makers to provide customers with integrated systems. Two- to four-page agreements laid out the terms of these alliances, which took a variety of forms. Husky might audit and certify a mold maker's operations, recommend a mold maker to a company buying a machine, or buy and resell the molds of a particular mold maker. A mold maker, in turn, might buy a Husky machine to operate in its test room and might purchase hot runners from Husky.

Hot runners. A complex mold often incorporated a "hot runner": a highly engineered system of manifolds and nozzles designed to channel hot resin into the cavities of the mold. Husky not only produced hot runners for its own molds but also sold hot runners to other mold makers. Though this business was small, Husky's sales force used the product line to learn processors' needs and to build relationships with new accounts. For instance, Husky sold hot runners to Gillette's Papermate division for several years before winning a machine contract and displacing two competitors.

Robotics. Husky produced robots which removed plastic parts from molds, sorted them, packaged them, and stacked them. The company made robots both for Husky machines and for machines made by others, though its robots were most easily and thoroughly integrated with its own machines. Prices ranged from $60,000 to $250,000 per robotic system.

Value-added services. Husky promoted itself as "a supplier of complete factory solutions for the plastics industry" rather than a simple vendor of equipment.[6] The company began in the 1990s to plan injection molding facilities for its customers, train customers, integrate production systems, and produce turnkey factories. Fees for such services were a small but growing part of Husky's revenue.

Husky typically tried to sell its products as integrated systems of machines, molds, hot runners, and robots. Among customers' engineers, Husky's systems were known for their speed, ruggedness, resin utilization, and durability. A Husky thinwall system, for instance, could mold 16 margarine containers in every 6-second cycle while a competitor's system might take 7 seconds to make as many containers. Speedy injection and clamping not only lowered the cycle time of a Husky system, but also allowed the processor to make a final product with a thinner wall.[2] The margarine container produced on a Husky machine might weigh 12 grams, 2 grams less than one made on a competing machine. Margarine containers were made from high-density polyethylene resin, which might cost 70¢ per kilogram.

Similarly, a Husky preform system might make a set of PET preforms for soda bottles with a cycle time 10-15% shorter than a competitor's system. **Exhibit 6**, based on a recent head-to-head competition at a customer's site, compares the performance of a Husky preform system to that of a major competitor's along a number of dimensions.

---

[2] With slower injection and clamping, a product's wall must be thicker. Otherwise, resin might solidify while seeping through the narrow portions of the mold cavity, causing part of the cavity to remain unfilled.

Husky was also known for charging a premium for its products. The Husky thinwall system described above might be priced at $400,000 versus $350,000 for a competing system. Husky charged roughly $1.2 million for the preform system described in **Exhibit 6**, while rivals might ask $1.0 million for a competing system. Across its product line, on machines producing comparable numbers of parts per cycle, it was not uncommon for Husky to charge a 10% to 20% price premium.

Production. Husky concentrated its manufacturing, development, and support facilities on two campuses, one in Bolton, Ontario (half an hour north of Toronto) and one in Dudelange, Luxembourg. Senior managers explained the thinking behind the campuses:[7]

> By clustering activities on major sites we maximize synergies between related businesses that serve the same industry. We create an environment that breathes excitement and drive, and we take advantage of economies of scale to provide services for our people. The campus is the ideal set-up to operate in a permanent mode of speed and flexibility…. By having a large people-base in one location, career moves do not uproot families…and we have ready space to build new facilities as soon as the need arises.

Near the Bolton campus, on what was otherwise rolling farmland interrupted only by strip malls, were a large number of smaller, related companies—mold makers, machine shops, and component providers—many founded by former Husky employees.

On each campus, Husky assembled molding systems on shop floors that were bright, open, air-conditioned, and spotless. The attention to order and to neatness in the company was legendary. Stories circulated about how Schad used to straighten draftsmen's T-squares at night, how one job applicant was rejected because his car's trunk was messy, and so on. The company prided itself on employing the latest tools and technology. Its heavily automated mold operation, for instance, stood in sharp contrast to the small, owner-operated machine shops that were common in the mold business. Gary Hughes, Husky's Senior Manager for the PET Market, described the difference:

> The contrast is between mold *manufacturer* and mold *maker*. We're a mold manufacturer. We manufacture a mold through a series of highly automated steps, and the guy who performs one step can't do the next and vice versa. Each step has a tight set of standards. Mold makers, in contrast, don't have the same kinds of standards. They're more like skilled artisans who can nurse a mold through a much less automated process from beginning to end. We've tried to take a craft business, invest in it, and turn it into more of a science.

Husky took a modular approach to system design and construction. With the help of sales people, customers selected from building blocks—injection units, clamps, controls, bases, robots. Husky then assembled the systems to order. The company focused on design and assembly, and it relied almost entirely on components purchased from outside vendors. Machine production volumes were low by industry standards, at roughly 200-300 machines per year.

The company tracked the production methods and products of its rivals closely, but had not analyzed their costs in detail. Husky's managers believed that the company incurred higher unit costs than competitors in many product lines, but in some, their investments made them more efficient than rivals.

Technology development and commercialization. Husky managers prided themselves on their willingness to take on the toughest technical challenges and their ability to bring new technologies to market rapidly. Accordingly, Schad had invested $25 million in the early 1990s to build Husky's Advanced Manufacturing Center (AMC). Opened on Schad's sixty-fifth birthday with a speech by Schad's friend Jane Goodall, the ethologist and authority on chimpanzees, the AMC was given a mandate to create "the injection molding factory of the future."[8]   Within its walls, new molding systems operated in a controlled, 24-hour production environment.   High partitions shielded secret projects from view.   No other company had such a facility, and some observers thought the investment was questionable at best.

Sales and service.   Husky deployed 300 people in 24 regional offices in 17 countries to find and serve customers in more than 70 countries.   See **Exhibit 7** for a list of some of Husky's largest customers.   Husky sold exclusively via its internal sales force and gave general managers in each region responsibility for both the local sales force and the local service technicians.   Top managers firmly believed that Husky's sales and service force was the strongest in the industry.   Mike Urquhart, Vice President for Service and Sales in the Americas, explained:

> We sell a line of premium-priced, premium-quality equipment.   This requires our sales people to have an in-depth knowledge of our equipment and its advantages over commodity machinery.   It's hard for independent agents to grasp our equipment and make a commitment to sell it.   Plus, many of our sales people used to be *service* people.   [Independent] agents, in contrast, tend to be true *sales* people, and the customer doesn't receive the same level of service and consultation.

Husky had begun to build Technical Centers in key locations to provide local technical support and training.   Centers were open in Atlanta, Los Angeles, Luxembourg, and Japan, and additional centers were slated for other locations.   In addition, Husky had deployed a system designed to ship spare parts to any location quickly.   A distribution center in Buffalo, New York, stocked 22,000 different items, including components for machines built in the early 1960s.

Reflecting its global approach to sales and service, Husky derived more than 95% of its sales from outside of Canada.   (See **Exhibit 8.**)   A 1994 report commissioned by the Ontario government gave Husky and the highly innovative suppliers that surrounded it in Bolton credit for "Canada's shift from a trade deficit to a surplus position in its plastics machinery account."[9]

Ownership and finance.   Husky was a privately held company, with Robert Schad and his family retaining 65% of the company's stock.   "Key employees," designated by the senior management team, were permitted to buy non-voting shares, and collectively, they owned 25% of the company.   To be identified as key, an individual had to demonstrate strong leadership potential and possess knowledge that could not be readily replaced.   Komatsu, the Japanese equipment maker, held the remaining 10% of the company, obtained when Husky was in need of capital in 1990.   At the time, Komatsu had begun manufacturing a line of small injection molding machines complementary to those offered by Husky, and the two companies planned to assist in the sales and marketing of each other's products.   Subsequently, however, Komatsu discontinued its line of injection molding machines and concentrated on its core businesses.

In 1995, long-term debt was 15% of total assets.   Husky's interest coverage ratio, or earnings divided by interest payments, was typically between 10 and 20.

Values.   Deeply imprinted on the firm were Schad's personal values—concern for the environment, devotion to personal health, dedication to hard work, egalitarianism, and perfectionism.

The firm's commitment to the environment was embodied in its Bolton campus.   Eighty-five percent of campus waste was recycled.   The landscape had been naturalized to eliminate the use of pesticides, cooling systems were modified to use ozone-friendly chemicals, and nighttime lighting was designed not to interfere with bird migration.   Nature prints adorned the walls.   In the cafeteria, utensils were placed at the *exit* so that diners would pick up only the utensils they needed.   Product development projects which used plastics in more environmentally responsible ways received special attention. Each year, the company donated 5% of after-tax profits to charities such as the World Wildlife Fund.

The campus environment was also designed to encourage personal wellness. A heavily-used fitness and wellness center employed, among others, a naturopathic doctor, a chiropractor, and a massage therapist. Cafeterias promoted vegetarian meals and offered no junk food; coffee cost 85¢ but herbal tea was free. Smoking had been banned decades earlier. A spacious, new child care center featured airy play spaces, heated hardwood floors, the latest learning technology, a high staff-to-child ratio, and extended hours.

Employees pointed out, however, that the long hours of the child care center reflected not just Husky's concern for its people, but also its expectation that they work hard. Managers described Husky's atmosphere as "intense," driven," and "unsentimental" and its leader as "an inspiration, a visionary, and a taskmaster."

Strict egalitarianism was the rule for all interactions. An employee council, in operation for more than 25 years, met regularly with Schad to air concerns openly. Everyone called each other by first name, no parking spaces were reserved, all cafeterias and washrooms were shared, and casual (but neat) dress was required. Company veterans noted, however, that Robert Schad was "Mr. Schad" until he circulated a memo instructing everyone to call him "Robert" or face a $5 fine. (Proceeds were donated to environmental charities.)

In recent years, Schad had taken vigorous steps to firm up the values of the company. Schad had worked with his senior managers first to articulate Husky's values and then to ensure that the values were reflected in company practice. **Exhibit 9** shows the purpose and values as stated by the top management team.

Schad and other managers were confident that the various environmental and health efforts would benefit the business. **Exhibit 10** shows the cost-benefit calculations which Schad presented to a conference convened by Canada's Ministry of the Environment and Energy. Closing the talk, Schad said,[10]

> There are some things in business that we cannot analyze to death. We have to know in our hearts that we are doing the right thing. And we have to invest in our vision. In fact, we only put the pay-back numbers on paper for today's presentation. Hopefully, it will make the accountants happy. We knew long before that our investment pays. Real energy does not come from logic, it comes from passion.

Competition

Husky faced a different set of competitors in each of its businesses. (See **Exhibit 2**.) In the machine business, leading rivals included the Mannesmann Group, Cincinnati Milacron, and Engel. In the mold market, Electra Form and R&D Tool & Engineering produced PET preform molds that competed with Husky's.

The Mannesmann Group. One of Germany's largest conglomerates, the Mannesmann Group produced a wide range of industrial equipment, automotive components, and steel tubes. In recent years, the company had invested heavily in telecommunications services and had shed non-core businesses. Injection molding businesses accounted for roughly 5% of total revenues. Mannesmann's engineering group, of which the injection molding businesses were a part, earned a return on gross assets in the low single digits. The telecommunications group earned a return in the 20-30% range.

Mannesmann had acquired an array of injection molding equipment vendors during the 1980s and 1990s. Group companies included Van Dorn, with facilities in the United States and Germany and roughly $399 million in injection molding machine revenue in 1996; Krauss Maffei (Germany, $276 million); Netstal (Switzerland, $181 million); and Billion (France, $51 million). Together, the Mannesmann companies at that time served a broader range of application markets than Husky.

The Mannesmann injection molding machine companies were run largely as independent businesses. They competed against one another for some customers, though geographic separation limited this competition to some degree. It was believed that the companies coordinated the production of a handful of components in order to attain economies of scale. Krauss Maffei, for instance, produced large extrusion screws for group companies, while Van Dorn manufactured small screws.

Among the Mannesmann companies, Netstal had the greatest market overlap with Husky. Acquired by Mannesmann in financial straits in the early 1990s, Netstal had invested in technology and had turned itself around. Specialized machines designed to make compact discs had proven very profitable and had helped put the company back on firm ground. Netstal's machines were, along with Husky's, among the most expensive in the business and enjoyed the luster of Swiss engineering. Some Husky managers considered Netstal "the only one who can challenge Husky on technology."

Cincinnati Milacron. In 1995, Cincinnati Milacron completed a three-year restructuring of its portfolio of businesses. The corporate makeover was intended to diversify the company away from its traditional base in the highly cyclical machine tool industry. By 1995, machine tools contributed only 25% of its revenue, while plastics machinery and industrial products contributed 34% and 41%, respectively.

Within the plastics equipment business, Cincinnati Milacron offered complete lines of machinery for three different processing technologies: injection molding, extrusion, and blow molding. Injection molding machines constituted two-thirds of its plastics equipment sales, and the company billed itself as "the largest U.S. producer of injection molding machines."[11] The company offered a broad line of standardized machines, rarely customizing machines for particular customers in substantial ways. Recent efforts to standardize products and tap economies of scale, according to management, had made Cincinnati Milacron "the lowest-cost U.S. producer of these machines."[12]

Cincinnati Milacron had bolstered its injection molding business with two recent acquisitions and a joint venture. In 1993, the company acquired Ferromatik of Germany, one of Europe's leading makers of injection molding machinery. The acquisition, managers claimed, brought the company high-end technology and a European distribution and service system. In January of 1996, Cincinnati Milacron purchased D-M-E, the largest U.S. producer of mold bases and supplies for the mold-making industry and a manufacturer of hot runners. With greater involvement in the mold-making business, the company expected to "achieve synergies in a number of areas, including manufacturing process, technology, marketing and distribution."[13] In May of 1995, Cincinnati Milacron established a joint venture with an Indian producer of injection molding machines. The venture aimed to make inexpensive, entry-level machines for the Asian and South American markets.

Engel. A privately held company based in Austria, Engel focused exclusively on injection molding machines and robots. Engel served the market for high-end technical applications such as cell phone casings. It enjoyed a strong reputation for its technology and its willingness to customize machines in the technical market segment. Tightly controlled by a family reputed to be among Austria's wealthiest, Engel was financially sound, highly secretive, and very conscious of costs.

Electra Form of Ohio and **R&D Tool & Engineering** of Kansas offered PET preform molds that competed with Husky's. Electra Form entered the market by, initially, refurbishing older PET molds, including those made by Husky. After using a mold for 3-5 years, a processor often wished to modify it, for instance, in order to use less resin. Husky had been too busy making new molds to retrofit its own molds. Electra Form, in contrast, had pursued the refurbishment business eagerly. Later, they offered brand new PET preform molds. Both Electra Form and R&D Tool & Engineering operated facilities that were smaller and less automated than Husky's, deployed less extensive sales and service networks, and set prices roughly 10% below Husky's. Neither offered injection molding machines. In addition to molds for PET preforms, Electra Form made machines to reheat preforms and blow-mold them into full bottles, molds for this second stage, and customized molds for special applications. R&D Tool & Engineering made molds for blow-molding, extrusion, and other injection molding applications.

Crisis and Decisions

At the end of July, 1995, Husky wrapped up a blockbuster fiscal year. Revenues were up 53% for the year, to $609 million. Net income, at $50 million, was twice the 1994 figure. Already, however, the order book and the sales force warned of serious trouble for the coming year. Demand for Husky systems was weak in the PET portion of the market.

The causes of the troubles were not altogether clear, but management suspected two culprits. First, the makers of PET resin appeared to have underestimated resin demand by a wide margin. They had added too little capacity, and PET prices had soared (**Exhibit 11**). In some cases, processors simply could not obtain resin. Processors halted their expansion plans for products made with PET and put orders for new equipment on hold. Now, resin makers were expanding capacity to make up for the PET shortfall, and Husky's management team expected PET supply to return to "normal" levels within 2-3 years.

Second, Schad noted, "our success had not gone unnoticed. We had come from being small to being a major player in a few short years. Our competitors decided to get into our businesses, especially the PET business." A series of rivals launched new products in Husky's core market segments. "These competitors do not have the specialized expertise that we have developed, but operate from a much lower cost base.... By modifying mainstream machines to suit the preform application, they won over customers who are willing to purchase less expensive technology...."[14]

Netstal, the Swiss member of the Mannesmann Group, had introduced new PET systems that some customers—particularly European customers—felt were of comparable quality to Husky's, at prices approximately 20% lower than Husky's. Rather than make molds itself, Netstal purchased molds from Otto Hofstetter, a Swiss mold maker. Netstal began to make inroads into the PET market, as did some smaller manufacturers. Husky's managers believed that its machines continued to perform relative to the best competition in the manner described above and shown in **Exhibit 6**, though they realized that Husky's performance advantage might have been even larger in the past. Increasingly, Husky sales people found themselves in the unfamiliar position of competing vigorously for business. A draft of the 1996 business plan concluded that "[t]he injection molding machine has become a commodity."

By January of 1996, Husky's management team was convinced that it had to alter the firm's strategy in a fundamental way. What the new direction should be, however, was still far from clear. A consensus existed that the company had to reduce its cost per unit, but there was little agreement

Authorized for use only in educational programs at McMaster University until Jun 07, 2017. Use outside these parameters is a copyright violation.

on how to do so. A related debate raged around Husky's pricing. Some proposed that Husky should drop its prices 10-20% *immediately,* in anticipation of cost savings. The sales force reveled at this notion while financial and manufacturing personnel revolted at it.

Economic pressures also brought Husky's mold-making businesses under closer scrutiny. With its highly automated, capital-intensive facilities, Husky seemed to enjoy a big advantage in the market for PET preform molds, which were a technically demanding product. The company also made molds for thinwall containers, other containers, and closures, however, and in these markets, Mom & Pop artisans were competing successfully with Husky.

As Schad reviewed the company's options, two books weighed heavily on his mind. Schad had recently read *Only the Paranoid Survive* by Intel's CEO Andy Grove, and he was convinced that Husky faced a "strategic inflection point"—a decisive moment brought on by major external change. *Built to Last,* by James Collins and Jerry Porras, persuaded Schad that companies survived or failed over the long haul on the strength of their values. Husky's response to its current predicament, Schad believed, would shape the company's character for years to come. His hope was that the response would mold a company and a management team built to last.

Exhibit 1: Size of Market for Injection Molding Equipment and Services by Application (US$ mm)

Application	Typical end-product	1993	1994	1995	1996E	1997E	1998E	Major competitors
PET packaging	Soda bottle	$346	454	755	649	1004	1153	**Husky**, Engel, Van Dorn, Toshiba, Netstal, Cincinnati Milacron, Electra Form, Otto Hofstetter
Containers	Yogurt cup	$301	321	346	368	391	416	**Husky**, Engel, Cincinnati Milacron, Krauss Maffei, Netstal
Closures	Bottle cap	$208	228	254	278	306	336	**Husky**, Engel, Cincinnati Milacron, Krauss Maffei, Van Dorn
Automotive	Bumper	$3,283	3,402	3,563	3,688	3,817	3,951	Cincinnati Milacron, Krauss Maffei, Ube, Engel
Technical	Electrical connector	$9,876	10,288	10,806	11,238	11,687	12,155	Arburg, Engel, Krauss Maffei, Sumitomo, Netstal, Cincinnati Milacron
Other		$3,005	3,102	3,247	3,346	3,448	3,553	
Total		$17,018	17,793	18,971	19,566	20,653	21,565	

Source: Company documents

Exhibit 2: Size of Market for Injection Molding Equipment and Services by Product (US$ mm)

Product category	1993	1994	1995	1996E	1997E	1998E	Major competitors
Small-tonnage† machines	$1,639	1,704	1,773	1,840	1,910	1,984	Arburg, Engel, Krauss Maffei*, Sumitomo, Netstal*, Cincinnati Milacron
Medium-tonnage† machines:							
PET preform	$156	205	316	248	413	475	**Husky**, Engel, Van Dorn*, Toshiba, Netstal*, Cincinnati Milacron
Thinwall	$42	43	45	47	48	50	**Husky**
Other medium-tonnage	$1,967	2,046	2,128	2,209	2,293	2,381	Engel, Cincinnati Milacron, Van Dorn*, Toshiba, Krauss Maffei*
Large-tonnage† machines	$492	511	532	552	573	595	North America: Cincinnati Milacron, HPM, Van Dorn* Europe: Krauss Maffei*, Battenfeld, Engel, Sandretto, MIR Asia: UBE, Mitsubishi, Toshiba, Meiki
Machine subtotal	$4,294	4,509	4,793	4,895	5,237	5,484	
PET preform molds	$144	189	303	285	397	456	**Husky**, Electra Form, Otto Hofstetter, R&D Tool & Engineering
Other molds	$11,553	12,012	12,491	12,969	13,468	13,986	Numerous competitors in particular niches
Hot runners	$443	469	536	552	601	639	**Husky**, Mold Masters, D.M.E.**, Dynisco (Eurotool, Kona)
Robotics	$583	615	656	667	743	784	Wittman, Sepro, Star, Yushin, Engel
Value added services	$176	183	191	199	207	215	
Total	$17,018	17,793	18,971	19,566	20,653	21,565	

† Small-tonnage machines have less than 150 tonnes of clamping force; medium-tonnage machines, 150-900 tonnes; and large-tonnage machines, more than 1,000 tonnes

* Member of the Mannesmann Group   ** D.M.E. owned by Cincinnati Milacron

Source: Company documents

Exhibit 3: Cost Structure of a Typical Injection-molded Plastic Item

Cost component	Portion of costs (%)
Resin	58
Labor	3
Facility (e.g., building, factory overhead)	15
Maintenance	1
Packaging	8
Equipment (e.g., depreciation)	7
Scrap (i.e., wasted resin)	2
Energy	6
Total	100

Source: Company documents

Exhibit 4: Principal Injection Molding Machine Competitors

Company	Husky	Battenfeld	Cincinnati Milacron	Engel	Billion	Mannesmann Group Krauss Maffei	Mannesmann Group Van Dorn	Mannesmann Group Netstal	Sumitomo
1996 machine sales (Est.)		$235 mm	$552 mm	$424 mm	$51 mm	$276 mm	$399 mm	$181 mm	$182 mm
Machines produced	Fewer than 300	1,500	2,000	2,700	260	900	2,340	500	1,600
Employees	1,700	1,500	4,000	2,800	280	1,500	2,200	635	800
Revenue / machine		$157 K	$276 K	$157 K	$196 K	$307 K	$171 K	$362 K	$114 K
Revenue / employee		$157 K	$138 K	$151 K	$182 K	$184 K	$181 K	$285 K	$228 K
Key application markets	PET preforms, thinwall packaging	Technical, medical, automotive, general purpose	Custom molders, construction, automotive, electrical, toys, housewares	Technical, appliance, automotive	Various applications	Automotive, technical, medical	Technical, medical, closures, thinwall, general purpose, automotive	Technical, medical, CDs, PET preform, thinwall	Technical, packaging, CDs
Ownership	Private	100% by public company, SMS AG of Germany	Public; 10% by company officers and directors	Private, family owned	100% owned by Krauss Maffei	100% owned by Mannesman Group	100% owned by Mannesman Group	90% owned by Krauss Maffei	Public; 20% Sumitomo financial companies
Other products	Molds, hot runners, robots, services	Plastics extrusion equipment	Plastics extrusion and blow molding equipment; machine tools; industrial consumables	None	None	Plastics extrusion machinery, process engineering; transport equipment, etc.	None	Downstream processing equipment for CDs	Heavy machinery, ship building, transmission equipment, machine tools, etc.
Headquarters	Canada	Germany	U.S.	Austria	France	Germany	Germany	Switzerland	Japan
Manufacturing locations	Canada, U.S., Luxembourg, Germany	Germany, Austria, U.S., Brazil, India	U.S. (2), Germany, India	Austria (3), Canada, U.S.; 3 more under development	France	Germany (2)	Germany (3), U.S. (5)	Switzerland	Japan
Sales and service	300 employees in 17 countries	Mixture of own sales people and agents on four continents	Agents on four continents; field service offices	Offices and agents on four continents	Little outside of France	Few agents; sales and service offices in seven countries	Offices in Europe; agents elsewhere	Own personnel in nine countries; agents elsewhere	Sales and service almost exclusively in Asia and North America

Source: Husky competitor analysis documents

98

Exhibit 5: Financial Results of Husky Injection Molding Systems

Year	Revenue (US$ mm)	Net income (US$ mm)	EOY Assets (US$ mm)	Return on sales (%)	Return on equity (%)
1988	127.6	4.6	66.4	3.6	39.9
1989	146.4	6.4	87.7	4.4	40.5
1990	173.4	2.1	120.1	1.2	5.0
1991	189.2	(5.7)	114.5	(3.0)	-15.9
1992	250.1	12.8	147.2	5.1	27.7
1993	307.9	16.3	186.0	5.3	27.1
1994	398.1	25.1	282.7	6.3	30.1
1995	608.7	50.1	443.1	8.2	37.8

Source: Company documents

Exhibit 6: Comparison of Preform Systems

	Husky	Major Competitor
System	PET preform system producing 48 preforms per cycle, for production of 20-ounce soft drink bottle	PET preform system producing 48 preforms per cycle, for production of 20-ounce soft drink bottle
Cycle time	10.4 seconds	11.8 seconds
Average operating hours per day	22.3 hours	18.9 hours
Weight of preform Average Standard deviation	24.39 gm 0.16 gm	24.42 gm 0.16 gm
Floor space occupied	343.1 square feet	351.8 square feet
Electricity consumption	Husky system used 0.137 kWh less of electricity per kilogram of preforms produced. Cost of electricity = 8¢ / kWh	
Number of surface blemishes visible on preform body	~ 5-10	~ 50
Pressure required to burst bottle Average Standard deviation	~ 205 psi ~ 5 psi	~ 205 psi ~ 20 psi
Approximate purchase price	$1.2 million	$1.0 million

Source: Case writer estimates based on Husky evaluation at customer site

[Handwritten calculations:]

22h 18m

10.4s   79 200
        1080s
        ———
        80 280s
= 7 719 prod.

1 kg = 35.274 oz re
0.57 kg = 20 oz = 48 preforms

0.863 / x = 1 / 0.08

18h 54m
64 800
  3240s
  ———
68 040
= 5766

Exhibit 7: Sample of Major Husky Customers

Company	Business
Alpla	Manufacture of plastics and plastic products; packaging materials
Ball Corporation	Manufacture of metal and plastic packaging, primarily for beverages and foods
Coca Cola Enterprises	Marketing, distribution, and bottling of beverage products
Continental PET	Manufacture of plastic bottles and other plastic products
Owens Brockway	Manufacture of glass containers, plastic closures
Plastipak Packaging	Manufacture of plastic bottles and other plastic items
Schmalbach-Lubeca	Manufacture of plastic and metal containers, cans, lids, and other packaging

Source: Company documents; OneSource

Exhibit 8: Husky Revenue by Region

	1994		1995	
Region	US$ mm	Percent	US$ mm	Percent
Canada	13.3	3.5	22.2	3.6
Rest of the Americas	270.6	70.3	393.4	64.6
Europe	86.6	22.5	141.0	23.2
Asia	14.6	3.8	52.0	8.5

Source: Company documents

Exhibit 9: Husky's Purpose and Values

Purpose: To be a role model of lasting business success based on our core values

Values:

- Make a contribution
- Proactive environmental responsibility
- Drive to do things much better
- Genuine care for all who are affected by what we do
- Uncompromising honesty

100

Exhibit 10: Cost-Benefit Estimates Concerning Environment, Health and Safety Initiatives

Costs
For child care development center; Environment, Health and Safety; cafeteria; and landscaping
Capital costs: Cn$10.8 mm Annual expenses: Cn$3.7 mm

Benefits Item	Annual savings (Cn$ mm)
Workers' compensation Consistently qualify for maximum rebate (50% of premium)	0.9
Low injury frequency 0.8 injuries per 200,000 hours worked vs. 5 for Husky's rate group Industry average cost per injury: $78,000	4.6
Low absenteeism rate 2.5 days per year per employee vs. industry average of 6.5 1.0 day per year per employee costs $500,000 (based on 1,400 people)	2.0
Low turnover rate 1.19% turnover vs. industry average of 5% Average cost to recruit and train an employee: $50,000	2.7
Recycling programs Generated $236,000 in 1996 Cost avoidance of $125,000	0.4
Energy audits Identified $525,000 in annual savings	0.5
Total	11.1

101

Exhibit 11: Price of PET Resin

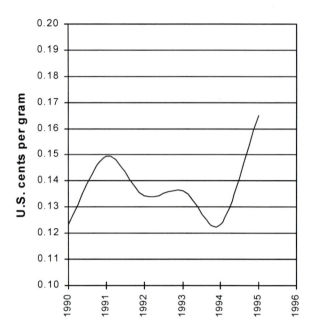

102

Notes

---

[1] All figures are in U.S. dollars unless stated otherwise.

[2] This section relies on material provided to the author by the company, especially the prospectus for Husky's 1998 initial public offering and drafts of documents related to the prospectus.

[3] Data from the American Plastics Council.

[4] This section draws on information provided by the company as well as B. Livesey, "Provide and Conquer," *The Globe and Mail Report on Business,* March 1997.

[5] Unless otherwise noted, all quotations of Husky managers were obtained from interviews conducted on December 3-4, 1997, August 20-21, 1998, and April 5, 1999.

[6] Husky Underwriter Information Package, Corporate Overview, p. 4.

[7] Husky Annual Report, 1997, p. 5.

[8] Husky Annual Report, 1997, p. 1.

[9] B. Livesey, "Provide and Conquer," *The Globe and Mail Report on Business,* March 1997.

[10] Robert Schad, "Building a Competitive Advantage Through Core Values," November 1997.

[11] Cincinnati Milacron 10-K, 1995, p. 9.

[12] Cincinnati Milacron 10-K, 1995, p. 9.

[13] Cincinnati Milacron 10-K, 1995, p. 10.

[14] Robert Schad, "Change or Die," *Team Husky* (internal newsletter), July 1997.

CHRISTOPHER A. BARTLETT
VINCENT DESSAIN
ANDERS SJÖMAN

IKEA's Global Sourcing Challenge: Indian Rugs and Child Labor (A)

In May 1995, Marianne Barner faced a tough decision. After just two years with IKEA, the world's largest furniture retailer, and less than a year into her job as business area manager for carpets, she was faced with the decision of cutting off one of the company's major suppliers of Indian rugs. While such a move would disrupt supply and affect sales, she found the reasons to do so quite compelling. A German TV station had just broadcast an investigative report naming the supplier as one that used child labor in the production of rugs made for IKEA. What frustrated Barner was that, like all other IKEA suppliers, this large, well-regarded company had recently signed an addendum to its supply contract explicitly forbidding the use of child labor on pain of termination.

Even more difficult than this short-term decision was the long-term action Barner knew IKEA must take on this issue. On one hand, she was being urged to sign up to an industry-wide response to growing concerns about the use of child labor in the Indian carpet industry. A recently formed partnership of manufacturers, importers, retailers, and Indian nongovernmental organizations (NGOs) was proposing to issue and monitor the use of "Rugmark," a label to be put on carpets certifying that they were made without child labor. Simultaneously, Barner had been conversing with people at the Swedish Save the Children organization who were urging IKEA to ensure that its response to the situation was "in the best interest of the child"—whatever that might imply. Finally, there were some who wondered if IKEA should not just leave this hornet's nest. Indian rugs accounted for a tiny part of IKEA's turnover, and to these observers, the time, cost, and reputation risk posed by continuing this product line seemed not worth the profit potential.

The Birth and Maturing of a Global Company[1]

To understand IKEA's operations, one had to understand the philosophy and beliefs of its 70-year-old founder, Ingvar Kamprad. Despite stepping down as CEO in 1986, almost a decade later, Kamprad retained the title of honorary chairman and was still very involved in the company's activities. Yet perhaps even more powerful than his ongoing presence were his strongly held values and beliefs, which long ago had been deeply embedded in IKEA's culture.

Kamprad was 17 years old when he started the mail-order company he called IKEA, a name that combined his initials with those of his family farm, Elmtaryd, and parish, Agunnaryd, located in the

Professor Christopher A. Bartlett, Executive Director of the HBS Europe Research Center Vincent Dessain, and Research Associate Anders Sjöman prepared this case. HBS cases are developed solely as the basis for class discussion. Certain details have been disguised. Cases are not intended to serve as endorsements, sources of primary data, or illustrations of effective or ineffective management.

forests of southern Sweden. Working out of the family kitchen, he sold goods such as fountain pens, cigarette lighters, and binders he purchased from low-priced sources and then advertised in a newsletter to local shopkeepers. When Kamprad matched his competitors by adding furniture to his newsletter in 1948, the immediate success of the new line led him to give up the small items.

In 1951, to reduce product returns, he opened a display store in nearby Älmhult village to allow customers to inspect products before buying. It was an immediate success, with customers traveling seven hours from the capital Stockholm by train to visit. Based on the store's success, IKEA stopped accepting mail orders. Later Kamprad reflected, "The basis of the modern IKEA concept was created [at this time] and in principle it still applies. First and foremost, we use a catalog to tempt people to visit an exhibition, which today is our store. . . . Then, catalog in hand, customers can see simple interiors for themselves, touch the furniture they want to buy and then write out an order."[2]

As Kamprad developed and refined his furniture retailing business model he became increasingly frustrated with the way a tightly knit cartel of furniture manufacturers controlled the Swedish industry to keep prices high. He began to view the situation not just as a business opportunity but also as an unacceptable social problem that he wanted to correct. Foreshadowing a vision for IKEA that would later be articulated as "creating a better life for the many people," he wrote: "A disproportionately large part of all resources is used to satisfy a small part of the population. . . . IKEA's aim is to change this situation. We shall offer a wide range of home furnishing items of good design and function at prices so low that the majority of people can afford to buy them. . . . We have great ambitions."[3]

The small newsletter soon expanded into a full catalog. The 1953 issue introduced what would become another key IKEA feature: self-assembled furniture. Instead of buying complete pieces of furniture, customers bought them in flat packages and put them together themselves at home. Soon, the "knockdown" concept was fully systemized, saving transport and storage costs. In typical fashion, Kamprad turned the savings into still lower prices for his customers, gaining an even larger following among young postwar householders looking for well-designed but inexpensive furniture. Between 1953 and 1955, the company's sales doubled from SEK 3 million to SEK 6 million.[4]

Managing Suppliers: Developing Sourcing Principles

As its sales took off in the late 1950s, IKEA's radically new concepts began to encounter stiff opposition from Sweden's large furniture retailers. So threatened were they that when IKEA began exhibiting at trade fairs, they colluded to stop the company from taking orders at the fairs and eventually even from showing its prices. The cartel also pressured manufacturers not to sell to IKEA, and the few that continued to do so often made their deliveries at night in unmarked vans.

Unable to meet demand with such constrained local supply, Kamprad was forced to look abroad for new sources. In 1961, he contracted with several furniture factories in Poland, a country still in the Communist eastern bloc. To assure quality output and reliable delivery, IKEA brought its know-how, taught its processes, and even provided machinery to the new suppliers, revitalizing Poland's furniture industry as it did so. Poland soon became IKEA's largest source and, to Kamprad's delight, at much lower costs—once again allowing him to reduce his prices.

Following its success in Poland, IKEA adopted a general procurement principle that it should not own its means of production but should seek to develop close ties by supporting its suppliers in a long-term relationship.[a] Beyond supply contracts and technology transfer, the relationship led IKEA to make loans to its suppliers at reasonable rates, repayable through future shipments. "Our objective is to develop long-term business partners," explained a senior purchasing manager. "We commit to doing all we can to keep them competitive—as long as they remain equally committed to us. We are in this for the long run."

Although the relationship between IKEA and its suppliers was often described as one of mutual dependency, suppliers also knew that they had to remain competitive to keep their contract. From the outset they understood that if a more cost-effective alternative appeared, IKEA would try to help them respond, but if they could not do so, it would move production.

In its constant quest to lower prices, the company developed an unusual way of identifying new sources. As a veteran IKEA manager explained: "We do not buy products from our suppliers. We buy unused production capacity." It was a philosophy that often led its purchasing managers to seek out seasonal manufacturers with spare off-season capacity. There were many classic examples of how IKEA matched products to supplier capabilities: they had sail makers make seat cushions, window factories produce table frames, and ski manufacturers build chairs in their off-season. The manager added, "We've always worried more about finding the right management at our suppliers than finding high-tech facilities. We will always help good management to develop their capacity."

Growing Retail: Expanding Abroad

Building on the success of his first store, Kamprad self-financed a store in Stockholm in 1965. Recognizing a growing use of automobiles in Sweden, he bucked the practice of having a downtown showroom and opted for a suburban location with ample parking space. When customers drove home with their furniture in flat packed boxes, they assumed two of the costliest parts of traditional furniture retailing—home delivery and assembly.

In 1963, even before the Stockholm store had opened, IKEA had expanded into Oslo, Norway. A decade later, Switzerland became its first non-Scandinavian market, and in 1974 IKEA entered Germany, which soon became its largest market. (See **Exhibit 1** for IKEA's worldwide expansion.) At each new store the same simple Scandinavian-design products were backed up with a catalog and offbeat advertising, presenting the company as "those impossible Swedes with strange ideas." And reflecting the company's conservative values, each new entry was financed by previous successes.[b]

During this expansion, the IKEA concept evolved and became increasingly formalized. (**Exhibit 2** summarizes important events in IKEA's corporate history.) It still built large, suburban stores with knockdown furniture in flat packages the customers brought home to assemble themselves. But as the concept was refined, the company required that each store follow a predetermined design, set up to maximize customers' exposure to the product range. The concept mandated, for instance, that the living room interiors should follow immediately after the entrance. IKEA also serviced customers with features such as a playroom for children, a low-priced restaurant, and a "Sweden Shop" for groceries that had made IKEA Sweden's leading food exporter. At the same time, the range gradually

---

[a]This policy was modified after a number of East European suppliers broke their contracts with IKEA after the fall of the Berlin Wall opened new markets for them. IKEA's subsequent supply chain problems and loss of substantial investments led management to develop an internal production company, Swedwood, to ensure delivery stability. However, it was decided that only a limited amount of IKEA's purchases (perhaps 10%) should be sourced from Swedwood.

[b] By 2005, company lore had it that IKEA had only taken one bank loan in its corporate history—which it had paid back as soon as the cash flow allowed.

3

expanded beyond furniture to include a full line of home furnishing products such as textiles, kitchen utensils, flooring, rugs and carpets, lamps, and plants.

The Emerging Culture and Values[5]

As Kamprad's evolving business philosophy was formalized into the IKEA vision statement, "To create a better everyday life for the many people," it became the foundation of the company's strategy of selling affordable, good-quality furniture to mass-market consumers around the world. The cultural norms and values that developed to support the strategy's implementation were also, in many ways, an extension of Kamprad's personal beliefs and style. "The true IKEA spirit," he remarked, "is founded on our enthusiasm, our constant will to renew, on our cost-consciousness, on our willingness to assume responsibility and to help, on our humbleness before the task, and on the simplicity of our behavior." As well as a summary of his aspiration for the company's behavioral norms, it was also a good statement of Kamprad's own personal management style.

Over the years a very distinct organizational culture and management style emerged in IKEA reflecting these values. For example, the company operated very informally as evidenced by the open-plan office landscape, where even the CEO did not have a separate office, and the familiar and personal way all employees addressed one another. But that informality often masked an intensity that derived from the organization's high self-imposed standards. As one senior executive explained, "Because there is no security available behind status or closed doors, this environment actually puts pressure on people to perform."

The IKEA management process also stressed simplicity and attention to detail. "Complicated rules paralyze!" said Kamprad. The company organized "anti-bureaucrat week" every year, requiring all managers to spend time working in a store to reestablish contact with the front line and the consumer. The workpace was such that executives joked that IKEA believed in "management by running around."

Cost consciousness was another strong part of the management culture. "Waste of resources," said Kamprad, "is a mortal sin at IKEA. Expensive solutions are often signs of mediocrity, and an idea without a price tag is never acceptable." Although cost consciousness extended into all aspects of the operation, travel and entertainment expenses were particularly sensitive. "We do not set any price on time," remarked an executive, recalling that he had once phoned Kamprad to get approval to fly first class. He explained that economy class was full and that he had an urgent appointment to keep. "There is no first class in IKEA," Kamprad had replied. "Perhaps you should go by car." The executive completed the 350-mile trip by taxi.

The search for creative solutions was also highly prized with IKEA. Kamprad had written, "Only while sleeping one makes no mistakes. The fear of making mistakes is the root of bureaucracy and the enemy of all evolution." Though planning for the future was encouraged, overanalysis was not. "Exaggerated planning can be fatal," Kamprad advised his executives. "Let simplicity and common sense characterize your planning."

In 1976, Kamprad felt the need to commit to paper the values that had developed in IKEA during the previous decades. His thesis, *Testament of a Furniture Dealer*, became an important means for spreading the IKEA philosophy, particularly during its period of rapid international expansion. (Extracts of the *Testament* are given in **Exhibit 3**.) Specially trained "IKEA ambassadors" were assigned to key positions in all units to spread the company's philosophy and values by educating their subordinates and by acting as role models.

4

In 1986, when Kamprad stepped down, Anders Moberg, a company veteran who had once been Kamprad's personal assistant, took over as president and CEO. But Kamprad remained intimately involved as chairman, and his influence extended well beyond the ongoing daily operations: he was the self-appointed guardian of IKEA's deeply embedded culture and values.

Waking up to Environmental and Social Issues

By the mid-1990s, IKEA was the world's largest specialized furniture retailer. Sales for the IKEA Group for the financial year ending August 1994 totaled SEK 35 billion (about $4.5 billion). In the previous year, more than 116 million people had visited one of the 98 IKEA stores in 17 countries, most of them drawn there by the company's product catalog, which was printed yearly in 72 million copies in 34 languages. The privately held company did not report profit levels, but one estimate put its net margin at 8.4% in 1994, yielding a net profit of SEK 2.9 billion (about $375 million).[6]

After decades of seeking new sources, in the mid-1990s IKEA worked with almost 2,300 suppliers in 70 countries, sourcing a range of around 11,200 products. Its relationship with its suppliers was dominated by commercial issues, and its 24 trading service offices in 19 countries primarily monitored production, tested new product ideas, negotiated prices, and checked quality. (See **Exhibit 4** for selected IKEA figures in 1994.) That relationship began to change during the 1980s, however, when environmental problems emerged with some of its products. And it was even more severely challenged in the mid-1990s when accusations of IKEA suppliers using child labor surfaced.

The Environmental Wake-Up: Formaldehyde

In the early 1980s, Danish authorities passed regulations to define limits for formaldehyde emissions permissible in building products. The chemical compound was used as binding glue in materials such as plywood and particleboard and often seeped out as gas. At concentrations above 0.1 mg/kg in air, it could cause watery eyes, headaches, a burning sensation in the throat, and difficulty breathing. With IKEA's profile as a leading local furniture retailer using particleboard in many of its products, it became a prime target for regulators wanting to publicize the new standards. So when tests showed that some IKEA products emitted more formaldehyde than was allowed by legislation, the case was widely publicized and the company was fined. More significantly—and the real lesson for IKEA—was that due to the publicity, its sales dropped 20% in Denmark.

In response to this situation, the company quickly established stringent requirements regarding formaldehyde emissions but soon found that suppliers were failing to meet its standards. The problem was that most of its suppliers bought from subsuppliers, who in turn bought the binding materials from glue manufacturers. Eventually, IKEA decided it would have to work directly with the glue-producing chemical companies and, with the collaboration of companies such as ICI and BASF, soon found ways to reduce the formaldehyde off-gassing in its products.[7]

A decade later, however, the formaldehyde problem returned. In 1992, an investigative team from a large German newspaper and TV company found that IKEA's best-selling bookcase series, Billy, had emissions higher than German legislation allowed. This time, however, the source of the problem was not the glue but the lacquer on the bookshelves. In the wake of headlines describing "deadly poisoned bookshelves," IKEA immediately stopped both the production and sales of Billy bookcases worldwide and corrected the problem before resuming distribution. Not counting the cost of lost sales and production or the damage to goodwill, the Billy incident was estimated to have cost IKEA $6 million to $7 million.[8]

These events prompted IKEA to address broader environmental concerns more directly. Since wood was the principal material in about half of all IKEA products, forestry became a natural starting point. Following discussions with both Greenpeace and World Wide Fund for Nature (WWF, formerly World Wildlife Fund) and using standards set by the Forest Stewardship Council, IKEA established a forestry policy stating that IKEA would not accept any timber, veneer, plywood, or layer-glued wood from intact natural forests or from forests with a high conservation value. This meant that IKEA had to be willing to take on the task of tracing all wood used in IKEA products back to its source.[9] To monitor compliance, the company appointed forest managers to carry out random checks of wood suppliers and run projects on responsible forestry around the world.

In addition to forestry, IKEA identified four other areas where environmental criteria were to be applied to its business operations: adapting the product range; working with suppliers; transport and distribution; and ensuring environmentally conscious stores. For instance, in 1992, the company began using chlorine-free recycled paper in its catalogs; it redesigned the best-selling OGLA chair—originally manufactured from beech—so it could be made using waste material from yogurt cup production; and it redefined its packaging principles to eliminate any use of PVC. The company also maintained its partnership with WWF, resulting in numerous projects on global conservation, and funded a global forest watch program to map intact natural forests worldwide. In addition, it engaged in an ongoing dialogue with Greenpeace on forestry.[10]

The Social Wake-Up: Child Labor

In 1994, as IKEA was still working to resolve the formaldehyde problems, a Swedish television documentary showed children in Pakistan working at weaving looms. Among the several Swedish companies mentioned in the film as importers of carpets from Pakistan, IKEA was the only high-profile name on the list. Just two months into her job as business area manager for carpets, Marianne Barner recalled the shockwaves that the TV program sent through the company:

> The use of child labor was not a high-profile public issue at the time. In fact, the U.N. Convention on the Rights of the Child had only been published in December 1989. So, media attention like this TV program had an important role to play in raising awareness on a topic not well known and understood—including at IKEA. . . . We were caught completely unaware. It was not something we had been paying attention to. For example, I had spent a couple of months in India learning about trading but got no exposure to child labor. Our buyers met suppliers in their city offices and rarely got out to where production took place. . . . Our immediate response to the program was to apologize for our ignorance and acknowledge that we were not in full control of this problem. But we also committed to do something about it.

As part of its response, IKEA sent a legal team to Geneva to seek input and advice from the International Labor Organization (ILO) on how to deal with the problem. They learned that Convention 138, adopted by the ILO in 1973 and ratified by 120 countries, committed ratifying countries to working for the abolition of labor by children under 15 or the age of compulsory schooling in that country. India, Pakistan, and Nepal were not signatories to the convention.[11] Following these discussions with the ILO, IKEA added a clause to all supply contracts—a "black-and-white" clause, as Barner put it—stating simply that if the supplier employed children under legal working age, the contract would be cancelled.

To take the load off field trading managers and to provide some independence to the monitoring process, the company appointed a third-party agent to monitor child labor practices at its suppliers in India and Pakistan. Because this type of external monitoring was very unusual, IKEA had some difficulty locating a reputable and competent company to perform the task. Finally, they appointed a well-known Scandinavian company with extensive experience in providing external monitoring of companies' quality assurance programs and gave them the mandate not only to investigate complaints but also to undertake random audits of child labor practices at suppliers' factories.

Early Lessons: A Deeply Embedded Problem

With India being the biggest purchasing source for carpets and rugs, Barner contacted Swedish Save the Children, UNICEF, and the ILO to expand her understanding and to get advice about the issue of child labor, especially in South Asia. She soon found that hard data was often elusive. While estimates of child labor in India varied from the government's 1991 census figure of 11.3 million children under 15 working[12] to Human Rights Watch's estimate of between 60 million and 115 million child laborers,[13] it was clear that a very large number of Indian children as young as five years old worked in agriculture, mining, quarrying, and manufacturing, as well as acting as household servants, street vendors, or beggars. Of this total, an estimated 200,000 were employed in the carpet industry, working on looms in large factories, for small subcontractors, and in homes where whole families worked on looms to earn extra income.[14]

Children could be bonded—essentially placed in servitude—in order to pay off debts incurred by their parents, typically in the range of 1,000 to 10,000 rupees ($30 to $300). But due to the astronomical interest rates and the very low wages offered to children, it could take years to pay off such loans. Indeed, some indentured child laborers eventually passed on the debt to their own children. The Indian government stated that it was committed to the abolition of bonded labor, which had been illegal since the Children (Pledging of Labour) Act passed under British rule in 1933. The practice continued to be widespread, however, and to reinforce the earlier law, the government passed the Bonded Labour System (Abolition) Act in 1976.[15]

But the government took a less absolute stand on unbonded child labor, which it characterized as "a socioeconomic phenomenon arising out of poverty and the lack of development." The Child Labour (Prohibition and Regulation) Act of 1986 prohibited the use of child labor (applying to those under 14) in certain defined "hazardous industries" and regulated children's hours and working conditions in others. But the government felt that the majority of child labor involved "children working alongside and under the supervision of their parents" in agriculture, cottage industries, and service roles. Indeed, the law specifically permitted children to work in craft industries "in order not to outlaw the passage of specialized handicraft skills from generation to generation."[16] Critics charged that even with these laws on the books, exploitive child labor—including bonded labor—was widespread because laws were poorly enforced and prosecution rarely severe.[17]

Action Required: New Issues, New Options

In the fall of 1994, after managing the initial response to the crisis, Barner and her direct manager traveled to India, Nepal, and Pakistan to learn more. Barner recalled the trip: "We felt the need to educate ourselves, so we met with our suppliers. But we also met with unions, politicians, activists, NGOs, U.N. organizations, and carpet export organizations. We even went out on unannounced carpet factory raids with local NGOs; we saw child labor, and we were thrown out of some places."

On the trip, Barner also learned of the formation of the Rugmark Foundation, a recently initiated industry response to the child labor problem in the Indian carpet industry. Triggered by a consumer awareness program started by human rights organizations, consumer activists, and trade unions in Germany in the early 1990s, the Indo-German Export Promotion Council had joined up with key

Indian carpet manufacturers and exporters and some Indian NGOs to develop a label certifying that the hand-knotted carpets to which it was attached were made without the use of child labor. To implement this idea, the Rugmark Foundation was organized to supervise the use of the label. It expected to begin exporting rugs carrying a unique identifying number in early 1995. As a major purchaser of Indian rugs, IKEA was invited to sign up with Rugmark as a way of dealing with the ongoing potential for child labor problems on products sourced from India.

On her return to Sweden, Barner again met frequently with the Swedish Save the Children's expert on child labor. "The people there had a very forward-looking view on the issue and taught us a lot," said Barner. "Above all, they emphasized the need to ensure you always do what is in the best interests of the child." This was the principle set at the heart of the U.N. Convention on the Rights of the Child (1989), a document with which Barner was now quite familiar. (See **Exhibit 5** for Article 32 from the U.N. Convention on the Rights of the Child.)

The more Barner learned, the more complex the situation became. As a business area manager with full profit-and-loss responsibility for carpets, she knew she had to protect not only her business but also the IKEA brand and image. Yet she viewed her responsibility as broader than this: She felt the company should do something that would make a difference in the lives of the children she had seen. It was a view that was not universally held within IKEA, where many were concerned that a very proactive stand could put the business at a significant cost disadvantage to its competitors.

A New Crisis

Then, in the spring of 1995, a year after IKEA began to address this issue, a well-known German documentary maker notified the company that a film he had made was about to be broadcast on German television showing children working at looms at Rangan Exports, one of IKEA's major suppliers. While refusing to let the company preview the video, the filmmaker produced still shots taken directly from the video. The producer then invited IKEA to send someone to take part in a live discussion during the airing of the program. Said Barner, "Compared to the Swedish program, which documented the use of child labor in Pakistan as a serious report about an important issue without targeting any single company, it was immediately clear that this German-produced program planned to take a confrontational and aggressive approach aimed directly at IKEA and one of its suppliers."

For Barner, the first question was whether to recommend that IKEA participate in the program or decline the invitation. Beyond the immediate public relations issue, she also had to decide how to deal with Rangan Exports' apparent violation of the contractual commitment it had made not to use child labor. And finally, this crisis raised the issue of whether the overall approach IKEA had been taking to the issue of child labor was appropriate. Should the company continue to try to deal with the issue through its own relationships with its suppliers? Should it step back and allow Rugmark to monitor the use of child labor on its behalf? Or should it recognize that the problem was too deeply embedded in the culture of these countries for it to have any real impact and simply withdraw?

Exhibit 1   IKEA Stores, Fiscal Year Ending August 1994

a. Historical Store Growth

	1954	1964	1974	1984	1994
Number of Stores	0	2	9	52	114

b. Country's First Store

Year	First Store (with city) Country	City
1958	Sweden	Älmhult
1963	Norway	Oslo
1969	Denmark	Copenhagen
1973	Switzerland	Zürich
1974	Germany	Munich
1975	Australia	Artamon
1976	Canada	Vancouver
1977	Austria	Vienna
1978	Netherlands	Rotterdam
1978	Singapore	Singapore
1980	Spain	Gran Canaria
1981	Iceland	Reykjavik
1981	France	Paris
1983	Saudi Arabia	Jeddah
1984	Belgium	Brussels
1984	Kuwait	Kuwait City
1985	United States	Philadelphia
1987	United Kingdom	Manchester
1988	Hong Kong	Hong Kong
1989	Italy	Milan
1990	Hungary	Budapest
1991	Poland	Platan
1991	Czech Republic	Prague
1991	United Arab Emirates	Dubai
1992	Slovakia	Bratislava
1994	Taiwan	Taipei

Source: IKEA website, http://franchisor.ikea.com/txtfacts.html, accessed October 15, 2004.

9

Exhibit 2   IKEA History: Selected Events

Year	Event
1943	IKEA is founded. Ingvar Kamprad constructs the company name from his initials (**I**ngvar **K**amprad), his home farm (**E**lmtaryd), and its parish (**A**gunnaryd).
1945	The first IKEA ad appears in press, advertising mail-order products.
1948	Furniture is introduced into the IKEA product range. Products are still only advertised through ads.
1951	The first IKEA catalogue is distributed.
1955	IKEA starts to design its own furniture.
1956	Self-assembly furniture in flat packs is introduced.
1958	The first IKEA store opens in Älmhult, Sweden.
1961	Contract with Polish sources, IKEA's first non-Scandinavian suppliers. First delivery is 20,000 chairs.
1963	The first IKEA store outside Sweden opens in Norway.
1965	IKEA opens in Stockholm, introducing the self-serve concept to furniture retailing.
1965	IKEA stores add a section called "The Cook Shop," offering quality utensils at low prices.
1973	The first IKEA store outside Scandinavia opens in Spreitenbach, Switzerland.
1974	A plastic chair is developed at a supplier that usually makes buckets.
1978	The BILLY bookcase is introduced to the range, becoming an instant top seller.
1980	One of IKEA's best-sellers, the KLIPPAN sofa with removable, washable covers, is introduced.
1980	Introduction of LACK coffee table, made from a strong, light material by an interior door factory.
1985	The first IKEA Group store opens in the U.S.
1985	MOMENT sofa with frame built by a supermarket trolley factory is introduced. Wins a design prize.
1991	IKEA establishes its own industrial group, Swedwood.

Source: Adapted from IKEA Facts and Figures, 2003 and 2004 editions, and IKEA internal documents.

Exhibit 3   "A Furniture Dealer's Testament"—A Summarized Overview

In 1976, Ingvar Kamprad listed nine aspects of IKEA that he believed formed the basis of the IKEA culture together with the vision statement "To create a better everyday life for the many people." These aspects are given to all new employees through a pamphlet titled "A Furniture Dealer's Testament." The following table summarizes the major points:

Cornerstone	Summarize Description
1. The Product Range—Our Identity	IKEA sells well-designed, functional home furnishing products at prices so low that as many people as possible can afford them.
2. The IKEA Spirit—A Strong and Living Reality	IKEA is about enthusiasm, renewal, thrift, responsibility, humbleness toward the task and simplicity.
3. Profit Gives Us Resources	IKEA will achieve profit (which Kamprad describes as a "wonderful word") through the lowest prices, good quality, economical development of products, improved purchasing processes and cost savings.
4. Reaching Good Results with Small Means	"Waste is a deadly sin."
5. Simplicity is a Virtue	Complex regulations and exaggerated planning paralyze. IKEA people stay simple in style and habits as well as in their organizational approach.
6. Doing it a Different Way	IKEA is run from a small village in the woods. IKEA asks shirt factories to make seat cushions and window factories to make table frames. IKEA discounts its umbrellas when it rains. IKEA does things differently.
7. Concentration—Important to Our Success	"We can never do everything everywhere, all at the same time." At IKEA, you choose the most important thing to do and finish that before starting a new project.
8. Taking Responsibility—A Privilege	"The fear of making mistakes is the root of bureaucracy." Everyone has the right to make mistakes; in fact, everyone has an obligation to make mistakes.
9. Most Things Still Remain to be Done. A Glorious Future!	IKEA is only at the beginning of what it might become. 200 stores is nothing. "We are still a small company at heart."

Source: Adapted by casewriters from IKEA's "A Furniture Dealer's Testament"; Bertil Torekull, "Leading by Design: The IKEA Story" (New York: Harper Business, 1998, p. 112); and interviews.

Exhibit 4   IKEA in Figures, 1993–1994 (fiscal year ending August 31, 1994)

a. Sales

Country/region	SEK billion	Percentage
Germany	10.4	29.70%
Sweden	3.9	11.20%
Austria, France, Italy, Switzerland	7.7	21.90%
Belgium, Netherlands, United Kingdom, Norway	7.3	20.80%
North America (U.S. and Canada)	4.9	13.90%
Czech Republic, Hungary, Poland, Slovakia	0.5	1.50%
Australia	0.4	1.00%
	35.0	

b. Purchasing

Country/region	Percentage
Nordic Countries	33.4%
East and Central Europe	14.3%
Rest of Europe	29.6%
Rest of the World	22.7%

Source: IKEA Facts and Figures, 1994.

Exhibit 5   The U.N. Convention on the Rights of the Child: Article 32

1. States Parties recognize the right of the child to be protected from economic exploitation and from performing any work that is likely to be hazardous or to interfere with the child's education, or to be harmful to the child's health or physical, mental, spiritual, moral, or social development.

2. States Parties shall take legislative, administrative, social, and educational measures to ensure the implementation of the present article. To this end, and having regard to the relevant provisions of other international instruments, States Parties shall in particular:

   (a)   Provide for a minimum age for admission to employment

   (b)   Provide for appropriate regulation of hours and conditions of employment

   (c)   Provide for appropriate or other sanctions to ensure the effective enforcement of the present article.

Source: Excerpt from "Convention on the Rights of the Child," from the website of the Office of the United Nations High Commissioner for Human Rights, available at http://www.unhchr.ch/html/menu3/b/k2crc.htm, accessed October 2005.

Endnotes

[1] This section draws on company histories detailed in Bertil Torekull, "Leading by Design—The IKEA Story" (New York: Harper Business, 1998), and on the IKEA website, available at http://www.ikea.com/ms/en_GB/about_ikea/splash.html, accessed October 5, 2005.

[2] Ingvar Kamprad, as quoted in Torekull, "Leading by Design—The IKEA Story," p. 25.

[3] Quoted in Christopher A. Bartlett and Ashish Nanda, "Ingvar Kamprad and IKEA," HBS No. 390-132 (Boston: Harvard Business School Publishing, 1990).

[4] Ibid.

[5] Ibid.

[6] Estimation in Bo Pettersson, "Han släpper aldrig taget," *Veckans Affärer*, March 1, 2004, pp. 30–48.

[7] Based on case study by The Natural Step, "Organizational Case Summary: IKEA," available at http://www.naturalstep.org/learn/docs/cs/case_ikea.pdf, accessed October 5, 2005.

[8] Ibid.

[9] "IKEA—Social and Environmental Responsibility Report 2004," p. 33, available at http://www.ikea-group.ikea.com/corporate/PDF/IKEA_SaER.pdf, accessed October 5, 2005.

[10] Ibid., pp. 19–20.

[11] Ratification statistics available on ILO website, page titled "Convention No. C138 was ratified by 142 countries," available at http://www.ilo.org/ilolex/cgi-lex/ratifce.pl?C138, accessed December 4, 2005.

[12] Indian Government Policy Statements, "Child Labor and India," available at http://www.indianembassy.org/policy/Child_Labor/childlabor_2000.htm, accessed October 1, 2005.

[13] Human Rights Watch figures, available at http://www.hrw.org/reports/1996/India3.htm, accessed October 1, 2005.

[14] Country Reports in Human Rights, U.S. State Department, February 2000, available at http://www.state.gov/g/drl/rls/hrrpt/2000/, accessed October 1, 2005.

[15] Indian Government Policy Statements, "Child Labor and India," available at http://www.indianembassy.org/policy/Child_Labor/childlabor_2000.htm, accessed October 1, 2005.

[16] Ibid.

[17] Human Rights Watch data, available at http://www.hrw.org/reports/1996/India3.htm, accessed October 1, 2005.

9-701-035

REV: JANUARY 5, 2009

MICHAEL G. RUKSTAD

DAVID COLLIS

The Walt Disney Company: The Entertainment King

I only hope that we never lose sight of one thing—that it was all started by a mouse.

— Walt Disney

The Walt Disney Company's rebirth under Michael Eisner was widely considered to be one of the great turnaround stories of the late twentieth century. When Eisner arrived in 1984, Disney was languishing and had narrowly avoided takeover and dismemberment. By the end of 2000, however, revenues had climbed from $1.65 billion to $25 billion, while net earnings had risen from $0.1 billion to $1.2 billion (see **Exhibit 1**). During those 15 years, Disney generated a 27% annual total return to shareholders.[1]

Analysts gave Eisner much of the credit for Disney's resurrection. Described as "more hands on than Mother Teresa," Eisner had a reputation for toughness.[2] "If you aren't tough," he said, "you just don't get quality. If you're soft and fuzzy, like our characters, you become the skinny kid on the beach, and people in this business don't mind kicking sand in your face."[3]

Disney's later performance, however, had been well below Eisner's 20% growth target. Return on equity which had averaged 20% through the first 10 years of the Eisner era began dropping after the ABC merger in 1996 and fell below 10% in 1999. Analysts attributed the decline to heavy investment in new enterprises (such as cruise ships and a new Anaheim theme park) and the third-place performance of the ABC television network. While profits in 2000 had rebounded from a 28% decline in 1999, this increase was largely due to the turnaround at ABC, which itself stemmed from the success of a single show: *Who Wants To Be a Millionaire*. Analysts were starting to ask: Had the Disney magic begun to fade?

The Walt Disney Years, 1923–1966

At 16, the Missouri farm boy, Walter Elias Disney, falsified the age on his passport so he could serve in the Red Cross during World War I. He returned at war's end, age 17, determined to be an artist. When his Kansas City-based cartoon business failed after only one year,[4] Walt moved to Hollywood in 1923 where he founded Disney Brothers Studio[5] with his older brother Roy (see **Exhibit 2**). Walt was the creative force, while Roy handled the money. Quickly concluding that he would never be a great animator, Walt focused on overseeing the story work.[6]

A series of shorts starring "Oswald, the Lucky Rabbit" became Disney Brothers' first major hit in 1927. But within a year, Walt was outmaneuvered by his distributor, which hired away most of

---

Disney's animators in a bid to shut Disney out of the Oswald franchise.[7] Walt initially thought he could continue making Oswald shorts with new animators and a new distributor, but after reading the fine print of his contract, he was devastated to learn that his distributor owned the copyright.

Desperate to create a new character, Walt modified Oswald's ears and made some additional minor changes to the rabbit's appearance. The result was Mickey Mouse. When Mickey failed to elicit much interest, Walt tried to attract a distributor by adding synchronized sound—something that had never been attempted in a cartoon.[89] His gamble paid off handsomely with the release of *Steamboat Willie* in 1928.[10] Overnight, Mickey Mouse became an international sensation known variously as "Topolino" (Italy), "Raton Mickey" (Spain), and "Musse Pigg" (Sweden). However, the company was still strapped for cash, so it licensed Mickey Mouse for the cover of a pencil tablet—the first of many such licensing agreements. Over time, as short-term cash problems subsided, Disney began to worry about brand equity and thus licensed its name only to "the best companies."[11]

The Disney brothers ran their company as a flat, nonhierarchical organization, in which everyone, including Walt, used their first names and no one had titles. "You don't have to have a title," said Walt. "If you're important to the company, you'll know it."[12] Although a taskmaster driven to achieve creativity and quality, Walt emphasized teamwork, communication, and cooperation. He pushed himself and his staff so hard that he suffered a nervous breakdown in 1931.[13] However, many workers were fiercely committed to the company.

Despite winning six Academy Awards and successfully introducing new characters such as Goofy and Donald Duck, Walt realized that cartoon shorts could not sustain the studio indefinitely. The real money, he felt, lay in full-length feature films.[14] In 1937, Disney released *Snow White and the Seven Dwarfs*, the world's first full-length, full-color animated feature and the highest-grossing animated movie of all time.[15] In a move that would later become a Disney trademark, a few *Snow White* products stocked the shelves of Sears and Woolworth's the day of the release.

With the success of *Snow White*, the company set a goal of releasing two feature films per year, plus a large number of shorts. Next, the company scaled up. The employee base grew sevenfold, a new studio was built in Burbank, and the company went public in 1940 to finance the strategy.

Disney survived the lean years of World War II and the failure of costly films like *Fantasia* (1940) by producing training and educational cartoons for the government, such as *How Disease Travels*.[16] Disney made no new full-length features during the war, but re-released *Snow White* for the first time in 1944, accounting for a substantial portion of that year's income.[17] Subsequently, reissuing cartoon classics to new generations of children became an important source of profits for Disney.

After the war, the company was again in difficult financial straits. It would take several years to make the next full-length animated film[18] (*Cinderella*, 1950), so Walt decided to generate some quick income by making movies such as *Song of the South* (1946) that mixed live action with animation.[19] Further diversification included the creation of the Walt Disney Music Company to control Disney's music copyrights and recruit top artists. In 1950, Disney's first TV special, *One Hour in Wonderland*, reached 20 million viewers at a time when there were only 10.5 million TV sets in the U.S.[20]

With the release of *Treasure Island* in 1950, Disney entered live-action movie production and, by 1965, was averaging three films per year. Most were live-action titles, such as the hits *Old Yeller* (1957), *Swiss Family Robinson* (1960), and *Mary Poppins* (1964), but a few animated films like *101 Dalmatians* (1961) were also made. To bolster the film business, Disney created Buena Vista Distribution in 1953, ending a 16-year-old distribution agreement with RKO. By eliminating distribution fees, Disney could save one-third of a film's gross revenues. And to further improve the bottom line, Disney avoided paying exorbitant salaries by developing the studio's own pool of talent.

2

Observed one writer: "Disney himself became the box office attraction—as a producer of a predictable family style and the father of a family of lovable animals."[21]

Disney expanded its television presence in 1954 with the ABC-produced television program *Disneyland* (followed the next year by the very popular *Mickey Mouse Club*, a show featuring pre-teen "Mouseketeers" as hosts). Walt hoped *Disneyland* would both generate financing and stimulate public interest in the huge outdoor entertainment park of the same name, which he had started designing two years earlier at WED Enterprises (WED being Walt's initials). This was kept separate from Disney Productions to provide an environment where Walt and his "Imagineers" could design and build the park free of pressure from film unions and stockholders.

The park was a huge risk for the company, as Disney had taken out millions of dollars in bank loans to build it. But the bet paid off. The enormous success of Disneyland, which opened in 1955, was a product of both technically advanced attractions and Walt's commitment to excellence in all facets of park operation. His goal had been to build a park for the entire family, since he believed that traditional parks were "neither amusing nor clean, and offered nothing for Daddy."[22] Corporate sponsorship was exploited to minimize the cost of upgrading attractions and adding exhibits.[23] To conserve capital, Disney also licensed the food and merchandising concessions. Once the park had generated sufficient revenue, the company bought back virtually all operations within the park.[24] Disneyland's success finally put the company on solid financial footing.[25]

With Disneyland still in its infancy, Walt dreamed of starting another theme park. In 1965, he secretly purchased over 27,000 acres of land near Orlando, Florida on which he planned to build Walt Disney World and EPCOT—an "experimental prototype community of tomorrow." However, Walt was never able to see his dream come to fruition; he died just before Christmas 1966. "He touched a common chord in all humanity," said former President Dwight Eisenhower. "We shall not soon see his like again."[26]

Walt Disney's philosophy was to create universal timeless family entertainment. A strong believer in the importance of family life, the company was always oriented to fostering an experience that families could enjoy together. As Walt Disney said, "You're dead if you aim only for kids. Adults are only kids grown up, anyway."

The huge number of "firsts" that the company could claim were a tribute to the success of this philosophy, but Disney recognized that they were not without risk. "We cannot hit a home run with the bases loaded every time we go to the plate. We also know the only way we can ever get to first base is by constantly going to bat and continuing to swing."

Disney attempted to retain control over the complete entertainment experience. Cartoon characters, unlike actors, could be perfectly controlled to avoid any negative imagery. Disneyland had been constructed so that once inside, visitors could never see anything but Disneyland. According to Walt, "The one thing I learned from Disneyland [is] to control the environment. Without that we get blamed for things that someone else does. I feel a responsibility to the public that we must control this so-called world and take blame for what goes on."[27]

The Post-Walt Disney Years, 1967–1984

The realization of Walt Disney World and EPCOT consumed Roy O. Disney, who succeeded his brother as chairman and lived just long enough to witness the opening of Walt Disney World in 1971. The theme park almost instantly became the top-grossing park in the world, pulling in $139 million from nearly 11 million visitors in its first year. Its two on-site resort hotels were the first hotels operated by Disney. To generate traffic in the park, Disney opened an in-house travel company to work with travel agencies, airlines, and tours. Disney also started bringing live shows, such as "Disney on Parade" and "Disney on Ice," to major cities all over the world.

The next major expansion was Tokyo Disneyland, announced in 1976. Although wholly owned by its Japanese partner, it was designed by WED Enterprises to look just like the U.S. parks. Disney received 10% of the gate receipts, 5% of other sales, and ongoing consulting fees.

Film output during the years of theme park construction declined substantially. Creativity in the film division seemed stifled. Rather than push new ideas, managers were often heard asking, "What would Walt have done?" The result was more sequels rather than new productions. To help stem the decline in its film division in the late 1970s and early 1980s, Disney introduced a new label, Touchstone, to target the teen/adult market, where film-going remained strong.

From 1980 to 1983, the company's financial performance deteriorated. Disney was incurring heavy costs at the time in order to finish EPCOT, which opened in 1982. It was also investing in the development of a new cable venture, The Disney Channel, launched in 1983. Film division performance remained erratic. As corporate earnings stagnated, Roy E. Disney (son of Roy O. Disney) resigned from the board of directors in March 1984. In the following months, corporate raiders Saul Steinberg and Irwin Jacobs each made tender offers for Disney with the intention of selling off the separate assets. However, oil tycoon Sid Bass invested $365 million, rescuing the company, reinstating Roy E. Disney to the board, and ending all hostile takeover attempts.[28]

Eisner's Turnaround, 1984–1993

Eisner takes the helm   Backed by the Bass group, Eisner, 42, was named Disney's chairman and chief executive officer, and Frank Wells was named president and chief operating officer in October 1984.[29] Eisner, a former president and chief operating officer of Paramount Pictures, had been associated with such successful films and television shows as *Raiders of the Lost Ark* and *Happy Days*. Wells, a former entertainment lawyer and vice chairman of Warner Brothers, was known for his business acumen and operating management skills. Roy E. Disney was named vice chairman. Eisner subsequently recruited Paramount executives Jeffrey Katzenberg and Rich Frank to be chairman and president, respectively, of Disney's motion pictures and television division.

Eisner committed himself to maximizing shareholder wealth through an annual revenue growth target and return on stockholder equity exceeding 20%. His plan was to build the Disney brand while preserving the corporate values of quality, creativity, entrepreneurship, and teamwork. Concerns that the new managers would neither understand nor maintain Disney's culture faded rapidly. The history and culture of the company and the legacy of Walt Disney were inculcated in a three-day training program at Disney's corporate university. As part of the training, all new employees, including executives, were required to spend a day dressed as characters at the theme parks as a way to develop pride in the Disney tradition.

Eisner viewed "managing creativity" as Disney's most distinctive corporate skill. He deliberately fostered tension between creative and financial forces as each business aggressively developed its market position. On the one hand, he encouraged expansive and innovative ideas and was protective of creative efforts in the concept-generation phase of a project. On the other hand, businesses were expected to deliver against well-defined strategic and financial objectives. All businesses (see **Exhibit 3**), including individual films and TV shows, were expected to have the potential for long-run profitability. Nevertheless, spending was readily approved if necessary to achieve creativity.

Revitalizing TV and movies   One of the new management's top priorities was to rebuild Disney's TV and movie business. Disney had stopped producing shows for network television out of

4

concern that it would reduce demand for the recently launched Disney Channel. But Eisner and Wells believed that a network show would help create demand by highlighting Disney's renewed commitment to quality programming. In early 1986, *The Disney Sunday Movie* premiered on ABC. According to Eisner, the show "helped to demonstrate that Disney could be inventive and contemporary. . . . It put us back on the map."[30] During this time, Disney produced the NBC hit sitcom *Golden Girls* and the syndicated non-network shows *Siskel & Ebert at the Movies* and *Live with Regis & Kathie Lee*. Eisner also created a syndication operation to sell to independent TV stations some of the TV programming that Disney had accumulated over 30 years.

Disney's movie division was nearly as moribund when Eisner and Wells took over. Disney's share of box office had fallen to 4% in 1984, lowest among the major studios, and Eisner contended that not one of the live-action movies that Disney had in development seemed worth making. However, in Eisner's first week at Disney, an agent called him with the script to what would become *Down and Out in Beverly Hills*, Touchstone's first R-rated movie. While Disney had risked alienating its core audience with the film, no backlash materialized.

Beginning with that movie, 27 of Disney's next 33 movies were profitable, and six earned more than $50 million each, including *Three Men and a Baby* and *Good Morning Vietnam*. For the industry as a whole, an estimated 60% of all movies lost money. By 1988, Disney Studios' film division held a 19% share of the total U.S. box office, making it the market leader. "Nearly overnight," said Eisner, "Disney went from nerdy outcast to leader of the popular crowd."[31] During this run, Disney began releasing 15 to 18 new films per year, up from two new releases in 1984. Releases under the Touchstone label were primarily comedies, with sex and violence kept to a minimum. Live-action releases under the Walt Disney label were designed for a contemporary audience but had to be wholesome and well plotted.

Katzenberg, who was known for his ability to identify good scripts, for his grueling work ethic (scheduling staff meetings for 10 p.m.), and for his dogged pursuit of actors and directors for Disney projects, convinced some of Hollywood's best talent to sign multideal contracts with Disney. Under Katzenberg, Disney pursued strong scripts from less established writers and well-known actors in career slumps and TV actors rather than the highest-paid movie stars. The emphasis was on producing moderately budgeted films rather than big-budget, special effects-laden blockbusters. Management held movie budgets to certain target ranges that acted as a "financial box" within which the creative talent had to operate. Films were closely managed to ensure that they would come in on time and near their target budgets, which were set below the industry average.[32]

Disney's animation division was slower to turn around, in part because animated movies took so long to produce. Disney decided to expand its animation staff and to accelerate production by releasing a new animated feature every 12 to 18 months, instead of every 4 to 5 years. Disney also invested $30 million in a computer animated production system (CAPS) that digitized the animation process, dramatically reducing the need for animators to draw each frame by hand. In 1988, Disney spent $45 million on *Who Framed Roger Rabbit*, a technically dazzling movie that combined animation with live action. The movie was uncharacteristically expensive for Disney, but the gamble paid off with the top earnings at the box office in 1988 ($220 million). Additional profits came from the merchandise, as the movie was Disney's first major effort at cross-promotion. By the time of the premiere, Disney had licensing agreements for over 500 Roger Rabbit products, ranging from jewelry to dolls to computer games. McDonald's and Coca-Cola also did promotional tie-ins.

Maximizing theme park profitability   Unlike Disney's television and movie business, Disney's theme parks had remained popular and profitable after the deaths of Walt and Roy Disney. However, the new management team updated and expanded attractions at the parks. Disney spent tens of millions of dollars on new attractions such as "Captain EO" (1986) starring Michael Jackson.

Investments in the parks were offset by attendance-building strategies designed to generate rapid revenue and profit growth (see Exhibit 4). These included for the first time national television ads, as well as special events, retail tie-ins, and media broadcast events. Disney also lifted restrictions on the numbers of visitors permitted into its parks, opened Disneyland on Mondays when it had previously been closed for maintenance, and raised ticket prices (see **Exhibits 5** and **6**). Despite the ticket hikes, market research showed that guests felt they received value for their money.

The Disney Development Company was established to develop Disney's unused acreage, primarily in Orlando, where only 15% of the 43 square miles had been exploited. It proceeded to aggressively expand its activities, which included a several-thousand-room hotel expansion at Disney World (and the company's first moderately priced hotel) and a $375 million convention center.

Coordination among businesses   As the business units expanded after 1984, overlaps among them began to emerge. Promotional campaigns with corporate sponsors in one business needed to be coordinated with similar initiatives by other Disney businesses. It was also unclear how, for example, to allocate the minute of free advertising granted to Disney during *The Disney Sunday Movie.*

Like many diversified companies, Disney employed negotiated internal transfer prices for any activity performed by one division for another. Transfer prices were charged, for example, on the use of any Disney film library material by the various divisions. While Eisner and Wells encouraged division executives to resolve conflicts among themselves, they made it clear that they were available to arbitrate difficult issues. Senior management's position was that disputes should be settled quickly and decisively so that business unit management could get on with their jobs.

Nevertheless, in 1987, a corporate marketing function was installed to stimulate and coordinate companywide marketing activities. A marketing calendar was introduced listing the next six months of planned promotional activities by every U.S. division. A monthly meeting of 20 divisional marketing and promotion executives was initiated to discuss interdivisional issues. A library committee was set up that met quarterly to allocate the Disney film library among the theatrical, video, Disney Channel, and TV syndication groups. An in-house media buying group was also established to coordinate media buying for the entire company.

Management also jointly coordinated important events, such as *Snow White's* 50th anniversary in 1987 and Mickey's 60th birthday the following year. A meeting of all divisions generated novel ideas, coordinated schedules, and built commitment and excitement for the year's theme. Plans were then coordinated by the five-person corporate events department. "I think our biggest achievement to date," said Eisner in 1987, "has been bringing back to life an inherent Disney synergy that enables each part of our business to draw from, build upon, and bolster the others."[33]

Expanding into new businesses, regions, and audiences   In the consumer products division, the Disney Stores (launched in 1987) pioneered the "retail-as-entertainment" concept, generating sales per square foot at twice the average rate for retail. The stores were designed to evoke a sense of having stepped onto a Disney soundstage. While children were the target consumers, the stores' merchandise mix of toys and apparel also included high-end collectors' items for Disney's grown-up fans. The consumer products division also entered book, magazine, and record publishing. Hollywood Records, a pop music label, was founded in 1989 for less than $20 million, the cost of making a single Hollywood movie. In 1990, Disney established Disney Press, which published children's books, and in 1991, the company launched Hyperion Books, an adult publishing label that printed, among others, Ross Perot's biography. Disney also established new channels of distribution through direct-mail and catalog marketing.

In its theme parks division, Disney's major project was Euro Disney, which opened in 1992 on 4,800 acres outside Paris. While Disney designed and developed the entire resort, it did not have majority ownership of the business. About 51% of Euro Disney S.C.A. shares had been sold on several European exchanges, leaving Disney a 49% ownership stake. Infrastructure, attractive financing, and other incentives from the French government, as well as a heavily leveraged financial structure, kept Disney's initial investment cost to $200 million on the $4.4 billion park. In return for operating Euro Disney, the company received 10% from ticket sales and 5% from merchandise sales, regardless of whether or not the park turned a profit.

The company was adamant about maintaining its adherence to the Disney formula for family recreation, pointing to Tokyo Disneyland as evidence of the formula's universal appeal. Despite important cultural differences, Tokyo Disneyland had defied its critics and performed well, welcoming its 100 millionth guest in 1992. The French were more suspicious, warning of a potential "Cultural Chernobyl,"[34] so Eisner enlisted a former professor of French literature to be Euro Disney president and oversee the park's development according to both Disney's specifications and French sensitivities. The project required compromise by the staff as well as the guests. French cast members were required to shave, for example,[35] while Disney gave in on the issue of alcohol in the park, making wine available in its restaurants.

The company had set its attendance target at 11 million visitors in the first year. During the summer, attendance was above the projected rate, but the park suffered a downturn as colder weather set in. Although Disney officials publicly emphasized their satisfaction with Euro Disney, the project required considerable fine-tuning. The company slashed hotel and admission prices, laid off workers, and deferred its management fees for two years.

At its other parks, Disney added attractions and stepped up expansion of its hotels and resorts to encourage longer stays and attract major conferences such that hotel occupancy rates at the resorts in Anaheim, Orlando, Tokyo, and Paris averaged well over 90% year-round.[36] In addition to the creation of the nightlife complex Pleasure Island[37] and a new water-based attraction, Typhoon Lagoon, Disney World grew with the construction of Splash Mountain and the expansion of the Disney-MGM Studios Theme Park. In California, Disneyland opened Toontown, a new section based on the *Roger Rabbit* movie. Between 1988 and 1994, the company spent over $1 billion on theme park expansion.

In movies, Disney began to release a series of highly profitable and critically successful animated features (see **Exhibit 7**). *The Little Mermaid* (1989) was followed by *Beauty and the Beast* (1991)—the first animated film ever nominated for a Best Picture Oscar—and by *Aladdin* (1992). In live action, having once felt the need to apologize publicly for the partial nudity in *Splash* (1984), Disney settled comfortably into the industry mainstream, releasing films like *Pretty Woman* through its Touchstone studio. Hollywood Pictures was then established in 1990 as the third studio under the Disney umbrella, and in 1993, the company acquired Miramax, an independent production studio making low-budget art films such as *Pulp Fiction* (1994). Disney increased its volume of movie output from 18 films a year in 1988—the most in Disney's history—to an ambitious 68 new films in 1994 (see **Exhibit 8**). However, between 1989 and 1994, fewer than half of the company's films grossed more than $20 million, and many earned less than half that amount.

As the home video industry grew, Buena Vista Home Video (BVHV) pioneered the "sell through" approach, marketing videos at low prices (under $30) for purchase by the consumer (instead of charging $75 and selling primarily to video rental stores). At 30 million copies, *Aladdin* in 1993 became the best-selling video of all time (followed by *Beauty and the Beast*). BVHV achieved the same market leadership role overseas, with marketing and distribution in all major foreign markets.

In 1992, Disney spent $50 million to acquire a National Hockey League expansion team based a few miles from Disneyland in Anaheim. Inspired by the box office popularity of a Disney movie, Eisner named the team The Mighty Ducks, the name of the team in the movie. Shortly thereafter came the sequel, *D2: The Champions*, featuring a soundtrack by Queen, produced by Disney's Hollywood Records label. The Mighty Ducks had a natural partner in Disney-owned KCAL-TV,[38] following a trend among media companies toward purchasing sports teams as a source of programming. Nor did the Ducks' prospects end with traditional sports marketing, given the potential for other cross-marketing opportunities. In 1993, 80% of the money spent on NHL merchandise went for "Duckwear."[39]

Late in 1993, Disney unveiled its first Broadway-bound theater production—a stage version of *Beauty and the Beast*. The $10 million show was a hit on Broadway. Although notoriously risky, Disney quickly recouped its estimated $400,000-per-week operating costs. Eisner and Katzenberg were directly involved in the production's development—offering creative guidance, calling for rewrites, and restaging scenes.[40] The following year, Disney made a $29 million deal to restore the New Amsterdam Theater on West 42nd Street in New York, giving a substantial boost to the city's beleaguered efforts to revive the district and giving Disney a home on Broadway. Eisner regarded theater as a long-term stand-alone business: "Our plans for the New Amsterdam Theater mark our expanding commitment to live entertainment."[41]

Turmoil and Transition, 1994–1995

At the beginning of 1994, Disney's projects seemed to be progressing satisfactorily. Disney's newest animated feature, *The Lion King*, would break box office records by year's end. Film revenues and related merchandise sales for *The Lion King* would eventually total more than $2 billion, with net income reaching $700 million. At the same time, Euro Disney (renamed Disneyland Paris in 1994) was finally getting on track after a Saudi prince and a number of European banks worked out a deal with the company by midyear to refinance the park, which had lost over $1 billion since 1992. Yet, a series of upheavals would rock the foundations of the company during the course of 1994.

On April 4, 1994, Disney President Wells was killed in a helicopter crash in Nevada. The loss of Wells created a void within the company that could not immediately be filled. As one observer put it, "[Wells] was a practical Sancho Panza to Eisner's mercurial Quixote, a tough-as-nails negotiator and lawyer-cum-numbers guy who freed Eisner to do what he does best—think creatively about everything from movies to international theme parks."[42] Eisner assumed the combined title of president and chairman while redistributing Wells's former responsibilities selectively among members of Disney's top management. Just weeks after Wells's death, Eisner, 52, underwent quadruple bypass heart surgery. Although Eisner barely let up following the surgery (running the company by phone within days after the procedure), the jockeying to replace Wells gained momentum. At the center of this was Katzenberg.

Katzenberg openly aspired to build on his success as head of the film division by assuming Wells's position as Disney president. Within Disney, Katzenberg reportedly was seen as a highly effective studio operative but not a corporate strategist, where he was at odds with Eisner about Disney's direction on such issues as music business expansion and theme park development.[43] After his bid for a corporate role was rebuffed by Eisner, Katzenberg left the company—the second step in dismantling the triumvirate widely considered to be responsible for Disney's resurgence after 1984. Katzenberg soon joined forces with director/producer Steven Spielberg and David Geffen of Geffen Records to form the entertainment company Dreamworks. Shortly after Katzenberg's departure, a series of key executives either left the company or changed roles.

8

Acquisition of ABC

In July 1995, Disney announced it was buying CapCities/ABC to own a programming distribution channel.[44] Without the input of investment bankers, Disney bought ABC for $19 billion in the second-largest acquisition in U.S. history. The acquisition made Disney the largest entertainment company in the U.S. and provided it with worldwide distribution outlets for its creative content. ABC included the ABC Television Network (distributing to 224 affiliated stations) and 10 television stations, the ABC Radio Networks (distributing to 3,400 radio outlets) and 21 radio stations, cable networks such as the sports channels ESPN and ESPN2, several newspapers, and over 100 periodicals.[45] The deal also transformed Disney from a company with a 20% debt ratio to one with a 34% debt ratio ($12.5 billion) after the takeover.

The merger was likened to a marriage between King Kong and Godzilla. Barry Diller observed that while Disney and CapCities/ABC were ideal partners, "the only negative [was] size. It's a big enterprise, and big enterprises are troublesome." Michael Ovitz, then chairman of talent firm Creative Artists Agency, said the merger gave Disney global access. But despite "synergy euphoria" in Hollywood and on Wall Street, some observers were skeptical about the merger due to the maturity of the network television business, the purchase price (22 times its estimated 1995 earnings), and the difficulties of creating synergy through vertical integration. Some suggested that synergy would be better "accomplished through nonexclusive strategic alliances between the companies."[46]

A year after the merger, there were press reports of a culture clash between executives at ABC and Disney. "Insiders say Disney's micro-management has left many at ABC unhappy and anxious," wrote one *Wall Street Journal* reporter. "The congenial atmosphere that once dominated the network's top ranks is gone; in its place is the high-pressure culture of Disney, which often pits executives against each other."[47] In addition, some ABC executives were uncomfortable with how ABC was being used to cross-promote Disney brands. ABC, for example, had aired a special on the making of the animated film, *The Hunchback of Notre Dame*, after the film opened to disappointing ticket sales.[48] According to *The Wall Street Journal*, the initiative came from ABC executives.[49] "The ABC people are a part of our team and they are interested in the well-being of the entire organization," said a Disney spokesman. "I think we'd have been faulted for *not* using that kind of synergy."[50]

ABC had also struck several deals with Disney rivals before the merger to develop programming. ABC and Dreamworks, for example, had agreed to finance jointly the cost of developing new TV shows. "We needed access to production talent," said one ABC executive of the deal.[51] Disney felt that such arrangements were no longer economical after the merger because Disney had its own production studio, and therefore terminated such agreements.[52]

Disney Slumps to the End of the Century

After acquiring ABC, Disney's financial performance began to deteriorate, particularly in 1998 and 1999. "It's impossible to predict the day that growth will be back," said Eisner. "I think it's coming, but it's not coming tomorrow. We have not given up our goal of 20% annual growth."[53] Disney's board of directors voted to cut Eisner's bonus from $9.9 million in 1997 to $5 million in 1998 and to $0 the following year. But growth returned in 2000—sooner than most analysts expected—on the strength of the company's broadcast and cable operations and its theme parks division.

ABC had been the top-rated network at the time of the merger but had fallen to third place. However, ABC returned to the top in 2000, largely due to the success of the prime-time game show, *Who Wants To Be a Millionaire*, which was broadcast three times a week and which raised the ratings of the shows airing immediately afterwards (see **Exhibit 9**). "Television networks have fixed costs," said one analyst. "So when the revenues begin to materialize, all that flows to the bottom line and that's great news for profits."[54] Furthermore, the cable operations were estimated, by 1999, to be worth more than the $19 billion Disney paid for the entire CapCities/ABC acquisition.[55] ESPN had become the most profitable TV network in the world, more profitable in absolute terms than the major broadcast networks. However, profitability was hurt by the rising cost of programming, especially sports. In 1998, ABC and ESPN paid $9 billion for the right to air NFL games through 2005.

In live-action films, Disney's approach to filmmaking had changed dramatically. Joe Roth, who replaced Katzenberg as head of Disney's live-action movies in 1994, began putting out big-budget, star-driven "event" movies such as *Con Air* (1997) and *Armageddon* (1998). "This is not a commodity business," said Roth. "The [movies] people will want to watch need to stand out."[56] He had also argued that the change was necessary because of the growing impact of international audiences, who were attracted to movies with big-name stars and with expensive special effects that transcended language barriers. In 1999, however, several costly box-office bombs led Roth to scale back budgets. When Roth had taken over in 1994, the average budget for a live-action Disney movie was $22 million (versus an industry average of $30 million).[57] That figure had risen to $55 million by 1999 (and an industry average of $52 million).[58] The cost of producing animated films had also risen rapidly in recent years.[59] *Tarzan* (1999) cost an estimated $170 million. These figures did not include marketing and distribution costs, which typically totaled over $50 million for a Disney animated film.[60]

Disney's home video division had been a major driver of growth during the 1990s, largely as a result of the decision to release its animated classics on video. By the end of the decade, however, revenues were dropping. Disney decided to make all but 10 of its animated films permanently available. The remaining 10—Disney's most popular animated titles—would follow the old rotation schedule. Only one would be on the shelves each year, and its release would be promoted by a companywide marketing campaign. Disney also expected the growing market for digital video discs (DVDs) to boost its home video division as consumers switched from VCRs to DVD players and repurchased the classic Disney titles on DVD.

Through 2000, Disney maintained its position as market leader in theme parks. The strategy in the theme park division was to turn all of its parks into destination resorts—places where tourists would spend more than one day. As of 2000, only Walt Disney World qualified. The average tourist spent three days at Walt Disney World but only one day at Disneyland, Disneyland Paris, and Tokyo Disneyland. The company believed that the key to turning a park into a destination resort was to build more than one park at a site. Walt Disney World, for example, included EPCOT, Disney-MGM Studios, and Disney's Animal Kingdom (each with separate admission gates). By 2002, Disney planned to open second parks at Disneyland (California Adventure in 2001), Tokyo Disneyland (DisneySea in 2001), and Disneyland Paris (Disney Studios in 2002). In November 1999, Disney announced that it was also forming a partnership with Hong Kong's government to build a new $3.6 billion theme park on an island six miles west of central Hong Kong, scheduled to open in 2005.

Disney also made a major push onto the Internet, with uneven results. In 1996, Disney began selling its products online, but in 1997 it failed in its launch of a subscription service called the Daily Blast. In 1999, Disney merged its Internet assets with the search engine Infoseek.[61] This entity operated Disney's Web sites (including Disney.com, ESPN.com, and ABCNews.com) and set up a portal called the GO Network (www.go.com), which was a gateway to the Web similar to Yahoo.[62] While Disney had planned to compete with the major portals, traffic at Go.com lagged behind that of its rivals. In response, Disney shut down the Go.com portal in 2001, laying off 20% of its 2,000 Internet employees. Disney said it would focus on e-commerce and on providing news and entertainment content through its individual Web sites. "You can view this as a strategy change," said one Disney executive. "[Go.com] did not have a leadership position. On the other hand, we have been extremely successful with our commerce and content sites."[63]

During the slump, Eisner concluded that Disney needed to pare back operations that had become bloated during the company's long run of success.[64] In 1999, Disney began a cost-cutting plan that was projected to save $500 million a year starting in 2001. Eisner refocused attention on the leaner marketing of products, reduced film budgets and output, and tightened cost control in its TV production unit.[65] He also conducted a major review of capital spending, with an eye toward eliminating businesses that could not show a healthy return. Club Disney, a chain of shopping mall play centers, was closed as a result, as were the ESPN Stores. Disney also began selling "non-strategic" assets such as Fairchild Publications, a magazine subsidiary acquired in the ABC deal.

Eisner's Strategic Challenges

Managing Synergies

Eisner believed that Disney's ability to leverage its brand and create value depended on corporate synergy. According to Eisner, the key to Disney's synergy was Disney Dimensions, a program held every few months for 25 senior executives from every business. As of 2000, over 300 people had been through the program, which Eisner described as a "synergy boot camp." Participants traveled to corporate headquarters in Burbank, Walt Disney World, and ABC in New York to learn about the company. They cleaned bathrooms, cut hedges, and played characters in the park. From 7 a.m. to 11 p.m. for eight days, participants were not allowed to handle their regular duties. Eisner explained:

> Everyone starts off dreading it. But by the third day, they love it. By the end of the eighth day, they have totally bonded. . . . When they go back to their jobs, what happens is synergy, naturally. When you want the stores to promote *Tarzan*, instead of the head of animation for *Tarzan* calling me, and me calling the head of the Disney Stores, what happens is the head of *Tarzan* calls the head of the stores directly.

Disney also had a synergy group, reporting directly to Eisner, with representatives in each business unit. The group's purpose was to "maximize synergy throughout the company . . . serve as a liaison to all areas, [and] keep all businesses informed of significant and potentially synergistic company projects and marketing strategies."[66] Divisions filed monthly operating reports in which they were expected to discuss new cross-divisional projects. Eisner was said to award larger bonuses to those who had been most committed to synergy. "This award system," said Dennis Hightower, a former Disney executive, "forced us to look left and right and to build bridges between divisions."[67] When business units clashed over production and marketing plans, Eisner stepped in to referee.

Synergy boosted revenues through cross-promotion. A prime example was Disney's leverage of its animated movie investments. Typically, in the year before a movie's release, creators from Disney animation made presentations to the heads of the consumer products, home video, and theme parks units. Participants then brainstormed on product options and reconvened monthly to update one another. Once divisions had their strategies in place, Disney approached its licensing partners, who paid a royalty for the privilege of marketing and selling the Disney brand. With the help of this cross-merchandising, Disney intended each new animated film to function as its own mini-industry. However, Disney claimed its primary focus remained entertainment, not licensing. "The film does come first," said a Disney spokesman. "Without the original product, the merchandise wouldn't come to anything."[68] The theme parks also worked to increase merchandise sales. Several years after the parks in Japan and Europe had opened, consumer product sales had more than tripled in Japan and risen 10-fold in Europe.[69]

Synergy affected the scope of Disney's business geographically, horizontally, and vertically. Geographically, the company sought to generate greater international sales, especially in Europe and Japan. In 1999, Disney generated about 21% of its revenue from abroad, while other global brands such as Coca-Cola and McDonald's had figures of 63% and 61%, respectively.[70] "If there's one single realm that can put our company back on the growth track, it is the overseas market," said Eisner.[71] "If we can drive per capita spending levels on Disney merchandise in Britain, France, Germany, Italy and Japan to 80% of the U.S. level, it would generate $2 billion a year in incremental annual revenue."[72] In 1999, consumers in Europe spent 40% as much, per capita, on Disney products as those in the United States. In Japan, the figure was 80%.[73] Disney planned to better integrate its overseas operations. In the past, each division had opened its own foreign office. Disney decided to consolidate its foreign offices under regional executives, including a CFO and brand manager. Part of the idea was to save money by renting shared office space and coordinating advertising, but the real focus was on creating more synergy through cross-promotion.

Horizontally, Disney sought to enter new types of entertainment. For example, it began developing new regional venues within the United States to make the Disney experience more accessible, including ESPN Zones -- sports restaurants with interactive sports attractions -- and DisneyQuests multistory facilities with a range of virtual and interactive attractions (such as elaborate video games) for both kids and adults. Similarly Disney expanded into cruise ships and educational retreats. The company packaged its cruises with visits to Disney World near its home port. Eisner said the company was unlikely to sell the ships even if they produced a low return on capital because they helped bring families to Disney World. The Disney Institute, opened in 1996 at Walt Disney World, focused on fitness and "adventures in learning" rather than purely on entertainment.[74] It catered to adults and families with older children by offering courses such as animation, landscape design, and culinary arts.

Vertically, the company's major initiatives involved the Internet and TV. Disney saw the Internet as a possible distribution channel for its film library and its sports and news programming, among other content. "Our goal is to lead in this space because we know that soon it will be where entertainment in the home consolidates," said Eisner.[75] In TV, ABC developed more of its own content—like a movie studio. Other studios began to wonder if ABC would still buy shows from them.[76] Eisner contended that if he heard about an interesting show while walking Disney's hallways, he would urge ABC to run it. If "it ends up being *ER*, then that is strategic planning," he said.[77]

Synergy also affected Disney's costs. In August 1999, Eisner merged Touchstone Television into a division of ABC to save an estimated $50 million a year[78] and increase cooperation. However, the restructuring involved moving a New York business to Los Angeles and, by some accounts, created a culture clash.[79] Synergy drove lower costs in theme parks as well. "It would make no more sense to build a completely different theme park in each new locale than it would to completely change the *Lion King* stage play every time it opened in a new city," a company report said.[80] With this rationale, the new Disney Studios Park next to Disneyland Paris included popular attractions from Disney-MGM Studios.

But synergy had its limits. For example, the effectiveness of movie tie-ins was dropping: "In the past decade, moviemakers have been able to wring ever-higher royalty rates from licensees of toys, clothing, and other goods. But the payoff has been shrinking. Mattel Inc. felt the pinch when several recent Disney pics . . . passed $100 million at the box office but did little for toy sales."[81]

In 1999, Disney decided to reduce the number of its licensed products by half, having reached a peak of over 4,000 in 1994. "This became far too many relationships to productively manage," said Eisner. "By having broader relationships with fewer licensees, we will be able to more effectively build new merchandise campaigns to strengthen such established characters as Winnie the Pooh."[82] As part of this strategy, the company decided to place less emphasis on merchandise tied to Disney's latest film releases and more emphasis on products featuring its core characters. For example, Disney launched a national TV ad campaign in fall 2000 promoting a new line of Mickey Mouse clothing.

Managing the Brand

As Disney entered new businesses, it increasingly faced the prospect of damaging its brand. Perhaps the most publicized example was the controversy over the ABC show *Ellen*. Sparked by the 1997 disclosure that the title character of the show was a lesbian, the Southern Baptists, the country's largest Protestant church, organized a boycott of all Disney products because Disney had departed from "traditional family values." In addition, Catholic groups objected to the Miramax movie *Priest* (1994), which featured a gay cleric; animal rights activists protested Disney's treatment of animals at the Animal Kingdom theme park; and Arab-Americans decried what they felt were stereotypical portrayals in the movie *Aladdin*.[83] Moreover, Disney's Hong Kong theme park had been delayed for two years because of *Kundun* (1997), a Disney movie about the Dalai Lama that the Chinese government found objectionable.

At the same time, some felt Disney was hamstrung by its wholesome image. The Disney Channel ranked a distant third in ratings for kids aged 2 to 11, behind Nickelodeon and Time-Warner's Cartoon Network. Both networks exploited Disney's emphasis on wholesome programming based on myths, history, and fairy tales by putting on more contemporary shows. "The Nickelodeon opportunity was to get inside the lives of today's kids," said Herb Scannell, Nickelodeon's president. "We've been contemporary. [Disney has] been traditional."[84] The same was perhaps true in the consumer products division. "Many of Disney's products were designed for a 'kinder, simpler time'—the days before video games," said one analyst.[85]

Managing Creativity

Disney had hired Michael Ovitz but he left with a $100 million-plus severance package after 14 ineffective months on the job. Noone was hired to replace him as president in 1996. In his autobiography, *Work in Progress*, Eisner talked about the importance of finding a president with a strong background in finance, dispute mediation, and labor relations who could free Eisner to focus on broad company issues and the creative side of Disney's businesses. He believed ABC Group Chairman Robert Iger was such a person and promoted him to president and COO in January 2000.

One of Eisner's traditional techniques for managing creativity was the "gong show," a weekly meeting in which Disney employees in each division would brainstorm for new ideas. However, the gong show had slowly fallen into disuse. Eisner explained:

> The Little Mermaid came out of a gong show, and so did Pocahontas. Lots of ideas came out of those meetings, and people had a great time. Gong shows still go on in the animation business, but they've sort of faded off in other parts of the company. That's part of getting big and successful. Suddenly, very, very important people don't want to put themselves into the position of getting "gonged." Not everybody likes having his or her idea dismissed.[86]

Disney had a strategic planning unit that was a financial check on Disney's various divisions. Put into place by Wells and former CFO Gary Wilson, the system encouraged conflict by pitting division managers against the strategic planning department. "You always have to fight your colleagues to show your worth," said one Disney executive.[87] Eisner's "feeling is that [if] you put a lot of smart people in a room and listen to them duke it out . . . the best idea will pop out," said another Disney executive.[88] Strategic planners were assigned to each of Disney's business units and reported to the head of strategic planning, who reported to Eisner. Some insiders felt that too much conflict was built into Disney's culture. "My rule of thumb was, if you ever have a meeting with more than five other people, you're in big trouble," said one Disney executive who had recently had a project rejected.[89]

Between 1994 and January 2000, approximately 75 high-level executives left the company.[90] Some observers wondered whether Disney was putting too much emphasis on controlling costs and thus driving away its creative talent. "It's not as fun a place as it used to be," said Ryan Harmon, a former Imagineer. "It's just money, money, money. The creative side doesn't rule anymore."[91] Other Disney executives cited Disney's combative culture and Eisner's increasingly autocratic management style as reasons for leaving.[92] Eisner countered that Disney's turnover was not unusual given the company's size and success. "Every headhunter head hunts Disney," he said. "Where would you go? You go to the companies that do very well. It may not be convenient, but it's a compliment."[93]

Disney's Strategy for Growth: Smart or Dumbo?

When Eisner arrived at Disney, there were 28,000 employees. By 2000, the number had ballooned to 110,000, reflecting Disney's ever-growing number of businesses. Did Disney still have a coherent strategy for its business mix? Did Eisner's 20% growth target still make sense, particularly when Disney faced ever-increasing competition across all its businesses (see **Exhibit 10**)?

Some observers worried that the company had simply become too large to accommodate Eisner's management style. "Can a [$25] billion enterprise, with its efforts flung throughout the world, be creatively run by a single person?" asked one executive at a rival studio. "It didn't get to be that business with one creative head."[94] Did Eisner—the man credited with Disney's rebirth—now need to change his approach to running his entertainment empire?

Exhibit 1 The Walt Disney Company Financial Data, 1983–2000 ($ millions)

	1983	1984	1985	1986	1987	1988	1989	1990	1991	1992	1993	1994	1995	1996[a]	1997	1998	1999	2000
Revenues																		
Theme parks and resorts	$1,031	$1,097	$1,258	$1,524	$1,834	$2,042	$2,595	$3,020	$2,794	$3,307	$3,441	$3,464	$3,960	$4,502	$5,014	$5,532	$6,139	$6,803
Studio Entertainment (film)	165	245	320	512	876	1,149	1,588	2,250	2,594	3,115	3,673	4,793	6,001	6,471	6,981	6,586	6,166	5,994
Consumer Products	111	110	123	130	167	247	411	574	724	1,082	1,425	1,798	2,151	3,688	3,782	3,165	2,954	2,622
Media Networks	0	0	0	0	0	0	0	0	0	0	0	0	0	4,078	6,522	7,433	7,970	9,615
Internet & Direct Marketing	0	0	0	0	0	0	0	0	0	0	0	0	NA	NA	174	260	206	368
Total	1,307	1,656	1,701	2,166	2,877	3,438	4,594	5,844	6,112	7,504	8,529	10,055	12,112	18,739	22,473	22,976	23,435	25,402
Operating Income																		
Theme parks and resorts	190	186	255	404	549	565	785	889	547	644	747	684	861	990	1,136	1,288	1,479	1,620
Studio Entertainment (film)	-33	1	34	52	131	186	257	313	318	508	622	856	1,074	895	1,079	749	154	110
Consumer Products	57	54	56	72	97	134	187	223	230	283	355	426	511	577	893	810	600	455
Media Networks	0	0	0	0	0	0	0	0	0	0	0	0	0	871	1,699	1,757	1,580	2,298
Internet & Direct Marketing	0	0	0	0	0	0	0	0	0	0	0	0	NA	NA	-56	-94	-93	-402[b]
Total	214	242	345	528	777	885	1,229	1,425	1,095	1,435	1,724	1,966	2,446	3,033	4,751	4,015	3,687	4,081
Selling, General, & Admin.	26	60	50	66	70	96	120	139	161	148	164	162	184	309	367	282	244	350[b]
Net Income	93	98	174	247	445	522	703	824	637	817	300	1,110	1,380	1,214	1,966	1,850	1,300	920
Total Assets	2,381	2,739	2,897	3,121	3,806	5,109	6,657	8,022	9,429	10,862	11,751	12,826	14,606	36,626	37,776	41,378	43,679	45,017
Ratios																		
Operating Margin (%)	14%	11%	17%	21%	25%	23%	24%	22%	16%	17%	18%	18%	19%	16%	18%	16%	13%	13%
ROA (%)	4%	4%	6%	8%	12%	10%	11%	10%	7%	8%	2%	9%	9%	3%	5%	4%	3%	2%
ROE (%)[c]	7%	9%	15%	17%	24%	25%	26%	25%	17%	19%	6%	21%	23%	11%	12%	10%	6%	4%
Total Debt/Assets	19%	31%	28%	18%	15%	9%	13%	20%	23%	20%	20%	23%	20%	34%	29%	30%	27%	22%
Stock Performance																		
Index Disney Stock	100	131	218	394	471	563	1,165	906	960	1,447	1,460	1,545	2,195	2,647	3,499	3,387	3,011	3,226
Index S&P 500	100	151	186	231	215	252	325	300	353	399	428	416	562	701	903	1,089	1,295	1,218

Source: Annual reports.

[a] Reorganization in 1996.

[b] Approximately half of SG&A was due to an increase in sales and marketing in the Internet division.

[c] ROE was −1.7% in 1940, 6.7% in 1945, 11.7% in 1950, 15.6% in 1955, −6.2% in 1960, 21.5% in 1965, 10.0% in 1970, 10.0% in 1975, 12.6% in 1980.

Exhibit 2 Disney Timeline and When Disney Entered New Businesses (exits are shaded)

Year	Event	Film	TV/Radio	Theme Parks	Consumer Products	Other
1923	**Walt Disney Productions founded**	Short cartoons				
1928	**Mickey Mouse introduced**					
1929	Mickey Mouse pencil tablets licensed				Tablet licensing	
1930	Mickey Mouse comic strip, comic book, and doll licensed				Comic book, doll licensing	Comic strips
1933	First music record licensed				Record licensing	
	Ingersoll makes Mickey Mouse watches				Watch licensing	
1934	*Le Journal de Mickey* published in France	Feature cartoons			International magazine	
1937	***Snow White and the Seven Dwarfs debuts***					
1940	Initial public stock offering					
	Disney studio moves to Burbank					
	Fantasia debuts (first stereo sound)					
1949	*Seal Island* (first true-life adventure short)				Record label—soundtracks	
	Walt Disney Music Co. formed					
1950	*Treasure Island* released	Live-action movies				
	One Hour in Wonderland airs		TV specials—children			
1952	WED Enterprises founded to design Disneyland					
1953	Buena Vista Distribution Co. formed	Film distribution				
1954	*Disneyland* TV show begins to air		TV series—children			
1955	**Disneyland opens**			Theme park		
	Mickey Mouse Club TV show premiers					
1966	**Walt Disney dies**					
1969	*Disney on Parade* tours					Arena shows
1971	**Walt Disney World opens**			Theme resort		
1980	Buena Vista Home Video division formed	Home video distribution				
1982	EPCOT Center opens					
1983	Tokyo Disneyland opens			Int'l theme park		
	Disney Channel debuts		Cable channel—kids			
1984	**Michael Eisner and Frank Wells hired**	Movies—adults				
	Touchstone label created					
	Arvida Corp. acquired			Real estate development		
1985	Disney produces *The Golden Girls* for NBC		TV programming—adults			
1986	Disney begins to syndicate TV programs		TV syndication			
1987	First Disney Stores open				Retail stores	
	KCAL, a Los Angeles TV station, purchased		TV stations			
	Arvida sold			Real estate development		
1989	Disney-MGM Studios Theme Park opens					
	Pleasure Island nightlife complex opens			Nightclubs		
	Hollywood Record label formed					
1990	First international Disney Store opens in London				Record label—pop music / International retail stores	
	Disney Press established				Book publishing—children	
	Mickey's Kitchens open					Fast food

Exhibit 2 (continued)

Year	Event	Film	TV/Radio	Theme Parks	Consumer Products	Other
1991	Time share started: Vacation Club			Time-shares		
	Hyperion Books established				Book publishing—adults	
1992	Euro Disney (later, Disneyland Paris) opens					
	Beauty and the Beast nominated for Best Picture					
	National Hockey League awards Disney a team					Hockey
	Mickey's Kitchens closed					Fast food
1993	Disney buys Miramax studios	Independent films—adults				
1994	**Wells, president and COO, dies**					
	Lion King debuts					
1995	Disney buys theater in Times Square					Theater operations
	Disney's first Broadway show, *Beauty and the Beast*					Broadway shows
	Disney announces ABC deal		TV and radio networks		Educational software and video games	Newspapers (four, as part of ABC deal)
	Company sets up Disney Interactive					
1996	Disney launches *Disney.com* Web site					Online shopping
	Disney buys 25% of Anaheim Angels baseball team					Baseball
	Disney Institute opens			Educational retreats		
1997	Town of Celebration, FL, opens to residents					Planned community
	Disney opens Wide World of Sports at Disney World			Sports complex		
	Club Disney opens at shopping malls			Indoor playparks		
	ESPN Stores open				Sports-themed retail	
	Disney buys Starwave, an Internet content provider					Internet content provider
	Disney starts Daily Blast, an online subscription service					Internet subscription service
1998	*Disney Magic* cruise ship sets sail			Cruise line		Newspapers
	Radio Disney, a radio network for children, debuts		Radio programming—children			
	Animal Kingdom, the fourth gate at Disney World, opens					
	Infoseek and Ultraseek acquired					Internet search engine, corporate intranets
	ESPN Zones opens					Sports-themed restaurants
	DisneyQuest opens					Regional interactive entertainment facilities
1999	Disney and Infoseek launch the GO Network portal					Internet portal
	Club Disneys and ESPN Stores close			Indoor playparks	Sports-themed retail	
2000	*Aida* debuts on Broadway					Mature-themed Broadway shows
	Disney buys 45% of CineNova in Europe		Int'l cable channel			
	Disney sells Ultraseek					Corporate intranets
2001	Disney shutters Go Network					Internet portal

Source: Compiled by casewriters.

Exhibit 3   Disney's Business Lines in 2000

MEDIA NETWORKS   Media Networks breaks down into two categories: Broadcasting and Cable Networks. Broadcasting includes the ABC Television Network, the company's ten television stations, the company's radio stations and the ABC Radio Network and Radio Disney. Cable Networks consists of the ESPN-branded cable networks, The Disney Channel and the start-up cable operations, including Toon Disney and beginning in January 2000, SoapNet.

Broadcasting
- ABC Television Network
- TV Stations
- ABC Radio Networks
- Radio Stations

Cable Networks & International
- ESPN
- Disney Channel
- Toon Disney
- SoapNet

STUDIO ENTERTAINMENT   Studio Entertainment ;principally includes the company's feature animation and live-action motion picture,home video, television and cable production, including syndication and pay TV, stage play and music production and distribution businesses.

Theatrical Films
- Walt Disney Pictures
- Touchstone Pictures
- Hollywood Pictures
- Miramax

Buena Vista Home Entertainment

Buena Vista Music Group
- Hollywood Records
- Mammoth Records
- Lyric Records

Theatrical Productions

Distribution
- Buena Vista
- Buena Vista International

Television Production
- Program Development
- First-Run Animation
- Live-Action Syndication
- Pay Televisions Services

Televentures

THEME PARKS AND RESORTS   Theme Parks and Resorts reflects the company's theme park and resort activities except Disneyland Paris, which is accounted for under the equity method and included in Corporate and Other Activities, its sports team franchises and its DisneyQuest and ESPN Zone regional entertainment businesses.

Walt Disney Attractions
- Disneyland Resort
- Walt Disney World Resort
- Disney Vacation Club
- Disney Cruise Line
- Tokyo Disneyland

Walt Disney Imagineering

Anaheim Sports
- Mighty Ducks of Anaheim
- Anaheim Angels

Disney Regional Entertainment
- DisneyQuest
- ESPN Zone

CONSUMER PRODUCTS   Consumer Products licenses the name "Walt Disney," as well as the company's characters, visual and literary properties, to various consumer manufacturers, retailers, show promoters and publishers throughout the world. The company also engages in direct retail distribution principally through The Disney Stores, and produces books and magazines for the general public in the United States and Europe. In addition, the company produces audio and computer software products for the entertainment market, as well as film, video and computer software products for the educational marketplace.

Merchandising Licensing

The Disney Store

Disney Publishing

Walt Disney Art Classics

Disney Interactive

INTERNET AND DIRECT MARKETING   Internet and Direct Marketing represents the operations of Disney's online activities and the Disney Catalog. After the fiscal year end, the Internet and Direct Marketing division combined with Infoseek to become Disney's Internet entity, GO.com.

Disney Online

ESPN Internet Group

ABC Internet Group

GO.com Commerce

GO.com International

GO Network

Source: The Walt Disney Company, *1999 Fact Book*, p. 4.

Note: In January 2001, Disney closed the GO.com portal.

Exhibit 4   Top 30 Amusement Parks Worldwide (attendance in millions)

Rank	Park and Location	1983 Attendance	1991 Attendance	1999 Attendance	CAGR 1983–1991	CAGR 1991–1999
1.	**Tokyo Disneyland[a]**	**10.2**	**15.8**	**17.5**	**5.6**	**1.3**
2.	**Magic Kingdom, Walt Disney World, FL[a]**	**12.6**	**18.0**	**15.2**	**4.5**	**(2.1)**
3.	**Disneyland, Anaheim, CA[a]**	**9.9**	**11.6**	**13.4**	**2.0**	**1.8**
4.	**Disneyland Paris[a]**	**N/O**	**N/O**	**12.5**	**N/O**	**N/O**
5.	**EPCOT, Walt Disney World, FL[a]**	**10.1**	**14.4**	**10.1**	**4.5**	**(4.3)**
6.	**Disney-MGM Studios, FL[a]**	**N/O**	**6.8**	**8.7**	**N/O**	**3.1**
7.	Everland, Kyonggi-Do, South Korea	N/A	N/A	8.6	N/A	N/A
8.	**Animal Kingdom, Walt Disney World[a]**	**N/O**	**N/O**	**8.6**	**N/O**	**N/O**
9.	Universal Studios Florida, Orlando	N/O	6.9	8.1	N/O	2.0
10.	Blackpool (England) Pleasure Beach	N/A	N/A	6.9	N/A	N/A
11.	Lotte World, Seoul, South Korea	N/O	4.5	6.1	N/O	3.9
12.	Yokohama (Japan) Sea Paradise	N/O	N/O	6.7	N/O	N/O
13.	Universal Studios, Universal City, CA	3.6	4.6	5.1	3.1	1.3
14.	SeaWorld Florida, Orlando	3.0	3.9	4.7	3.3	2.4
15.	Huis Ten Bosch, Sasebo, Japan	N/O	N/O	4.0	N/O	N/O
16.	Nagashima Spa Land, Kuwana, Japan	N/O	N/O	4.0	N/O	N/O
17.	Busch Gardens, Tampa Bay, FL	3.0	2.9	3.9	(0.4)	3.8
18.	Six Flags Great Adventure, Jackson, NJ	3.1	3.0	3.8	(0.4)	3.0
19.	SeaWorld California, San Diego	2.9	3.8	3.6	3.4	(0.7)
19.	Knott's Berry Farm, Bueno Park, CA	3.2	4.0	3.6	2.8	(1.3)
21.	Universal's Islands of Adventure, Orlando	N/O	N/O	3.4	N/O	N/O
22.	Paramount's Kings Island, OH	2.6	2.9	3.3	1.4	1.6
23.	Cedar Point, Sandusky, OH	2.4	3.0	3.3	2.8	1.2
23.	Morey's Piers, Wildwood, NJ	N/A	N/A	3.3	N/A	N/A
23	Ocean Park, Hong Kong	N/A	2.5	3.3	N/A	3.5
26.	Six Flags Magic Mountain, Valencia, CA	2.5	3.2	3.2	3.1	0
27.	Suzuka (Japan) Circuit	N/O	N/O	3.2	N/O	N/O
28.	Tivoli Gardens, Copenhagen, Denmark	5.0	4.0	3.1	(2.8)	(3.1)
28.	Six Flags Great America, Gurnee, IL	2.3	2.6	3.1	1.5	2.2
30.	Santa Cruz Beach Boardwalk, CA	2.3	3.0	3.0	3.4	0

Source: *Amusement Business, Los Angeles Times, Toronto Globe & Mail, The San Diego Union-Tribune,* and *The Wall Street Journal.*

N/A—Not available.
N/O—Not yet open.

[a]Worldwide Disney theme park attendance grew at a CAGR of 5.7% from 1983 to 1991 and at a CAGR of 3.2% from 1991 to 1999. Attendance at Disney's Florida theme parks grew at a CAGR of 7.1% from 1983 to 1991 and at a CAGR of 1.0% from 1991 to 1999. Attendance at Walt Disney World and Disneyland grew at a CAGR of 4.8% between 1983 and 1987.

Exhibit 5   Annual Increase in Adult Ticket Prices (%)

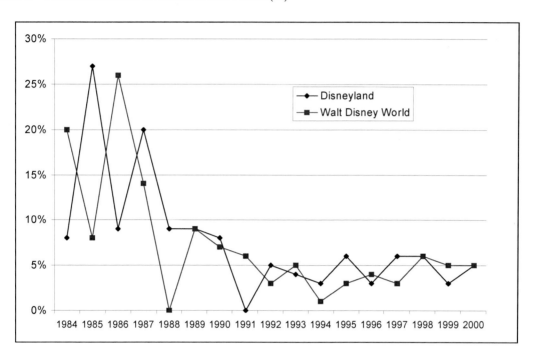

Source: Walt Disney Co. and *Amusement Business.*

Note: Between 1983 and 1987, ticket price increases at the parks accounted for about $300 million of incremental revenue.

Exhibit 6   Average Adult Admission Prices at Select U.S. Parks

Park and Location	1985	1990	1995	2000	CAGR 1985–1990	CAGR 1990–2000
Six Flags Great America, Gurnee, IL	$14	$20	$26	$39	7.4	6.9
Six Flags New England, Agawam, MA	12	17	22	33	7.2	6.9
Cedar Point, Sandusky, OH	14	20	27	38	7.4	6.6
Paramount's Kings Island, Kings Island, OH	14	21	27	39	8.4	6.4
SeaWorld Florida, Orlando	15	25	36	46	10.8	6.3
Paramount's Carowinds, Charlotte, NC	13	19	26	35	7.9	6.3
Dorney Park, Allentown, PA	12	17	25	31	7.2	6.2
Knott's Berry Farm, Buena Park, CA	13	21	29	38	10.1	6.1
Paramount's Kings Dominion, Doswell, VA	14	20	28	36	7.4	6.1
Six Flags Over Texas, Arlington	14	20	28	36	7.4	6.1
Six Flags Magic Mountain, Valencia, CA	14	22	29	39	9.5	5.9
Busch Gardens, Williamsburg, VA	15	21	29	37	7.0	5.8
Six Flags Great Adventure, Jackson, NJ	15	23	31	40	8.9	5.7
Worlds of Fun, Kansas City, MO	13	19	25	32	7.9	5.4
Disneyland, Anaheim, CA	**17**	**28**	**33**	**41**	**10.5**	**3.9**
Walt Disney World, Lake Buena Vista, FL	**20**	**33**	**39**	**46**	**10.5**	**3.4**

Source: Compiled by casewriters from *Amusement Business* data and *Los Angeles Times, Toronto Globe & Mail, San Diego Union-Tribune,* and *The Wall Street Journal.*

Note: In 1983, adult one-day tickets for Disney World and Disneyland were $15 and $12, respectively.

Exhibit 7   Top-Grossing Animated Films of All Time

Rank	Movie	Inflation-Adjusted U.S. Box-Office Revenue (millions of 2000 dollars)	U.S. Revenue (unadjusted)	Revenue Outside U.S. (unadjusted)	Year of Original Release	Creative Producer	Studio
1	Snow White	572	185	n/a	1937	Walt Disney	Walt Disney
2	101 Dalmatians	552	153	71	1961	Walt Disney	Walt Disney
3	The Jungle Book	454	136	64	1967	Walt Disney	Walt Disney
4	Fantasia	436	76	n/a	1940	Walt Disney	Walt Disney
5	The Lion King	393	313	459	1994	Jeffrey Katzenberg	Walt Disney
6	Sleeping Beauty	381	52	n/a	1959	Walt Disney	Walt Disney
7	Bambi	370	103	165	1942	Walt Disney	Walt Disney
8	Pinocchio	354	84	n/a	1940	Walt Disney	Walt Disney
9	Cinderella	328	91	n/a	1950	Walt Disney	Walt Disney
10	Lady and the Tramp	293	94	n/a	1955	Walt Disney	Walt Disney
11	Aladdin	275	217	285	1992	Jeffrey Katzenberg	Walt Disney
12	Toy Story 2	254	246	240	1999	John Lasseter	Pixar/Disney
13	Peter Pan	240	87	n/a	1953	Walt Disney	Walt Disney
14	Toy Story	232	192	167	1995	John Lasseter	Pixar/Disney
15	Who Framed Roger Rabbit?	200	157	195	1988	Jeffrey Katzenberg	Walt Disney
16	A Bug's Life	182	163	195	1998	John Lasseter	Pixar/Disney
17	Beauty and the Beast	182	146	207	1991	Jeffrey Katzenberg	Walt Disney
18	Tarzan	177	171	264	1999	Bonnie Arnold	Walt Disney
19	Pocahontas	171	142	206	1995	James Pentecost	Walt Disney
20	The Little Mermaid	148	112	111	1989	Jeffrey Katzenberg	Walt Disney
21	Dinosaur	138	138	180	2000	Pam Marsden	Walt Disney
22	Mulan	135	121	183	1998	Pam Coats	Walt Disney
23	Hunchback of Notre Dame	118	100	226	1996	Don Hahn	Walt Disney
24	Hercules	113	99	152	1997	R. Clements, A. Dewey, and J. Musker	Walt Disney
25	The Prince of Egypt	113	101	117	1998	Jeffrey Katzenberg	Dreamworks
26	The Rugrats Movie	113	101	40	1998	D. Beece, A. Hecht, G. Csupo, and A. Klasky	Nickelodeon/ Paramount
27	Space Jam	107	90	135	1996	D. Falk, K. Ross, D. Goldberg, J. Medjuck, and Reitman	Warner Bros.
28	Chicken Run	107	107	65	2000	Jeffrey Katzenberg	Dreamworks
29	Antz	102	91	80	1998	P. Cox, B. Lewis, A. Warner, and J. Katzenberg	Dreamworks
30	Pokemon: The First Movie	89	86	70	1999	N. Grossfield, M. Kubo, and T. Kawaguchi	Shogakukan

Source: www.boxofficereport.com, Independent Movie Data Base (www.imdb.com).

Note: Out of the top 100 grossing films of all time (including both animated and non-animated movies), Paramount and Fox distributed 16 each; Disney, 14; Universal and Warner, 13 each; MGM/UA, 12; Sony (under the Columbia and TriStar labels), 11; RKO, 2; and Avco, Selznick, and Orion, 1 each.

Exhibit 8   Domestic Box-Office Market Shares in Percent (with number of movie releases in parentheses)[a]

Distributor	1985	1988	1990	1991	1992	1993	1994	1995	1996	1997	1998	1999	1999 Box-Office Revenues ($ million)
Disney[b]	**4 (NA)**	**19.4 (18)**	**16.7 (35)**	**15.1 (43)**	**20.5 (47)**	**19.2 (60)**	**23.1 (68)**	**27.5 (75)**	**25.2 (85)**	**21.0 (68)**	**21.9 (71)**	**23.0 (66)**	**1,263.0**
Warner[c]	17 (NA)	11.2 (31)	17.5 (40)	17.9 (46)	21.9 (43)	21.9 (50)	22.3 (NA)	22.9 (NA)	20.7 (59)	17.1 (60)	18.7 (56)	20.2 (48)	1,061.0
Universal[d]	15 (NA)	9.8 (20)	13.1 (21)	11.0 (23)	11.7 (22)	13.9 (22)	12.5 (NA)	12.5 (NA)	8.4 (19)	9.9 (14)	5.5 (18)	13.0 (23)	954.0
Paramount	11 (NA)	15.2 (19)	14.9 (17)	12.0 (21)	9.9 (20)	9.3 (15)	13.9 (NA)	10.0 (NA)	12.6 (25)	11.8 (28)	15.8 (19)	11.0 (18)	855.0
Fox[e]	10 (NA)	11.6 (14)	13.1 (20)	11.6 (20)	14.2 (24)	10.7 (21)	9.4 (NA)	7.6 (NA)	12.5 (19)	11.2 (24)	10.6 (16)	11.0 (21)	794.0
Sony[f]	19 (NA)	9.3 (36)	13.9 (34)	20.0 (27)	19.1 (20)	17.5 (39)	9.2 (NA)	12.8 (NA)	11.1 (40)	20.4 (37)	10.9 (41)	9.0 (31)	652.0
MGM/UA[g]	8 (NA)	10.3 (21)	2.8 (15)	2.3 (16)	1.2 (9)	1.8 (12)	2.8 (NA)	6.2 (NA)	5.1 (20)	2.5 (17)	2.9 (18)	4.0 (13)	310.0
Dreamworks	—	—	—	—	—	—	—	—	—	1.7 (3)	6.9 (7)	4.0 (9)	310.0
Total	**84.0**	**86.8**	**92.0**	**89.9**	**98.5**	**94.3**	**93.2**	**94.5**	**95.6**	**93.9**	**93.2**	**79.2**	**5,889.0**

Source: Standard & Poor's, *Variety, Hollywood Reporter.*

NA: Not available.

[a] Some data approximated by Standard & Poor's and casewriter.

[b] Includes Disney and Touchstone/Hollywood labels, as well as separately run studio, Miramax—maker of lower-budget movies—that Disney acquired in 1993. From 1996 to 1999, Miramax averaged 38 releases per year and a 6% market share.

[c] Includes Warner Bros. label and New Line, a separately run studio that makes lower-budget movies. From 1996 to 1999, New Line averaged 29 movie releases per year and a 6% market share.

[d] Owned by Vivendi Universal.

[e] Owned by News Corp., includes Fox and Fox Searchlight labels.

[f] Includes Sony Pictures, Sony Pictures Classics, and Columbia Pictures labels and used to include TriStar (which was folded into Columbia in the late 1990s).

[g] Includes MGM, United Artists (UA), and Goldwyn labels.

Exhibit 9   Most-Watched TV Networks and Programs, 1980–1999

Rank	Network[a]	Program	Rank	Network[a]	Program
1980–81			**1990–91**		
1	CBS (19.8)	Dallas (CBS)	1	NBC (12.7)	Cheers (NBC)
2	ABC (18.2)	60 Minutes (CBS)	2	ABC (12.5)	60 Minutes (CBS)
3	NBC (16.6)	The Dukes of Hazzard (CBS)	3	CBS (12.3)	Roseanne (ABC)
4		Private Benjamin (CBS)	4	FOX (6.4)	A Different World (NBC)
5		M*A*S*H (CBS)	5		The Cosby Show (NBC)
1981–82			**1991–92**		
1	CBS (19.0)	Dallas (CBS)	1	CBS (13.8)	60 Minutes (CBS)
2	ABC (18.1)	Dallas (CBS)	2	NBC (12.3)	Roseanne (ABC)
3	NBC (15.2)	60 Minutes (CBS)	3	ABC (12.2)	Murphy Brown (CBS)
4		Three's Company (ABC)	4	FOX (8.0)	Cheers (NBC)
4		NFL Football (CBS)	5		Home Improvement (ABC)
1982–83			**1992–93**		
1	CBS (18.2)	60 Minutes (CBS)	1	CBS (13.3)	60 Minutes (CBS)
2	ABC (17.7)	Dallas (CBS)	2	ABC (12.4)	Roseanne (ABC)
3	NBC (15.1)	M*A*S*H* (CBS)	3	NBC (11.0)	Home Improvement (ABC)
3		Magnum P.I. (CBS)	4	FOX (7.7)	Murphy Brown (CBS)
5		Dynasty (ABC)	5		Murder, She Wrote (CBS)
1983–84			**1993–94**		
1	CBS (18.0)	Dallas (CBS)	1	CBS (14.0)	Home Improvement (ABC)
2	ABC (17.2)	Dynasty (ABC)	2	ABC (12.4)	60 Minutes (CBS)
3	NBC (14.9)	The A Team (NBC)	3	NBC (11.0)	Seinfeld (NBC)
4		60 Minutes (CBS)	4	FOX (7.2)	Roseanne (ABC)
5		Simon & Simon (CBS)	5		Grace Under Fire (ABC)
1984–85			**1994–95**		
1	CBS (16.9)	Dynasty (ABC)	1	ABC (12.0)	Seinfeld (NBC)
2	NBC (16.2)	Dallas (CBS)	2	NBC (11.5)	ER (NBC)
3	ABC (15.4)	The Cosby Show (NBC)	3	CBS (11.1)	Home Improvement (ABC)
4		60 Minutes (CBS)	4	FOX (7.7)	Grace Under Fire (ABC)
5		Family Ties (NBC)	5	UPN (3.4)	Monday Night Football (ABC)
1985–86			**1995–96**		
1	NBC (17.5)	The Cosby Show (NBC)	1	NBC (11.7)	ER (NBC)
2	CBS (16.7)	Family Ties (NBC)	2	ABC (10.6)	Seinfeld (NBC)
3	ABC (14.9)	Murder, She Wrote (CBS)	3	CBS (9.6)	Friends (NBC)
4		60 Minutes (CBS)	4	FOX (7.3)	Caroline in the City (NBC)
5		Cheers (NBC)	5	UPN (3.1)	Monday Night Football (ABC)
1986–87			**1996–97**		
1	NBC (17.8)	The Cosby Show (NBC)	1	NBC (10.5)	ER (NBC)
2	CBS (15.8)	Family Ties (NBC)	2	CBS (9.6)	Seinfeld (NBC)
3	ABC (14.1)	Cheers (NBC)	3	ABC (9.2)	Friends (NBC)
4		Murder, She Wrote (CBS)	4	FOX (7.7)	Suddenly Susan (NBC)
5		Night Court (NBC)	5	UPN (3.2)	Naked Truth (NBC)
1987–88			**1997–98**		
1	NBC (16.0)	The Cosby Show (NBC)	1	NBC (10.2)	Seinfeld (NBC)
2	ABC (13.7)	A Different World (NBC)	2	CBS (9.6)	ER (NBC)
3	CBS (13.4)	Cheers (NBC)	3	ABC (8.4)	Veronica's Closet (NBC)
4		Growing Pains (ABC)	4	FOX (7.1)	Friends (NBC)
5		Night Court (NBC)	5	WB (3.1)	Monday Night Football (ABC)
1988–89			**1998–99**		
1	NBC (15.9)	The Cosby Show (NBC)	1	CBS (9.0)	ER (NBC)
2	ABC (12.9)	Roseanne (ABC)	2	NBC (8.9)	Friends (NBC)
3	CBS (12.5)	Roseanne (ABC)	3	ABC (8.1)	Frasier (NBC)
3		A Different World (NBC)	4	FOX (7.0)	Monday Night Football (ABC)
5		Cheers (NBC)	5	WB (3.2)	Veronica's Closet (NBC)
1989–90			**1999–00**		
1	NBC (14.6)	Roseanne (ABC)	1	ABC (9.3)	Who Wants To Be a Millionaire (ABC)
2	ABC (12.9)	The Cosby Show (NBC)	2	CBS (8.6)	Who Wants To Be a Millionaire (ABC)
3	CBS (12.2)	Cheers (NBC)	3	NBC (8.6)	Who Wants To Be a Millionaire (ABC)
4		A Different World (NBC)	4	FOX (5.9)	ER (NBC)
5		Funniest Home Videos (ABC)	5	UPN (2.7)	Friends (NBC)

Sources: 2000 Nielsen Media Research (2000 Report on Television) and www.entertainmentscene.com.

[a]Ranked by average prime-time Nielsen ratings.

23

141

Exhibit 10   Business Lines of Disney Competitors

	Disney	AOL-Time Warner	Viacom-CBS	Bertelsmann	Vivendi-Universal	News Corp.	Sony[a]
Broadcast TV stations	✓	✓	✓			✓	
Broadcast TV network	✓	✓	✓	✓		✓	
Cable distribution systems	✓	✓					
Cable networks	✓	✓	✓	✓	✓	✓	✓
Satellite TV				✓	✓	✓	✓
Film production	✓	✓	✓	✓	✓	✓	✓
Film library	✓	✓	✓	✓	✓	✓	✓
Movie theaters				✓	✓		✓
Music	✓	✓		✓	✓		✓
Radio	✓		✓	✓	✓		
Publishing	✓	✓	✓	✓	✓	✓	
Internet	✓	✓	✓	✓	✓	✓	✓
Theme parks	✓	✓	✓		✓	✓	✓
Retailing	✓	✓	✓	✓	✓	✓	
Audio/video players				✓	✓		✓
2000 Revenues[b] ($ billions)	$25.4	$36.2	$20.0	$15.7[d]	$17.7[e]	$14.2	$10.0[c]
Pretax Income ($ millions)	2,633.0	8,400.0	560.6	NA	613.0	1,724.0	2,381.2
Net Income ($ millions)	1,196.0	(3,500)	(816.1)	NA	246.0	1,921.0	1,097.6
Avg. 5-year ROE	8.9	(18.2)/3.1	4.4	NA	7.6/15.0	7.0	9.0
Avg. 10-year ROE	15.0	NA	0.3	NA	9.8/11.6	7.4	8.2

Source: *The Economist*; annual reports; Standard & Poor's; OneSource; Bloomberg.

[a]Sony Corporation of America.

[b]Bertelsmann figure is from the fiscal year ended June 30, 2000.

[c]Includes only the media portions of the company. The total was $64.5 billion.

[d]The company is privately held.

[e]Includes only the media portions of the company. The total was $48.4 billion.

Endnotes

[1] Robert La Franco, "Eisner's Bumpy Ride," *Forbes*, July 5, 1999, p. 50.

[2] Joe Flower, *Prince of the Magic Kingdom* (New York: John Wiley & Sons, 1991), p. 143.

[3] John Huey, "Eisner Explains Everything," *Fortune*, April 17, 1995.

[4] In 1922, Disney and Ub Iwerks started Laugh-O-Grams, which went out of business in 1923. After Walt moved to Hollywood, he persuaded Iwerks to join his new company a year later.

[5] The name of the studio was changed to Walt Disney Productions in 1929.

[6] Dave Smith and Steven Clark, *Disney: The First 100 Years* (New York: Hyperion, 1999), p. 16.

[7] Among the primary animators, only Ub Iwerks remained loyal to Disney.

[8] Robert De Roos, "The Magic Worlds of Walt Disney," in *Disney Discourse* (Eric Smoodin, ed., New York, Routledge, 1994), p. 52.

[9] Walt even sold his car to help finance the soundtrack.

[10] Bob Thomas, *Building a Company* (New York: Hyperion, 1998), pp. 60–62.

[11] Dave Smith and Steven Clark, *Disney: The First 100 Years* (New York: Hyperion, 1999), p. 26.

[12] Joe Flower, *Prince of the Magic Kingdom* (New York: John Wiley & Sons, 1991), p. 55. In the 1990s, organization charts were still uncommon at Disney. People were expected to know how the organization worked without reference to charts.

[13] Dave Smith and Steven Clark, *Disney: The First 100 Years* (New York: Hyperion, 1999), p. 30.

[14] Douglas Gomery, "Disney's Business History: A Reinterpretation," in *Disney Discourse* (Eric Smoodin, ed., New York, Routledge, 1994), p. 72.

[15] *Snow White* had not been nominated for an Oscar in 1938 for Best Picture. However, at the 1939 awards show, the Academy of Motion Picture Arts and Sciences awarded the movie an honorary full-size Oscar along with seven miniature Oscars.

[16] Douglas Gomery, "Disney's Business History: A Reinterpretation," in *Disney Discourse* (Eric Smoodin, ed., New York, Routledge, 1994), pp. 73–74.

[17] Dave Smith and Steven Clark, *Disney: The First 100 Years* (New York: Hyperion, 1999), p. 57.

[18] The company had found that it could produce a full-length animated film only once every three or four years, rather than the two per year that it had initially tried for.

[19] Dave Smith and Steven Clark, *Disney: The First 100 Years* (New York: Hyperion, 1999), pp. 59–60.

[20] Ibid., p. 70.

[21] "The Walt Disney Company (A)," HBS No. 388-147 (Boston: Harvard Business School Publishing, 1988), p. 4.

[22] Ibid., p. 3.

[23] Dave Smith and Steven Clark, *Disney: The First 100 Years* (New York: Hyperion, 1999), p. 64.

[24] The company also established a division to create its own nonlicensed products specifically for Disneyland.

[25] Douglas Gomery, "Disney's Business History: A Reinterpretation," in *Disney Discourse* (Eric Smoodin, ed., New York, Routledge, 1994), p. 76.

[26] Dave Smith and Steven Clark, *Disney: The First 100 Years* (New York: Hyperion, 1999), p. 101.

[27] "The Walt Disney Company (A)," HBS No. 388-147, p.14.

[28] Howard Rudnitsky, "Creativity, With Discipline," *Forbes*, March 6, 1989, p. 41.

[29] In 1986, the company changed its name to The Walt Disney Company.

[30] Michael D. Eisner and Tony Schwartz, *Work in Progress* (New York: Random House, 1998), p. 152.

[31] Ibid., p. 157.

[32] Disney also sought to spread the risk of film production by offering shares in limited partnerships. Through Silver Screen Partners II and III, nearly half a billion dollars was raised to expand film and television production activities. The limited partners shared the financial cost of producing a movie but were residual claimants on the profit stream with a highly leveraged position.

[33] "The Walt Disney Company (A)," HBS No. 388-147, p. 1.

[34] *Newsweek*, April 13, 1992, p. 67.

[35] "The Walt Disney Company (B)," HBS No. 794-129, p. 2.

[36] "Mickey Mouse to Get Lai'ed," via hotelchatter.com, accessed September 2008.

[37] The rationale for Pleasure Island was that Disney World's adult visitors needed more things to do at night. Opened in 1989, the complex was a six-acre nightlife haven featuring dance clubs, shopping boutiques, and restaurants. Early performance was below par. One of the problems was the pricing policy. Each club had a separate cover charge, which discouraged guests from moving between venues, leaving the streets of Pleasure Island empty. Disney instituted a single

adult-rate admission charge for the entire area, revamped the less successful clubs, and began holding a nightly "New Year's Eve" outdoor celebration. Managers had monthly "in-costume" duties to keep them in closer touch with guests and to give them insights into how to improve operations. For example, additional food and beverage stations appeared, and layout was rearranged to better suit the waiters and waitresses. Disney also began advertising heavily in the local media, cultivating the one-third of guests who came for a night out from the surrounding Orlando area.

[38] KCAL was later sold because Disney acquired a second station in Los Angeles as part of the ABC deal. Owning both stations would have been a violation of FCC rules.

[39] *The Wall Street Journal*, July 12, 1995, p. B2.

[40] Jeremy Gerard, "Disney's New Dream: 42nd Street Fantasia," *Variety*, February 7–13, 1994, p. 57.

[41] Ibid.

[42] Michael D. Eisner and Tony Schwartz, *Work in Progress* (New York: Random House, 1998), p. 157.

[43] Richard Turner, "Is Walt Disney Ready to Rewrite Its Own Script?" *The Wall Street Journal*, August 26, 1994, p. B1.

[44] Disney had previously considered buying CBS or NBC. Disney terminated negotiations with General Electric, which owned NBC, due to widely disparate bids. And although CBS chairman Larry Tisch had publicly maintained that his network was not for sale, Disney was, according to Eisner, in talks with CBS right up until the ABC deal was announced.

[45] The ABC deal made Disney the nation's sixth-largest TV station owner and the third-largest radio station owner.

[46] *The Wall Street Journal*, August 4, 1995, p. A8.

[47] Elizabeth Jensen and Thomas King, "World of Disney Isn't So Wonderful for ABC," *The Wall Street Journal*, July 12, 1996, p. B1.

[48] Ibid.

[49] The show had already been running on the Disney Channel.

[50] Elizabeth Jensen and Thomas King, "World of Disney Isn't So Wonderful for ABC," *The Wall Street Journal*, July 12, 1996, p. B1.

[51] Ibid.

[52] Complicating the relationship, Dreamworks partner Katzenberg was still in the midst of a lawsuit with Disney, in which he was arguing that he had been guaranteed a percentage of all the future profits of the projects he had initiated while working there. In 1999, a settlement was reached giving Katzenberg $250 million.

[53] Dwight Oestricher, "Disney's Eisner Vows that Growth Will Return," *Dow Jones News Service*, November 4, 1999.

[54] Sharon Epperson, "Third Quarter Turns Out to Be Magical for Disney," *CNBC News Transcripts*, August 3, 2000.

[55] Disney's 1999 annual report, p. 8.

[56] Ronald Grover, "At Disney, There's Life After Toons," *BusinessWeek*, November 11, 1996, p. 102.

[57] Ibid.

[58] "1999 US Economic Review," MPA Worldwide Market Research, p. 16.

[59] While Disney maintained its dominance in animation, the company had failed to repeat the enormous success of *The Lion King* (1994). The 10 animated films that followed were all less profitable. Moreover, three of the company's biggest hits over this time were not created by Disney but by Pixar, a Northern California studio specializing in computer-generated imagery (CGI) acclaimed for both its technical wizardry and its storytelling skill. Disney had a deal to distribute five Pixar films through 2007, sharing the profits 50-50. To make CGI films like Pixar's, Disney built a $70 million digital studio. *Dinosaur* (2000) was Disney's first CGI film, but while the film was lauded for its special effects, it was derided by movie critics for its weak dialogue and plot. Disney had faced an assault over the past several years as Dreamworks, Fox, and Warner Brothers all tried to produce full-length animated films, but without Disney-level success. In 2000, Fox closed its animation studio, deciding to focus instead on CGI animation of the kind produced by Pixar. After several costly failures, Warner Brothers' animated division scaled back production, opting for lower-quality animation and movies based on established brands such as *Pokemon 2000* (which fared poorly). Only Dreamworks remained committed to matching Disney with several new films in the works, some traditionally animated, some computer generated. In the latter category was *Chicken Run*, one of only three non-Disney animated films in history to earn $100 million at the U.S. box office.

[60] Claudia Eller, "Disney Chief Lets Out a Roar Amid Anxiety Over Costly 'Dinosaur,'" *Los Angeles Times*, May 12, 2000, p. C1.

[61] The Internet Group had its own tracking stock and listed its results separately from the rest of Disney.

[62] And like Yahoo and AOL, the GO Network offered e-mail, chat rooms, a search engine, and stock and weather updates.

[63] Ronna Abramson, "Disney Puts a Stop to Go.com," TheStandard.com, January 29, 2001.

[64] Bruce Orwall, "Eisner Moves to Slow Down Disney Spending," *The Wall Street Journal*, August 16, 1999, p. B1.

[65] In 1999, Disney set up a new group called Strategic Sourcing to cut its procurement costs. Its function was to negotiate better terms from the vendors that supplied Disney with the $9 billion worth of goods and services it purchased each year. For example, Disney calculated that it used 110 million shopping bags and gift boxes per annum. By standardizing box and bag

sizes and by consolidating and leveraging its purchasing power, Disney estimated that it was able to save $1.5 million a year. In taking this approach with all its purchases, Disney projected that the Strategic Sourcing program would save it $300 million a year by 2004 (1999 annual report, p. 5).

[66] Disney's Web site, www.disney.com.

[67] "Disney's 'The Lion King' (B): The Synergy Group," HBS Case No. 899-042.

[68] "Disney Roars in Kingdom of Movie Merchandise," *Los Angeles Times*, August 11, 1994.

[69] 1999 annual report, p. 7. Figures compare sales levels two years before each park opened with sales five years after.

[70] Marc Gunther, "Eisner's Mouse Trap," *Fortune*, September 6, 1999, p. 116.

[71] David Germain, "Disney Earnings Drop as Revenue Slump Continues," *AP Business Wire*, November 4, 1999.

[72] Christopher Parkes, "Disney Chief Draws on the Past," *The Financial Times*, November 6–7, 1999.

[73] 1999 annual report, p. 12.

[74] When Harvard gave Walt an honorary master's degree in 1938, Walt remarked, "I try to entertain, not educate: an important part of education is stimulating an interest in things." (Cynthia Rossano, "Honoris Causa," *Harvard Magazine*, May–June 2001, p. H28.)

[75] Suzy Wetlaufer, "Common Sense and Conflict: An Interview with Disney's Michael Eisner," *Harvard Business Review*, January–February 2000, p. 124.

[76] Disney had only moderate success selling shows to other networks, producing *The PJs* on Fox and *Felicity* on the WB Network but few others.

[77] Bruce Orwall, "Michael Eisner's New Agenda," *The Wall Street Journal*, January 26, 2000, p. B1.

[78] Disney's 1999 annual report, p. 34.

[79] "Two Sharks in a Fishbowl," *The Economist*, September 13, 1999, p. 67.

[80] 1999 annual report, p. 7.

[81] Kathleen Morris, "This *Phantom* is a Menace to Toymakers," *BusinessWeek*, July 19, 1999, p. 42.

[82] 1999 annual report, p. 3.

[83] Paul Farhi, "Commercial KO'd by Offensive Punch Line," *The Washington Post*, June 26, 1999, p. C7.

[84] Marc Gunther, "Eisner's Mouse Trap," *Fortune*, September 6, 1999, p. 107.

[85] Bruce Orwall, "From its ABC to its DVDs, Disney is Seeing Brighter Picture," *The Wall Street Journal*, March 27, 2000, p. B1.

[86] Suzy Wetlaufer, "Common Sense and Conflict: An Interview with Disney's Michael Eisner," *Harvard Business Review*, January–February 2000, p. 117.

[87] Frank Rose, "The Eisner School of Business," *Fortune*, July 6, 1998, p. 29.

[88] Ibid.

[89] Ibid.

[90] Claudia Eller and James Bates, "It's Quitting Time Again at Disney," *Los Angeles Times*, January 13, 2000, p. A1.

[91] Bernard J. Wolfson, "Creative Brain Drain at Disney?" *The Orange County Register*, October 20, 1999, p. C1.

[92] Claudia Eller and James Bates, "It's Quitting Time Again at Disney," *Los Angeles Times*, January 13, 2000, p. A1.

[93] Ibid.

[94] Bernard Weinraub, "Clouds Over Disneyland," *The New York Times*, April 9, 1995, sec. 3, p. 12.

9-316-101
NOVEMBER 1, 2015

YOUNGME MOON

Uber: Changing the Way the World Moves

Uber is evolving the way the world moves. By seamlessly connecting riders to drivers through our apps, we make cities more accessible, opening up more possibilities for riders and more business for drivers. From our founding in 2009 to our launches in hundreds of cities today, Uber's rapidly expanding global presence continues to bring people and their cities closer.

— From the Uber website, November 2015

In late 2015, Uber was among the most high-profile new companies of its generation. Founded just six years ago, the company connected passengers to drivers at an unprecedented scale, using point-to-point software enabled by smartphone technology.

Customers raved about Uber's reliability and convenience. The breathtaking efficiency of its value proposition had fueled astonishing growth: It was now said to be booking 2 million[1] rides a day, and although it did not report revenues as a private company, analysts estimated Uber's net commission from drivers would come in between $1.5 billion and $2 billion[2] in 2015.

But if there was an adage about disruptive technology companies — "move fast and break things" — few companies embodied this adage better than Uber. Not only did the company endure frequent customer criticisms about its surge pricing policy, Uber was constantly battling government regulators, taxi companies, and critics who charged that they were playing fast and loose with the legal system. Barry Korengold, President of the San Francisco Cab Drivers Association, described Uber this way: "I think of them as robber barons. They started off by operating illegally, without following any of the regulations and unfairly competing. And that's how they became big — they had enough money to ignore all the rules."[3]

Still, by late 2015, there was no denying the global phenomenon that Uber had become. Like Google, its brand name was already in regular use as a verb. It had more than a million active drivers and operated in more than sixty countries and 330 cities around the world. It was valued by investors at $51 billion, which made the young startup more valuable than two-thirds of the companies on the Fortune 500. At the same time, the company was also being credited (along with a handful of other startups) with ushering in what was being called the on-demand economy, in which people used their

---

[1] Chafkin, Max. *What Makes Uber Run*, Fast Company, Oct 2015.

[2] Kosoff, Maya. *New Revenue Figures Show $50 billion Uber is Losing a Lot of Money*. Business Insider, Aug 5, 2015.

[3] Swisher, Kara. *Man and Uber Man*. Vanity Fair, Dec 2014.

Professor Youngme Moon prepared this case. This case was developed from published sources. Funding for the development of this case was provided by Harvard Business School and not by the company. HBS cases are developed solely as the basis for class discussion. Cases are not intended to serve as endorsements, sources of primary data, or illustrations of effective or ineffective management.

smartphones to connect to a distributed workforce that delivered everything from hot meals, housekeeping services, to groceries, at a moment's notice.

The Origins of Uber

The idea for Uber originated in 2008 when Travis Kalanick and Garrett Camp, both serial entrepreneurs who had successfully sold their most recent startups, were in Paris, casting about for their next business idea. Inspired by their difficulties in finding a taxi in the snow, the two began plotting a smartphone app that would solve the problem of summoning a car service. Once back in San Francisco, Camp bought the domain name UberCab.com and convinced Kalanick to run the company. UberCab officially launched in 2010 as a private luxury car service catering to San Francisco and Silicon Valley executives.

In the company's early days, customers wishing to use the service had to email Kalanick for a code to gain access to the app. After entering their credit card information on the app, customers could then summon a private black car with the press of a button. The app allowed passengers to track the car's approach; once the chauffeur picked up the rider, the built-in GPS guided the chauffeur to the rider's destination. The cost of the ride was automatically charged to the customer's preloaded credit card at the end of the ride, with no tipping required. Uber kept 20% of the gross fare as commission; the chauffeur kept the rest.

For executives accustomed to having to book an expensive private car service well in advance of needing a ride, or alternatively, to walk onto the street and hail a cab, the convenience, spontaneity, and efficiency afforded by UberCab was a revelation. Not long after launch, the prominent angel investor Chris Sacco tweeted: "Rolling in an @ubercab. Eat your heart out Robin Leach."[4] The tweet's sentiment captured the instant affinity first-time users typically felt for the service.

In October 2010, just months after launch, the company received cease-and-desist orders from both the California Public Utilities Commission and the San Francisco Municipal Transportation Agency, demanding that the company immediately cease "all advertisements and operations" for operating without a taxi license—or else face fines of $1,000 and 90 days in jail for every day it stayed in business. (See **Exhibit 1**.) But because Kalanick believed that Uber was not in the taxi business—it simply provided the software platform to connect town car chauffeurs and drivers—he just changed the company name to Uber and otherwise ignored the order.

Over the next few months, the company's momentum grew. As the company began attracting a steady stream of customers and drivers, investors began flocking in as well. In February 2011, Uber raised $11 million in a financing round led by Benchmark that valued the company at $60 million. Additional investments over the next few years came in from high-profile firms like Menlo Ventures, Google Ventures, Fidelity and BlackRock. By May 2013, Uber was valued at $330 million. Later that same year, it was valued at more than $3 billion. By the summer of 2014, it was valued at more than $18 billion. By late 2015, it had raised a cumulative total of $8 billion and was valued at $51 billion.[5]

As for the business itself, because Uber was a private company, its financial performance was a bit of a guessing game. In 2013, Uber's gross annual revenue was leaked to be roughly $500 million, with

---

[4] Swisher, Vanity Fair.

[5] Source: Crunchbase.

net revenue of more than $100 million.[6] In 2014, net revenue was said to have grown to more than $400 million[7] and a year later, the company was believed to have more than doubled that. As for profitability, Uber was widely assumed to be taking a loss. But it was also believed that Uber was profitable in dozens of its more mature cities and was simply managing its overall income statement to prioritize for expansion and growth over profitability. Uber as much as confirmed this in a sarcastic response to media outlets: "Shock, horror, Uber makes a loss. It's the case of Business 101: You raise money, you invest money, you grow (hopefully), you make a profit and that generates a return for investors."[8]

How Uber Worked

Uber should feel magical to the customer. They just push the button and the car comes. But there's a lot going on under the hood to make it happen.

— CEO Travis Kalanick[9]

Uber was a remarkably easy service for customers to use. To access Uber, customers simply had to download the app, create an account, and input their credit card information. When they were ready to summon a car, they simply opened the app and pressed a button. The app displayed available drivers in the nearby location, and usually responded within seconds that a driver was on its way.

As the driver headed to pick up a customer, the customer could track the driver's progress on a map. The app allowed customers to view the name of the driver and the driver's quality rating, which ranged from 1 to 5 stars. Customers could reject a driver with a low rating; they could also contact the driver via phone or text if necessary (with the driver's actual phone number cloaked). The car would generally arrive within minutes. Once the driver picked up the passenger, the driver could navigate to the destination using Uber's built-in GPS system.

At the end of the ride, no cash would exchange hands; instead, the fare was automatically deducted from the customer's account. An email receipt was sent to the customer when the trip was completed, at which point the customer was encouraged to rate the driver. (See **Exhibit 2** for screenshots of the app.)

Uber's prices were determined by the time and distance of the trip as measured by GPS. Uber's black town car service (UberBlack) was typically priced lower than the cost of a private limousine service, but 40% to 100% higher than a comparable cab ride.[10] During times of peak ridership—which could include rush hour, bad weather, or special occasions—Uber would put something called "Surge Pricing" into effect, which would raise the price anywhere from 1.5x to 7x of normal. Although the precise algorithm behind these surges remained a mystery, Uber claimed they went into effect automatically whenever demand in a given area exceeded supply.

When surge pricing was in effect, customers were notified immediately upon opening the app. Before they could summon a ride, they had to acknowledge the surge pricing, and type the precise

---

[6] Kosoff.

[7] Eric Newcomer and Jing Cao, "Uber Bonds Term Sheet Reveals $470 Million in Operating Losses," BloombergBusiness report, June 29, 2015. (bloom.bg/1M9YtAj)

[8] DeAmicis, Carmel. *Yes, Uber Lost a Lot of Money. (And It Will Lose More.)* Re/code, Aug 5, 2015. (on.recode.net/1kqAouv)

[9] Wohlsen, Marcus. *What Will Uber Do With All That Money From Google.* Wired. Jan 3, 2014.

[10] *We Did The Math: Uber vs. Taxi.* Business Insider report. Oct 6, 2014. (read.bi/1Mb1H38)

amount of the surge increase into the app to ensure they knew they were being charged a higher price. (See **Exhibit 3** for screenshots of surge pricing in effect.) The company's commission remained a flat 20% regardless of the price charge. As Kalanick put it, "What you are aiming for is the equilibrium of supply and demand. A perfect day is when you set an all-time record for trips per hour with zero surges."[11]

On the driver's side, Uber's system worked in reverse. When a customer summoned a car, nearby drivers had the option to respond, and had the right to refuse to pick up passengers whose ratings were low. They also had the option to contact the customer by phone or text if necessary (with the customer's actual phone number cloaked). The driver app had additional features as well. It had "heat maps" that gave drivers visibility into the areas where they were most likely to find passengers. It had an earnings icon that displayed a breakdown of the money they were making, separating out take-home pay. It had a feedback icon that displayed how passengers were rating them, including any comments passengers may have left. (See **Exhibit 4** for screenshots of Uber's driver app.)

Meanwhile, at Uber's San Francisco headquarters, a software tool called God View offered Uber managers a real-time display of all of the city's Uber vehicles—represented as tiny cars on a map—on the move, while tiny eyeballs on the same map displayed the location of potential customers looking at the Uber app on their smartphones. Uber used sophisticated data analysis to determine the best locations for drivers to wait for pickups. This was a massive effort on Uber's part; the company employed a large data science team of PhDs from fields ranging from nuclear physics to computational biology to hone the algorithms that kept Uber humming at maximum efficiency.

Uber's Driver Model

Uber drivers were independent contractors rather than regular permanent employees of Uber. As contract workers, they did not receive health benefits, retirement, disability, vacation leave, unemployment or injured workers compensation; they were simply paid for the business they generated driving passengers.[12] Uber took a flat percentage commission fee on all fares and in 2015 this fee had been raised: Uber's cut now ranged from 20% to 30% of the gross fare, depending on the city and the circumstances. Drivers kept the remainder.

Uber did not own its cars; instead, it served as a referral or dispatch system for drivers who drove their own cars. For the company's UberBlack town car service, the company relied on a network of established, licensed limousine drivers who applied to be part of its system. A growing number of U.S. limousine companies (estimates ranged from 20%-40%) allowed their drivers to participate in Uber.[13] To become an UberBlack driver, drivers had to be professional chauffeurs with a commercial license and commercial auto insurance. Their vehicles had to fit Uber's criteria for black car service. They also had to have clean driving records and undergo background checks at both the state and federal level.

---

[11] Malik, Om. *Uber is the New Google*. Fast Company, June 2014.

[12] Uber was facing lawsuits for treating its drivers as independent contractors. It was not alone in this regard; many other prominent "sharing economy" companies were facing similar lawsuits over the same issue. Uber's response to these lawsuits was to argue that the classification was appropriate, because the company was simply connecting contractors with customers through its technology platform. In fact, many cab drivers were also independent contractors for the taxi industry. Uber additionally noted that its drivers often preferred the flexibility that came with the classification, because it meant they could work for multiple employers and set their own schedules.

[13] Limousine, Charter & Tour Factbook, May 2014.

In 2013, Uber introduced uberX, a cheaper version of Uber that allowed non-professional drivers to apply to use the platform using their personal vehicles. Riding uberX generally tended to save passengers 10% off the cost of a taxi. The criteria for being an uberX driver were less stringent than that for UberBlack: Drivers had to be at least 21 years old, with a personal license and personal auto insurance that covered using the vehicle for commercial purposes. They had to possess clean driving records, pass background checks, and drive a midsize or full-size 4-door vehicle in good condition. Drivers were also expected to have an iPhone, although if they didn't have one, Uber would rent them one for $10 per week.

By 2015, Uber offered additional service options as well: uberXL for passengers who wanted the low cost of uberX service but needed a larger vehicle to fit up to six passengers; UberSUV for passengers who wanted UberBlack service but required an SUV. (See **Exhibit 5** for a comparison of a subset of the different Uber services. See **Exhibit 6** for expenses incurred by typical uberX drivers.)

When Uber prepared to launch in a new city, it would send two advance teams into the area six weeks in advance: One team was charged with building market awareness about Uber's impending entry into the market; the other was charged with recruiting drivers for the service.[14] This second team would aggressively pitch potential drivers on the advantages of driving for Uber: Drivers could set their own hours; they could earn a good income; they were guaranteed automatic payment upon completion of each fare; and they could participate in a system in which misbehaving passengers could be suspended from the system. In addition, Uber often granted these drivers bonus incentives to drive for Uber, particularly in their first year of driving. As for potential drivers who did not own a car, Uber offered favorable loan terms to help them purchase the vehicles necessary to drive for the company.

(See **Exhibits 7** and **8** for additional information on the number and earnings of UberBlack versus uberX drivers.)

The Competition

Uber competed directly against the taxi industry, which operated differently across countries. In the United States, most taxicabs required a license (or "medallion") to operate. Some cities controlled the number of available taxis through their medallion systems. For example, the number of cabs in New York had remained constant for decades despite significant increases in the population. San Francisco was another city that capped the number of taxi medallions even as the population had increased. By contrast, cities like Washington DC allowed anyone to operate a cab as long as they obtained a license and operated according to regulations.

The distinction between taxicabs and livery vehicles ("for hire" vehicles such as limousines and black town cars) was significant. Only taxicabs could be hailed on the streets, and only taxicabs could be dispatched immediately after a telephone call to a dispatcher. In some cases, a prearranged taxi pickup could be requested in advance, but such pickup arrangements were generally perceived to be unreliable by customers.

Taxis were generally required to have a distinctive appearance and to make it clear whether or not they were "in service." The price of a cab fare was based on the time and distance of the trip and was regulated by an official taximeter, although exceptions to this existed—the price of trips to/from established destinations (e.g., airports) was often fixed, for example.

---

[14] Lagorio-Chafkin, Christine. *Resistance is Futile*. Inc. Magazine, July/August 2013.

Complaints about taxicabs were widespread. Riders often found the cars to be in poor repair (seatbelts not working, seats ripped), unclean and generally unpleasant. Some cabs accepted credit cards, but others did not. Cab drivers were known to talk on the phone or even text while driving, and often needed to be given directions to the destination (as not all of them were equipped with GPS). Some cabs blared music and/or advertisements during the ride. Catching a cab generally required standing outside and trying to hail one that drove by. This tended to be a hit-or-miss proposition: In some parts of the city, cabs were easily hailed; in other areas, cabs were nowhere to be found. It was generally accepted that cabs tended to avoid certain areas of certain cities. It was also accepted that they were hard to catch at night.

Becoming a taxi driver was a complicated process due to regulatory constraints. Because the number of medallions was capped in some cities, their prices had soared in recent years. In New York, for example, the price of a medallion had skyrocketed, reaching a height in 2013 when an auction of 200 medallions netted the city a total of $200 million. There were other hurdles as well. In London, potential drivers had to pass a "knowledge test" of the city's streets to attain a license. Although GPS had probably made the test obsolete, the requirement persisted and it would sometimes take up to four years for an individual to pass the test successfully.

Some drivers owned their own medallions, but because of their high price, many were purchased by companies that operated fleets of taxis. Owners would buy them for their investment value, and then lease their vehicles to other drivers. New York medallion owners were known to charge drivers on a daily or weekly basis to lease a licensed vehicle, and were often able to lease the car for two shifts a day, doubling profitability. In cities such as New York, it could cost cab drivers—who often worked as independent contractors—as much as $75,000 a year to rent a medallion.

Once lease payments were deducted, a typical driver made somewhere around $130 per shift. The median annual income for a full-time taxi driver tended to range from $27,000 to $41,000 with a rough median of about $33,000, although this figure varied depending on location and company.[15] As David S. Yasskey, NYC Taxi Commissioner, put it: "Like a lot of the economy, the taxi industry has become a winner-take-all industry where the profits at the top are very large and the wages at the bottom are grindingly low."[16] (**Exhibits 9** through **11** provide additional information on the characteristics and earnings of Uber drivers versus taxi drivers and chauffeurs.)

Given this context, it was perhaps not surprising that some taxi drivers were defecting to Uber. A 2014 *BusinessWeek* article described one San Francisco taxi driver who, weary of paying $400 a week to lease his cab, had recently made the switch. After an hour of orientation, Uber had handed him an iPhone with its driver app and had sent him out on the road. "No one under the age of 40 with a smartphone is going out and getting a cab anymore," the driver was quoted as saying. "I say if you can't beat 'em, join 'em."[17] The article also described how the driver was now receiving a stream of offers from Uber, offering discounts on new cars and other perks.

Uber also faced competition from livery services that provided limousines and black town cars. In the United States, livery services tended to be regulated by state agencies. In most cities, these vehicles could not be hailed on the street, nor could they respond immediately to pick-up requests; rather, they had to be prearranged at least an hour in advance. Cars were generally unavailable on short notice.

---

[15] Salary.com report: www1.salary.com/Taxi-Driver-Salary.html

[16] Flegenheimer, Matt. "$1 Million Medallions Stifling the Dreams of Cabdrivers," New York Times, Nov. 14, 2013.

[17] Stone, Brad. *Invasion of the Taxi Snatchers: Uber Leads an Industry's Disruption.* BloombergBusiness, Feb 20, 2014.

6

These services tended to charge based on time, with a preset minimum. They also tended to be expensive.

The typical limo driver earned between $11 and $12 an hour, plus tips. In some cases, these drivers owned their own vehicles and worked as independent contractors for the limousine company; in other cases, the limo company would provide vehicles to a staff of employed chauffeurs.

Finally, Uber faced newer competition from other ride-sharing services such as Lyft and Sidecar. These companies allowed any non-professional driver with a vehicle to pick up passengers using their apps. Some of these companies had garnered positive momentum, but none had achieved the popularity and growth of Uber.

A Battle of Words, Regulation, and Public Relations

Although there was no disputing Uber's market momentum, controversy swirled around the company on a regular basis.

Uber versus the Taxi Industry

Within months after Uber's launch, regulators, politicians, and the taxi industry had begun fighting back against Uber, and by 2015, the battle was in full force. The response took on many forms: In some countries such as the Netherlands and South Korea, Uber was banned or treated as an illegal taxi service. In other countries where Uber operated, taxi drivers would sometimes go on strike to protest their government's failure to regulate ride-sharing businesses. These strikes occasionally erupted into violence, inflaming public opinion and headlining global news coverage.

One long-time taxi driver who managed a seven-car fleet in Houston fumed: "For 30 years I've done physicals, drug tests, keeping myself in order so I can keep my license. And now this company's just going to come in here, charge 20 percent, and let [their drivers] go?" He recently told his older son, who occasionally drove for uberX: "When you're out there for a few hours, you're stealing food from the mouth of a guy who's out there eight or nine hours — who's a professional."[18]

In reality, the legality of Uber's business was unclear. Although laws existed to regulate the taxi and limousine industries, Uber's service had unique characteristics that made comparison difficult. The fact was, the technology that was core to Uber's network represented an unprecedented disruption that city and country regulators were ill equipped to deal with. Most laws had been written before the existence of software that could coordinate real-time ride-sharing on a massive scale. Most regulations had been written before regulators could conceive of a time when passengers could summon rides from devices kept in their pockets.

Still, some of the charges leveled at the company from its critics appeared to have some weight. For example, one of the criticisms was that Uber was putting non-professional drivers on the road. This was at least partially true: While UberBlack drivers were commercially licensed professional drivers, uberX drivers were not. What wasn't clear was whether, as critics claimed, the company was actually risking lives by putting these uberX drivers on the road. Uber claimed that its background checks for drivers were more thorough than that of the taxi industry, but given the variability in how different

---

[18] Kim, E. Tammy. *The Taxi Wars: Uber is 'Destroying the Taxi Industry.'* Al Jazeera, Sept 16, 2015. (bit.ly/1iBHZoS).

---

taxi companies vetted their drivers, this was impossible to verify. (See **Exhibit 12** for driver requirements for different industries.)

Critics also claimed that Uber's prices were unfairly designed to kill off competition. Kalanick, not known for being diplomatic, responded by calling the taxi industry a "protectionist scheme" that "prefers not to compete at all and likes things the way they are."[19] In a blog post, he expanded on this by writing, "Our opponent—the Big Taxi cartel—has used decades of political contributions and influence to restrict competition, reduce choice for consumers, and put a stranglehold on economic opportunity for drivers."[20]

On its side, Uber had defenders among the many former taxi drivers who were now driving for the company. Bloomberg BusinessWeek spoke to one former cab driver who had little sympathy for the yellow cab operators complaining about Uber: "He bitterly recalls having to wait for hours in the garages of a local car company before Uber entered the scene, as dispatchers decided whether they had a spare car to give him. 'It's their fault,' he says. 'They made it so hard.'"[21]

In addition, Uber had legions of defenders among its customer base. One reporter described his personal experience switching from taxis to Uber this way:

> I've lived in New York City's outer boroughs for a decade, first in Brooklyn and now in Queens, and I can tell you that Uber has made life dramatically easier on those who can't afford a Manhattan apartment or to live especially close to a subway stop. Back in the old days, if you wanted to take a taxi home . . . the city's iconic yellow cabs generally flat-out refused to take you to a borough. If you managed to get in the cab, they might simply drive around in circles, with the meter running, until you got out, miles away from your destination. And they also routinely racially profiled passengers and refused to take anyone to neighborhoods like Harlem that are predominantly African American.[22]

Yet another journalist, writing for Business Insider, headlined his piece: "Uber has changed my life and as God is my witness I will never take a taxi again."[23]

Uber's Surge Pricing Model

In addition to waging battles with regulators and the taxi industry, Uber also had to contend with persistent complaints about its surge pricing model.

Dynamic pricing was not a novel concept; it was used on a regular basis by a wide array of companies, including hotels, airlines, movie theatres, and nightclubs. But Uber's surge pricing had invited a particularly high degree of negative attention as a result of several specific incidents. On New Year's Eve in 2011, Uber prices had surged to 7x normal rates, stunning and infuriating revelers. Then in 2013, when winter snow storms had battered the East Coast, surge pricing had again raised the ire of customers when Jessica Seinfeld, the wife of comedian Jerry Seinfeld, posted to Instagram a screen

---

[19] Stone.

[20] Swisher, Kara. *Uber Hires Top Obama Advisor David Plouffe as New 'Campaign Manager.'* Re/code, Aug 19, 2014. (on.recode.net/1iFFlhE)

[21] Stone.

[22] Chafkin, Max. *Admit It, You Love Uber.* Fast Company, Oct 2015.

[23] Edwards, Jim. *Uber Has Changed My Life And As God Is My Witness I Will Never Take a Taxi Again.* Business Insider, Jan 22, 2014. (read.bi/1H57FWl)

---

shot of her $415 Uber bill with a caption that read in part "#OMG #neverforget #neveragain #real." Others had piled on, sharing similar experiences and accusing Uber of exploiting customers. As a result of the controversy, Uber vowed not to exceed 2.8x its normal rates during any future state of emergency. But the anger had mounted once again when, during the 2014 Sydney hostage crisis, Uber's algorithms automatically put surge pricing into effect in the surrounding neighborhoods, resulting in fares 4x normal. The company later apologized and refunded the surcharges.

Still, Uber refused to back down from its overall policy of surge pricing when demand peaked. The company's argument was simple: Surge pricing was necessary to lure drivers on the road to meet demand during busy times. As Kalanick put it, "people would love to have 100% reliability at a fixed price all the time. I get it. That is not possible."[24] Elsewhere he added, "Because this is so new, it's going to take some time for folks to accept it. There's 70 years of conditioning around the fixed price of taxis."[25]

Uber's Aggressive Market Tactics

Aside from the specific complaints leveled by critics against Uber, there was also a more generalized perception that Uber engaged in overly aggressive market tactics. When Uber entered a new market, it typically just ignored local regulations and began operating its service without waiting for permission. It also had a reputation for cutthroat competitive tactics. In one case, Uber was caught trying to slow down the service of one of its ride-sharing competitors by ordering and cancelling cars en masse (Uber later apologized for the tactic).[26] The company was also known for attempting to poach drivers from other ride-sharing services by deploying its sales representatives to order rides and then try to convince the drivers to defect to Uber with offers of monetary bonuses and other incentives.

Kalanick himself had come under personal criticism for being overly combative in his words and approach. He seemed to acknowledge the criticism at a celebration for the company's fifth birthday when he said, "I realize I can come across as a somewhat fierce advocate for Uber. I also realize some people have used a different a-word to describe me."[27] Indeed, by late 2015, there were concerns that the company's was simply moving *too* aggressively—with its fast-moving forays into new markets, with its disdain for regulatory concerns, with its disregard for consumer complaints about pricing— and as a result, was attracting more than its share of backlash from regulators, industry incumbents, and a public wary of its aggression.

In 2014, Uber hired David Plouffe to head the company's public policy and communications function. Plouffe was the high-powered political strategist best known for being the campaign genius behind Obama's 2008 presidential campaign. When asked whether he was hired to repair Uber's image problem, Plouffe replied, "I don't subscribe to the idea that the company has an image problem. I actually think when you are a disrupter you are going to have a lot of people throwing arrows."[28]

---

[24] Stone.

[25] Bilton, Nick. *Taxi Supply and Demand, Priced by the Mile*. New York Times, Jan 8, 2012.

[26] Stone.

[27] *Uber: Driving Hard*. The Economist, June 13, 2015.

[28] Swisher, Vanity Fair.

Kalanick added, "What we maybe should've realized sooner was that we are running a political campaign and the candidate is Uber. And this political race is happening in every major city in the world. And because this isn't about a democracy, this is about a product, you can't win 51 to 49. You have to win 98 to 2.[29]

Looking Ahead

As Uber prepared to close out 2015, it had a number of reasons to be optimistic about its future. For one thing, it had just won a high-profile transportation skirmish in New York City: Over the summer, Mayor de Blasio had threatened to place a cap on the number of vehicles Uber could operate in the city. In response, Uber had spent heavily on advertisements blasting the Mayor for being in the pocket of the cab industry. It had also introduced a feature in its app called "de Blasio view," that showed NYC riders the lengthy wait times they would have to endure if de Blasio's legislation passed. A number of celebrities had weighed in to support Uber on social media (Ashton Kutcher, Kate Upton, Neil Patrick Harris, and others), and New York Governor Cuomo had even chimed in, calling Uber "one of the great inventions of this new economy."[30] Mayor de Blasio had finally caved, agreeing to delay any cap pending further study of the issue.

Other signs of Uber's momentum were more subtle and yet intriguing nonetheless. Some real estate experts, for example, were reporting that because Uber was making transportation more reliable and affordable in some cities, they were seeing a real estate resurgence in these dense locations. A few public health studies were reporting a reduction in drunk driving as a result of Uber.[31] Perhaps most interestingly, the price of a NYC taxi medallion had dropped precipitously (down 40%) in the past year, a sure indication that the market for taxi licenses had become bearish as a result of Uber's presence.[32]

At the same time, the company continued to clash with regulators and courts in multiple countries around the world, including Germany, Spain, Colombia, France, Australia, Italy, Denmark, China, and England. And anti-Uber protests, sometimes violent, continued to flare up in in cities from Paris to Madrid.

This didn't seem to be deterring the company, however, as it continued to hew to its philosophy of brazenly entering and operating in these markets whenever possible, despite the legal ambiguities. Uber was putting a particular amount of energy into conquering two of the world's largest markets, China and India. And it was actively experimenting with new services, including the following:

- Uber had recently launched a concept called UberPOOL in select cities. UberPOOL was a service that paired riders on the same route and charged them a reduced price. In San Francisco the UberPOOL offering accounted for as much as 50% of all trips on some days. Kalanick noted: "We want to get to the point that using Uber is cheaper than owning a car. Transportation that's

---

[29] Ibid.

[30] Flegenheimer, Matt. *De Blasio Administration Dropping Plan for Uber Cap, For Now.* New York Times, July 22, 2015.

[31] Chafkin.

[32] *New York City's Yellow Cab Crisis.* CNN, July 21, 2015. (cnnmon.ie/1l6Olcg)

10

as reliable as running water."[33] Kalanick was hinting the company might one day expand UberPOOL to include buses, which he referred to as the "ultimate carpool machine."[34]

- Uber had recently started a driverless-car initiative, and had jumpstarted the initiative by poaching dozens of members of Carnegie Mellon's robotics department, doubling their salaries and offering them six-figure bonuses.[35]

- In some cities, Uber was experimenting with a lunch-delivery service called UberEATS; in other cities, it was exploring a food delivery service called UberFRESH. In Manhattan, it was experimenting with a bicycle courier service called UberRUSH.

Kalanick explained the company's approach this way: "We like to think of Uber as the cross between lifestyle and logistics, where lifestyle is what you want and logistics is how you get it there." He added: "If we can get you a car in five minutes, we can get you *anything* in five minutes." [36]

---

[33] Swisher, Vanity Fair.

[34] Chafkin.

[35] Ibid.

[36] Video and Transcript: Uber's Travis Kalanick. Fortune, July 23, 2013. (for.tn/1H593Iv)

Exhibit 1   Cease and Desist Order

STATE OF CALIFORNIA   Arnold Schwarzenegger, Governor
PUBLIC UTILITIES COMMISSION
505 Van Ness Ave.
San Francisco CA 94102

October 19, 2010   File: None
                                                    Case: PSG-3018

UberCab, Inc.
Attn: Ryan Graves
182 Howard St., Ste. 8
San Francisco CA 94105

NOTICE TO CEASE AND DESIST

This letter places you on notice to cease and desist immediately all advertisements and operations as a for hire passenger carrier without a valid authority in force with the Commission. Continued violations of law may result in criminal prosecutions and termination of telephone service.

UberCab's website states that it collects the fees from the passenger and pays the limousine company for the transportation. This is a prime carrier/subcarrier relationship with the companies providing the transportation. In this role, UberCab, Inc. is required to have a charter party carrier permit issued by the Public Utilities Commission.

Pursuant to Public Utilities Code sections 5371, 5411, and 5415, any carrier which operates and/or advertises after revocation of their authority is guilty of a misdemeanor which is punishable by a fine of up to $1,000 or by imprisonment in the county jail for up to three months, or both. Each day of continued violations is a separate and distinct offense.

In addition, Public Utilities Code section 5386.5 states in part, "No charter-party carrier of passengers shall advertise its services, or in any manner represent its services, as being a taxicab or taxi service." The name UberCab itself is representative of a taxicab service and thus prohibited under this code section.

To obtain an application and/or view information regarding the CPUC requirements for reapplying to reinstate your authority and operating a passenger carrier company, visit the Commission website or contact the License Section at (800) 877-8867.

http://www.cpuc.ca.gov/PUC/transportation/passengers

If you have any questions regarding this letter, I can be reached at

Very truly yours,

Investigator, Badge #
Consumer Protection and Safety Division
Transportation Enforcement Section

CC: Ed Rouquette, Supervising Investigator

Source: Uber website. (newsroom.uber.com/2010/10/ubers-cease-desist/).

Exhibit 2   Screenshots from the Uber App

Source: Uber.

Exhibit 3   Screenshots of Surge Pricing in Effect

Source: Uber.

Exhibit 4   Screenshot of Uber's Driver-Side App

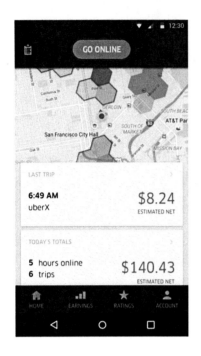  

Source: Uber.

Exhibit 5   A Comparison of a Subset of the Different Uber Services

Service	Description
UberBlack and UberSUV	Uber's luxury service. Commercially registered and insured livery vehicles, typically a black luxury sedan or SUV. Drivers must be professional livery drivers—they must have a commercial license, commercial insurance—and must own a high-end black luxury sedan or SUV.
uberX	Uber's low-priced service. Drivers are not professional livery drivers and a commercial license is not required. Drivers must be 21 or older with a clean driving record, and must own a model 2000 car (2005 in some cities) or newer and pass an independent vehicle inspection. Drivers must also have a clean driving history and pass a background check. Typical vehicles: Honda Accord, Toyota Camry, Ford Escort.
uberXL	Slightly higher fare price than uberX. Vehicles seat at least six passengers. Vehicles are ordinary minivans and SUVs (Honda Pilot, Dodge Caravan, etc.). Driver requirements are the same as for uberX.
UberSelect (aka UberPlus)	Only available in some cities. Uber's mid-luxury service. Priced are lower than UberBlack, but higher than uberX. Drivers are not professional livery drivers and a commercial license is not required, but they must own a luxury sedan (Mercedes, BMW, Audi) that seats up to four riders.
UberPOOL	Only available in some cities. Passengers share rides with other passengers and split the cost. Because of the carpooling nature of the ride, passengers may not be picked up first or dropped off first. An even cheaper option than uberX.

Source: Uber.

Exhibit 6   Estimated Driver Expenses for Typical uberX Driver

Miles Traveled: 40,000 Miles		
	New York City 2014 Toyota Camry	San Francisco 2014 Toyota Prius
MPG	25	48
$/gallon	$3.72	$4.18
Depreciation	$5,774	$7,763
Fuel	$5,952	$3,483
Maintenance	$679	$919
Insurance	$2,676	$2,012
	$15,080	**$14,177**

Source: Data provided by Uber to Salmon, Felix. *The Economics of Everyone's Private Driver*. Medium, June 1, 2014. (bit.ly/1MfTNsQ).

Note: Assumes driver drives 40 hours a week and a total of 40,000 miles a year. Note that in most cases, the IRS allows individuals to deduct businesses expenses from business income. Typical deductions included gas, insurance, fees, repairs, mobile phone charges, depreciation, etc.

Exhibit 7   Active U.S. Uber Drivers by Type of Service (UberBlack vs. uberX)

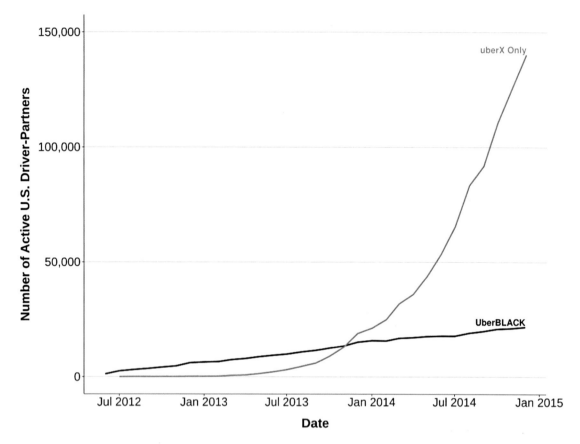

Source: Uber website (ubr.to/1GPVxZt). From a study commissioned by Uber: Hall, Jonathan and Alan Krueger. *An Analysis of the Labor Market for Uber's Driver-Partners in the United States*. Published Jan 22, 2015.

Note: Sample consists of all U.S. UberBlack and uberX drivers making at least four trips in any month.

Exhibit 8   Distribution and Median Hourly Earnings of uberX Drivers versus UberBlack Drivers, by Hours Worked (October 2014)

	1 to 15 hours/week		16 to 34		35 to 49		Over 50	
	Percent of drivers	Earnings per hour	Percent of drivers	Earnings per hour	Percent of drivers	Earnings per hour	Percent of drivers	Earnings per hour
UberBlack	29%	$20.87	32%	$20.85	19%	$21.67	20%	$20.76
uberX	55%	$16.89	30%	$18.08	10%	$18.31	5%	$17.13

Source: Uber website. (ubr.to/1GPVxZt). From a study commissioned by Uber: Hall, Jonathan and Alan Krueger. *An Analysis of the Labor Market for Uber's Driver-Partners in the United States*. Published Jan 22, 2015.

Note: Data aggregated at the driver-week level. Figures exclude incentive payments that are offered to new drivers in some markets. Earnings are net of Uber fees but do not adjust for driver expenses.

Exhibit 9   Characteristics of Uber Drivers vs. Taxi Drivers/Chauffeurs and All Workers

	Uber Drivers	Taxi Drivers and Chauffeurs	All Workers
Age 18-29	19.1%	8.5%	21.8%
30-39	30.1%	19.9%	22.5%
40-49	26.3%	27.2%	23.4%
50-64	21.8%	36.6%	26.9%
65+	2.7%	7.7%	4.6%
Female	13.8%	8.0%	47.4%
Less than HS	3.0%	16.3%	9.3%
High School	9.2%	36.2%	21.3%
Some College/Associate	40.0%	28.8%	28.4%
College Degree	36.9%	14.9%	25.1%
Postgraduate Degree	10.8%	3.9%	16.0%
Previous experience working as a driver	49%	NA	NA

Source: Uber website. (ubr.to/1GPVxZt). From a study commissioned by Uber: Hall, Jonathan and Alan Krueger. *An Analysis of the Labor Market for Uber's Driver-Partners in the United States*. Published Jan 22, 2015.

Note: Uber data from a BSG study conducted December 2014 by Benenson Strategy Group, using a survey of Uber drivers in 20 markets that represent 85% of Uber's US drivers. All other data from the American Community Survey, which is based on nationally representative data. The ACS data pertain to the same 20 Uber markets as the BSG survey, and are for 2012 and 2013.

Exhibit 10   Comparison of Hours Worked by Uber Drivers vs. Taxi Drivers/Chauffeurs

	Uber Drivers	Taxi Drivers and Chauffeur)
1-15 hours/week	51%	4%
16-34	30%	15%
35-49	12%	46%
50+ hours/week	7%	35%

Source: Uber website. (ubr.to/1GPVxZt). From a study commissioned by Uber: Hall, Jonathan and Alan Krueger. *An Analysis of the Labor Market for Uber's Driver-Partners in the United States*. Published Jan 22, 2015. Taxi driver/chauffeur data from the 2012-2013 American Community Survey.

Note: Data for Uber drivers pertain to each week when they worked at least one hour in Oct 2014. ACS hours based on "usual hours worked per week in past 12 months."

Exhibit 11   Comparison of Median Hourly Earnings of Uber Drivers vs. Drivers/Chauffeurs

	Uber Drivers	OES Taxi Drivers/Chauffeurs
Boston	$20.29	$12.92
Chicago	$16.20	$11.87
Washington DC	$17.79	$13.10
Los Angeles	$17.11	$13.12
New York	$30.35	$15.17
San Francisco	$25.77	$13.72
Average Across All 20 BSG Survey Markets	$19.19	$12.90

Source: Uber website. (ubr.to/1GPVxZt). From a study commissioned by Uber: Hall, Jonathan and Alan Krueger. *An Analysis of the Labor Market for Uber's Driver-Partners in the United States*. Published Jan 22, 2015. OES (Occupational Employment Statistics) data from the Bureau of Labor Statistics.

Note: Data aggregated to the driver-month level and medians of hourly earnings reported for Uber's drivers who drove at least one hour a week during the month of October 2014. Earnings per hour are net of Uber fees but do not adjust for driver expenses. For OES Taxi Drivers and Chauffeurs: OES data from May 2013. OES average for all areas in last row is weighted by the number of taxi drivers and chauffeurs in the 20 BSG market areas. The figure reported for Uber in the last row is the weighted average of median earnings per hour in the 20 market areas surveyed, where weights are the number of taxi drivers and chauffeurs in the market area.

Exhibit 12   Driver Requirements across Industries

UBER
- Minimum Age 21
- 2000 or newer (2005 in some cities)
- Pass Background Check

TAXI
- Minimum Age 21
- Pay Application Fee
- Pass Background Check
- Get Fingerprinted

BUS
- Minimum Age 22
- Pass Background Check
- 3 week training program

HEAVY TRUCK
- Minimum Age 21
- Commercial license
- Pass physical test
- Private Truck Driving School or 3-6 Month Truck Driving Course

DELIVERY TRUCK
- Pass Physical
- Ability to operate a manual transmission
- Commercial License

COURIER, MESSENGER (15)
- Ability to lift 75 pounds
- High school diploma

Source: Uber. (www.uber.com/driver-jobs).

9-384-049
REV: MARCH 16, 2011

E. TATUM CHRISTIANSEN

RICHARD T. PASCALE

Honda (A)

The two decades from 1960 to 1980 witnessed a strategic reversal in the world motorcycle industry. By the end of that period, previously well-financed American competitors with seemingly impregnable market positions were faced with extinction. Although most consumers had an initial preference to purchase from them, these U.S. manufacturers had been dislodged by Japanese competitors and lost position despite technological shifts that could have been emulated as competition intensified.

The Japanese invasion of the world motorcycle market was spearheaded by the Honda Motor Company. Its founder, Soichiro Honda, a visionary inventor and industrialist, had been involved peripherally in the automotive industry prior to World War II. However, Japan's postwar devastation resulted in the downsizing of Honda's ambitions; motorcycles were a more technologically manageable and economically affordable product for the average Japanese. Reflecting Honda's commitment to a technologically based strategy, the Honda Technical Research Institute was established in 1946. This institute, dedicated to improvements in internal combustion engines, represented Honda's opening move in the motorcycle field. In 1947, Honda introduced its first A-type, 2-stroke engine.

As of 1948, Honda's Japanese competition consisted of 247 Japanese participants in a loosely defined motorcycle industry. Most competitors operated in ill-equipped job shops, adapting clip-on engines for bicycles. A few larger manufacturers endeavored to copy European motorcycles but were hampered by inferior technology and materials that resulted in unreliable products.

Honda expanded its presence in the fall of 1949, introducing a lightweight 50cc, 2-stroke, D-type motorcycle. Honda's engine at 3 hp was more reliable than most of its contemporaries' engines and had a superior stamped metal frame. This introduction coincided closely, however, with the introduction of a 4-stroke engine by several larger competitors. These engines were both quieter and more powerful than Honda's. Responding to this threat, Honda followed in 1951 with a superior 4-stroke design that doubled horsepower with no additional weight. Embarking on a bold campaign to exploit this advantage, Honda acquired a plant, and over the next two years it developed enough manufacturing expertise to become a fully integrated producer of engines, frames, chains, sprockets, and other ancillary parts crucial to motorcycle performance.

Dr. Richard T. Pascale of Stanford Graduate School of Business prepared this case with the collaboration of Professor E. Tatum Christiansen of Harvard Business School. This case was developed from published sources. HBS cases are developed solely as the basis for class discussion. Cases are not intended to serve as endorsements, sources of primary data, or illustrations of effective or ineffective management.

Note: This case is based largely on HBS No. 587-210, "Note on the Motorcycle Industry—1975," and on a published report of the Boston Consulting Group, "Strategy Alternates for the British Motorcycle Industry," 1975.

Motorcycle manufacturers in the Japanese industry tended to minimize risk by investing in one winning design and milking that product until it became technologically obsolescent. Beginning in the 1950s, Honda began to depart from this pattern—seeking simultaneously to (1) offer a multiproduct line, (2) take leadership in product innovation, and (3) exploit opportunities for economies of mass production by gearing designs to production objectives. Most notably, in 1958 Honda's market research identified a large, untapped market segment seeking a small, unintimidating motorcycle that could be used by small-motorcycle businesses for local deliveries. Honda designed a product specifically for this application: a step-through frame, automatic transmission, and one-hand controls that enabled drivers to handle the machine with one hand while carrying a package in the other. The 50cc Honda was an explosive success. Unit sales reached 3,000 per month after six months on the market. Deciding to make this the product of the future, Honda gambled, investing in a highly automated 30,000-unit-per-month manufacturing plant—a capacity 10 times in excess of demand at the time of construction.

Honda's bold moves set the stage for a yet bolder decision—to invade the U.S. market. The following section depicts the sequence of events as taken from a Harvard Business School case on the motorcycle industry.[1]

In 1959 . . . Honda Motor Company . . . entered the American market. The Japanese motorcycle industry had expanded rapidly since World War II to meet the need for cheap transportation. In 1959, Honda, Suzuki, Yamaha, and Kawasaki together produced some 450,000 motorcycles. With sales of $55 million in that year, Honda was already the world's largest motorcycle producer. . .

In contrast to other foreign producers who relied on distributors, Honda established a U.S. subsidiary, American Honda Motor Company, and began its push in the U.S. market by offering very small lightweight motorcycles. The Honda machine had a three-speed transmission, an automatic clutch, five horsepower (compared with two and a half for the lightweight motorcycle then sold by Sears, Roebuck), an electric starter, and a step-through frame for female riders. Generally superior to the Sears lightweight and easier to handle, the Honda machines sold for less than $250 retail, compared with $1,000–$1,500 for the bigger American or British machines.

Honda followed a policy of developing the market region by region, beginning on the West Coast and moving eastward over a period of four to five years. In 1961 it lined up 125 dealers and spent $150,000 on regional advertising. Honda advertising represented a concerted effort to overcome the unsavory image of motorcyclists that had developed since the 1940s, given special prominence by the 1953 movie *The Wild Ones*, which starred Marlon Brando as the surly, destructive leader of a motorcycle gang. In contrast, Honda addressed its appeal primarily to middle-class consumers and claimed, "You meet the nicest people on a Honda." This marketing effort was backed by heavy advertising, and the other Japanese exporters also invested substantial sums: $1.5 million for Yamaha and $0.7 million for Suzuki.

Honda's strategy was phenomenally successful. Its U.S. sales rose from $500,000 in 1960 to $77 million in 1965. By 1966, Honda, Yamaha, and Suzuki together had 85% of the U.S. market. From a negligible position in 1960, lightweight motorcycles had come to dominate the market.

The transformation and expansion of the motorcycle market during the early 1960s benefited British and American producers as well as the Japanese. British exports doubled between 1960 and 1966, while Harley-Davidson's sales increased from $16.6 million in 1959 to $29.6 million in 1965. Two press reports of the mid-1960s illustrate these traditional manufacturers' interpretation of the Japanese success:

---

[1] D. Purkayastha and R. Buzzell, "Note on the Motorcycle Industry—1975," HBS No. 578-210, pp. 5–7.

"The success of Honda, Suzuki, and Yamaha in the States has been jolly good for us," Eric Turner, chairman of the board of BSA Ltd., told *Advertising Age.* "People here start out by buying one of the low-priced Japanese jobs. They get to enjoy the fun and exhilaration of the open road and frequently end up buying one of our more powerful and expensive machines." The British insist that they're not really in competition with the Japanese (they're on the lighter end). The Japanese have other ideas. Just two months ago Honda introduced a 444cc model to compete, at a lower price, with the Triumph 500cc. [*Advertising Age,* December 27, 1965]

"Basically we do not believe in the lightweight market," says William H. Davidson, son of one of the founders and currently president of the company (Harley-Davidson). "We believe that motorcycles are sports vehicles, not transportation vehicles. Even if a man says he bought a motorcycle for transportation, it's generally for leisure time use. The lightweight motorcycle is only supplemental. Back around World War I, a number of companies came out with lightweight bikes. We came out with one ourselves. We came out with another one in 1947 and it just did not go anywhere. We have seen what happens to these small sizes." [*Forbes,* September 15, 1966]

Meanwhile, the Japanese producers continued to grow in other export markets. In 1965, domestic sales represented only 59% of Honda's total of $316 million, down from 98% in 1959. Over the same period, production volume had increased almost fivefold, from 285,000 to 1.4 million units. In Europe, where the Japanese did not begin their thrust until the late 1960s, they had captured a commanding share of key markets by 1974.

In short, by the mid-1970s the Japanese producers had come to dominate a market shared by European and American producers 20 years earlier. . . .

It was often said that Honda created the market for the recreational uses of motorcycles through its extensive advertising and promotional effort.

The company achieved a significant product advantage through a heavy commitment to R&D and advanced manufacturing techniques. Honda used its productivity-based cost advantage and R&D capability to introduce new models at prices below those of competitive machines. New products could be brought to market very quickly; the interval between conception and production was estimated to be only 18 months. Honda was also reported to have a "cold storage" of designs that could be introduced if the market developed. . . .

Since 1960, Honda had consistently outspent its competitors in advertising. It had also established the largest dealership network in the U.S. On average, Honda dealers were larger than their competitors. In new markets, Honda had been willing to take short-term losses in order to build up an adequate selling and distribution network.

In 1975, the Boston Consulting Group was retained by the British government to diagnose the British motorcycle industry and the factors contributing to its decline. The remainder of this case, reflecting on Honda's strategy, consists of excerpts from that report:[2]

The market approach of [Honda] has certain common features which, taken together, may be described as a "marketing philosophy." The fundamental feature of this philosophy is the emphasis it places on market share and sales volume. Objectives set in these terms are regarded as critical, and defended at all costs.

---

[2] Boston Consulting Group, "Strategy Alternatives for the British Motorcycle Industry," Her Majesty's Stationary Office, London, 30 July 1975, pp. 16–17, 23, 39–43, 54–55.

The whole thrust of the marketing program . . . is towards maintaining or improving market share position. . . . We have seen some ways in which this goal is pursued. It is worth adding, as an example of how pervasive this objective is . . . that in an interview with a Honda personnel director, we were told that the first question a prospective Honda dealer is asked is the level of his market share in his local area. "I don't know why, but this company places an awful lot of emphasis on market share" was the comment. . . . We shall return to the reasons why market shares are critical for commercial success in the industry.

We were also told by representatives of [Honda] that their primary objectives are set in terms of sales volume rather than short-term profitability. Annual sales targets—based on market share penetration assumptions and market growth prospects—are set, and the main task of the sales company is to achieve these targets. The essence of this strategy is to grow sales volume at least as fast or faster than any of your competitors.

A number of more specific policies follow from this general philosophy, and our descriptions of each of the Japanese competitors provide ample examples of these policies:

1. Products are updated or redesigned whenever a market threat or opportunity is perceived.

2. Prices are set at levels designed to achieve market share targets and will be cut if necessary.

3. Effective marketing systems are set up in all markets where serious competition is intended, regardless of short-term cost.

4. Plans and objectives look to long-term payoff.

The results of these policies for the Japanese competitors have, of course, been spectacularly successful. Over the last fifteen years, the rates of growth of the four major Japanese companies have been as shown in **Table A**.

Table A   Growth of Japanese Production

	Production in 1959 (000 units)	Production in 1974 (000 units)	Average Annual Growth Rate (% p.a.)
Honda	285	2,133	14
Yamaha	64	1,165	21
Kawasaki	10	355	27
Suzuki	96	840	16

Source: Japan Automobile Industry Association.

Selling and distribution systems   We have so far discussed market share as a function of the product features and prices of particular models. Market share across all cc classes is also influenced by what we shall call the selling and distribution system (s and d system). Within the s and d system we include all the activities of the marketing companies (or importers) in each national market:

*   Sales representation at the dealer level

*   Physical distribution of parts and machines

*   Warranty and service support

4

- Dealer support

- Advertising and promotion

- Market planning and control

We also include the effects of the dealer network established by the marketing companies:

- Numbers and quality of dealers

- Floor space devoted to the manufacturers' products

- Sales support by dealers

The s and d system supports sales of the manufacturer across the whole model range, and its quality affects market shares in each cc class where the manufacturer is represented. **Table B** compares the s and d systems of the four full-line Japanese manufacturers in the USA, and shows that high market shares both overall *and* in each cc class go with high levels of expenditure on s and d and with extensive dealer networks.

The interaction between product-related variables and s- and d-related variables is complex. The better the product range in terms of comprehensiveness, features, and price, and the more sophisticated the s and d system of the sales company, the easier it will be to attract good dealers. This is because good products, which are well supported at the marketing company level, lead to good retail sales. Equally, good dealers themselves improve retail sales, and active competition between dealers can lead to retail discounting which acts as a volume-boosting price cut to the public. The manufacturers' products and s and d system therefore influence sales both directly, at retail, and proximately, through their effect on the dealer network.

In particular cc categories, each manufacturer's position is substantially influenced by its specific product offerings. For example, Kawasaki are strong in the 750cc-and over class due to the Z-1, and Yamaha have been weak due to its poor 750cc model. Outstanding products obtain market shares that are unusually high for a manufacturer, and weak products lead to atypically low market shares. For products of average attraction, however, market shares seem to move towards some equilibrium level. For each manufacturer, this level in the USA appears to be:

Honda	40–50%
Yamaha	15–25%
Kawasaki	10–15%
Suzuki	9–12%

As overall market leaders, the Japanese have dominated pricing in the motorcycle industry. It is therefore appropriate to begin this analysis by examining the extent to which the experience curve concept appears to explain the performance of the Japanese. Unfortunately, it is impossible directly to determine unit cost performance data for competitors, since the data are not publicly available. Sources can be found, however, for unit price and production volume data. Over the long term, price behavior is a useful guide to movements in the underlying costs, and so an experience curve analysis on prices can be extremely revealing.

Japanese price performance   In **Figure A**, price experience curves are drawn for the Japanese motorcycle industry as a whole, based on aggregate data collected by MITI. These curves show price reduction performance of a consistent nature for each of the size ranges of motorcycle considered, the rate of price reduction being most rapid of all in the largest range, 126–250cc, which is following an experience curve slope of 76%. The other slopes are more shallow, at 81% and 88%, but there is no mistaking the fact that real prices are descending smoothly over time. These experience-based price reductions clearly go a long way towards explaining the historical competitive effectiveness of the Japanese in the marketplace in small and medium motorcycles.

Table B   The Selling and Distribution Systems of Japanese Companies in the U.S.A.

	Est'd Total S&D Expenditure by Sales Company 1974 ($m)	Advertising Expenditure 1972 ($m)	Dealers 1974		1974 % Share of Total Market (units)	Lowest % Share of Any cc Class	Highest % Share of any cc Class
			Numbers	Units Sold per Dealer			
Honda	90–100	8.1	1,974	220	43	34	61
Yamaha	40–45	4.2	1,515	135	20	4	34
Kawasaki	30–35	2.2	1,018	127	13	9	19
Suzuki	25–30	3.0	1,103	98	11	5	16

Source: R.L. Rolk, *Motorcycle Dealer News*, Ziff-Davis Market Research Dept., BCG estimates.

For the purposes of strategy development ... it is [helpful] to look more closely at price performance in the larger bike models. The Honda CB 750 has been the pacesetter in superbikes in terms of both market penetration and pricing. In **Figure B**, price experience curves are plotted for this product and for two other large Honda bikes. The prices of other Japanese manufacturers have been broadly comparable to Honda's in the equivalent size range (they usually tend if anything to price at a slight premium relative to Honda), so that we may use Honda as a good "benchmark" for the Japanese competition in big bikes in general.

Figure A   Japanese Motorcycle Industry: Price Experience Curves, 1959–1974

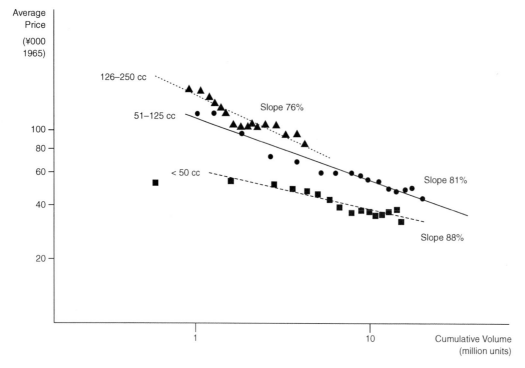

Source: MITI.

6

Figure B   Honda Large Bikes: Price Experience Curves

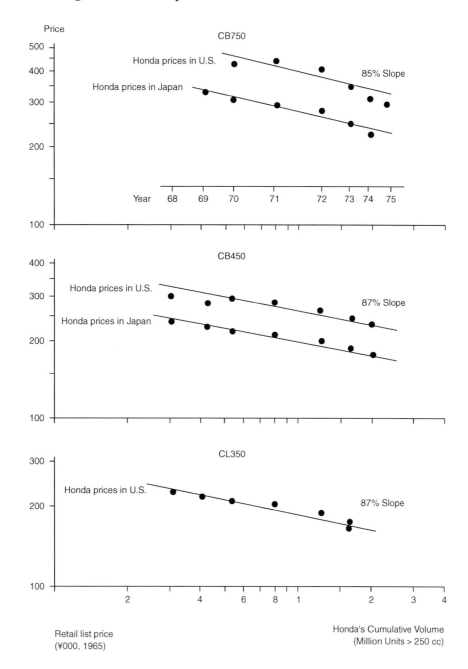

Retail list price
(¥000, 1965)

Honda's Cumulative Volume
(Million Units > 250 cc)

It is clear from **Figure B** that price performance in the large bikes has been consistent with that in small: real prices have declined along experience curve slopes in the region of 85%–87%. This has also been true of the price in the United States, when converted into yen terms.

An interesting feature of the curves is that the prices in the United States are so much higher than [those] of the same products in Japan. As shown in **Table C**, the premiums are high across almost the entire range of bikes and are far larger than seems necessary, even allowing for the extra costs

7

incurred for duty, freight, and packing in shipping bikes from Japan to the United States. This certainly suggests that there is no possibility that the Japanese are "dumping" their products in the U.S. market: quite the reverse. Furthermore, it may well indicate that competitive though the Japanese have been in the United States, based on the downward trends in their real price levels over time, there may well be plenty of scope for them to be even more competitive in the future if seriously challenged in that market. They could simply reduce their margins on exports to the United States to levels more in line with those enjoyed in their domestic business.

Table C   Honda Price Premium, USA vs. Japan

Premium on retail list prices, 1974

Model	Japan Price		U.S. Price ($)	Premium
	¥000	$ Equiv.		
CB 750	395	1411	2024	43%
CB 550	355	1268	1732	37%
CB 450	303	1082	1471	36%
CB 360	253	904	1150	26%
CB 350	275	982	1363	39%
MT 250	218	779	965	24%
MT 125	158	564	743	32%
CB 125	166	593	640	8%

Premium allowing for freight, duty and packing

CB 750, U.S. retail price 1975 = $2112
             Price to dealer $1584 (75% of 2112)
             Price to distributor $1373 (65%)

             Japan list price   ¥440,000 or
                              $1517 (equivalent)
             Price to distributor $ 986 (65%)
             Ocean freight to LA   60
             Duty   63 (3% U.S. Retail Price)
             Packaging costs   40
                         $ 163

Thus, indicated price to U.S. distributor for equal manufacturer's margin to that on bikes sold in Japan
                     = $ 986 + 163
                     $1149

Thus, premium in U.S.A. even after allowing for freight, duty and packing
                     = (1373/1149 - 1) × 100
                     = 20%

Note: The versions of the smaller bike models shipped to the States may be slightly more expensive than their Japanese equivalents (extra lighting, etc.). The versions of the larger bikes are, however, reported to be identical in both markets.

Japanese cost performance   The implication of the downward trends in real prices for the Japanese is, of course, that there have been underlying experience-based cost reductions: that the decline has not been accounted for simply by a reduction in margins. ... However, the major Japanese manufacturers have been continuously profitable, and this suggests that cost reductions have indeed taken place in parallel with real price reductions. On the other hand, all the Japanese motorcycle manufacturers also make a significant proportion of products other than motorcycles (in 1974 about 35% of Honda's turnover, and about 40% of Suzuki's, was accounted for by cars; of Yamaha Motor's turnover about 40% was in products such as boats and snowmobiles). It is, perhaps, reasonable to question whether these products are sufficiently profitable to "subsidize" the motorcycle business.

. . . It seems clear that . . . none of [the three major Japanese] manufacturers is subsidizing the motorcycle business from other businesses. Indeed, Honda was actually losing money in its car business in 1974, which suggests that their motorcycle business that year may have shown returns of the order of 20% (BIT) compared with the 12.4% return earned by the company overall. The overall inference from this profit performance must be that each manufacturer has indeed achieved an experience curve effect on costs in parallel with those achieved on price. The existence of this experience curve effect in the motorcycle industry has important strategy implications.

Competitive Strategy Implications

As we have discussed, failure to achieve a cost position—and hence cost reductions over time–equivalent to your competitors' will result in commercial vulnerability. At some point your competitors will start setting prices which you cannot match profitably, and losses will ensue. The strategic importance of the experience curve is that it explains clearly the two possible long-term causes of uncompetitive costs:

- Relative growth: failure to grow as rapidly as competitors, thereby progressing more slowly than them along the experience curve.

- Relative slopes: failure to bring costs down the characteristic experience curve slope achieved by competitors. . . .

Summary

From the perspective of the writers of the BCG study, a fundamental cause for the Japanese success was their high productivity. The motorcycle industry was exhibiting the effects that differences in growth rates, volume, and level of capital investment among competitors can have on relative costs. The high rates of growth and levels of production achieved by the Japanese manufacturers resulted in their superior productivity. In terms of value added per employee, Honda outperformed Western competitors by as much as four times. Even the smaller Japanese competitors were able to outperform their Western counterparts by a factor of two or three.

The BCG report also countered the common argument that the relatively inexpensive Japanese labor was the primary source of competitive advantage. The Japanese competitors in fact had higher labor costs than companies in the West. Their relative high growth and scale caused total costs to drop quickly enough to support regular pay increases and price decreases at the same time.

Essentially the argument presented by BCG was that the Japanese emphasis on market share as the primary objective led to high production volume, improved productivity, low costs, and in the long term to higher profitability than their competitors.

9-384-050
REV: MARCH 16, 2011

E. TATUM CHRISTIANSEN

RICHARD T. PASCALE

Honda (B)

Soichiro Honda, an inventive genius with a legendary ego, founded the Honda Motor Co., Ltd., in 1948. His exploits have received wide coverage in the Japanese press. Known for his mercurial temperament and bouts of "philandering,"[1] he is variously reported to have tossed a geisha out a second-story window,[2] climbed inside a septic tank to retrieve a visiting supplier's false teeth (and subsequently placed the teeth in his own mouth),[3] appeared inebriated and in costume before a formal presentation to Honda's bankers requesting financing vital to the firm's survival (the loan was denied),[4] hit a worker on the head with a wrench,[5] and stripped naked before his engineers to assemble a motorcycle engine.[6]

Company Background

Postwar Japan was in desperate need of transportation. Motorcycle manufacturers proliferated, producing clip-on engines that converted bicycles into makeshift "mopeds." Soichiro Honda was among these, but his prior experience as an automotive repairman provided neither the financial, managerial, nor technical basis for a viable enterprise.

Soichiro Honda viewed "technology" as the vehicle through which Japanese society could be restored and the world made a better place in which to live. Reflecting the intensity of this commitment, he established the Honda Technical Research Institute in 1946. The term institute was somewhat misleading, since the organization was composed of himself and a few associates and had no practical means of support. Under this organizational umbrella, he began to tinker, and, as a means of livelihood, he purchased 500 war surplus engines and retrofitted them for bicycle use. Lacking marketing know-how, he entered into an exclusive arrangement with a distributor, who packaged a motorcycle conversion kit for bicycles. The Honda Motor Company was formed. Further

---

[1] Sakiya, Tetsuo. "The Story of Honda's Founders," *Asahi Evening News*, June 1-August 29, 1979, Series #2 and #3.

[2] Interviews with Honda executives, Tokyo, Japan, July 1980.

[3] Sakiya, Tetsuo. *Honda Motor: The Men, The Management, The Machines*, Kadonsha International. Tokyo, Japan, 1982, p 69; also Sakiya, "Honda's Founders," Series #4.

[4] Sakiya, "Honda's Founders," Series #7 and #8.

[5] Sakiya, *Honda Motor*, p. 72.

[6] Sakiya, "Honda's Founders," Series #2.

Dr. Richard T. Pascale of Stanford Graduate School of Business wrote this case with the collaboration of Professor E. Tatum Christiansen of Harvard Business School. It is based largely on internal Honda sources and interviews with founders of Honda Motor Co., Ltd., and the Japanese management team that founded Honda of America. HBS cases are developed solely as the basis for class discussion. Cases are not intended to serve as endorsements, sources of primary data, or illustrations of effective or ineffective management.

tinkering led, in turn, to the introduction of the "A-design"—a 2-stroke, 50cc engine. The engine had numerous defects, and sales did not materialize. Scraping by on occasional orders, the company lost money in 1947 and grossed $55,000 in 1948.

In 1949, Soichiro Honda turned to friends. Raising $3,800, he developed and introduced the 2-stroke, D-type engine. This engine, generating 3 hp, was more reliable than most on the market and enjoyed a brief spurt of popularity. Recruiting a work force of 70 employees, Honda produced engines one at a time and approached an annualized production rate of 100 units per month by the end of 1949.

Success was short-lived, however. Honda's exclusive distributor elected to artificially limit sales to 80 units per month in order to maintain high margins. Soichiro Honda was irate and vowed to avoid such dependencies in the future. In late 1949 he set out to raise additional financing but suffered a second setback when competitors leapfrogged the 2-stroke design and introduced quieter and more powerful 4-stroke engines.

A classic dilemma now faced the struggling enterprise. Honda's engine was obsolete, and his distribution system held him at ransom. Without additional financing he could not correct these deficiencies, and banks and investors did not regard him as a sound management risk.

In late 1949, an intermediary urged him to accept a partner—Takeo Fujisawa. Fujisawa was prepared to invest 2 million yen (about $7,500). More important, Fujisawa brought financial expertise and marketing strengths.

Despite Fujisawa's presence, the firm continued to falter. No further capital could be raised in 1950. Fujisawa pressed his partner to quit tinkering with his noisy 2-stroke engine and join the industry leaders with a 4-stroke design, since it was clear that competition had threatened Honda with extinction. At first too proud to accept this counsel, in 1951 he unexpectedly unveiled a breakthrough design that doubled horsepower over competitive 4-stroke engines. With this innovation, the firm was off and putting, and by 1952 demand was brisk.[7]

Honda's superior 4-stroke engine enabled Fujisawa to raise $88,000 in 1952. With these funds, Fujisawa committed to reduce dependency on suppliers and distributors by becoming a full-scale motorcycle manufacturer. To forestall technological obsolescence, he encouraged Honda to stay abreast of technological developments. He also sought more flexible channels of distribution. Unfortunately, Honda was a relatively late entrant; the best Fujisawa could do was to arrange for several distributors to carry Honda as a secondary line. He compensated for weak product positioning by going directly to the consumer with advertising.

In late 1952 a sewing machine plant was purchased and converted to a crude motorcycle factory. Neither partner had managerial or manufacturing experience, and there was no real plan other than to work as long as necessary each day to keep up with orders. Honda's more powerful engine and superior stamped motorcycle frame created considerable interest, and demand remained strong. Employment leaped from 150 in 1951 to 1,337 by the end of 1952. Honda integrated into the production of chains, sprockets, and motorcycle frames. Altogether, these factors greatly complicated the management task. There were no standardized drawings, procedures, or tools. For several years the plant was, in effect, a collection of semi-independent "activities" sharing the same roof. Nonetheless, by the beginning of 1959 Honda had become a significant participant in the industry, with 23% market share (see *Exhibit 1).*

---

[7] Sakiya, *Honda Motor,* pp. 71–72.

Honda's successful 4-stroke engine eased the pressures on Fujisawa by increasing sales and providing easier access to financing. For Soichiro Honda, the higher-horsepower engine opened the possibility of pursuing one of his central ambitions in life: to build and to race a high-performance, special-purpose motorcycle—and win. Winning provided the ultimate confirmation of his design abilities. Racing success in Japan came quickly. As a result, in 1959 he raised his sights to the international arena and committed the firm to winning at Great Britain's Isle of Man—the "Olympics" of motorcycle racing.[8] Again, Honda's inventive genius was called into play. Shifting most of the firm's resources into this racing effort, he embarked on studies of combustion that resulted in a new configuration of the combustion chamber, which doubled horsepower and halved weight. Honda leapfrogged past European and American competitors—winning in one class, then another, winning the Isle of Man manufacturer's prize in 1959, and sweeping the first five positions by 1961.[9]

Throughout the 1950s, Fujisawa sought to turn his partner's attention from enthusiasm with racing to the more mundane requirements of running an enterprise. By 1956, as the innovations gained from racing had begun to pay off in vastly more efficient engines, Fujisawa pressed Honda to adapt this technology for a commercial motorcycle.[10] He had a particular segment in mind. Most motorcyclists in Japan were male, and the machines were used primarily as an alternative form of transportation to trains and buses. However, a vast number of small commercial establishments in Japan still delivered goods and ran errands on bicycles. Trains and buses were inconvenient for these activities. The purse strings of these small enterprises were controlled by the Japanese wife—who resisted buying conventional motorcycles because they were expensive, dangerous, and hard to handle. Fujisawa challenged his partner: Can you use what you've learned from racing to come up with an inexpensive, safe-looking motorcycle that can be driven with one hand (to enable carrying packages)?[11]

The First Breakthrough

In 1958 the Honda 50cc Supercub was introduced—with an automatic clutch, 3-speed transmission, automatic starter, and the safe, friendly look of a bicycle (without the stigma of the outmoded mopeds). As a rule of thumb, a 50cc engine is 50% cheaper to make than a 100cc engine. Achieving high horsepower with a small engine thereby reaps automatic cost savings—making the new bike affordable. Innovative design provided a cost advantage without requiring Honda to manufacture more efficiently than its competitors. (This was fortunate since the firm, having expanded into three plants in the 1950s, had still not achieved a well-integrated production process.)

Overnight, Honda was overwhelmed with Supercub orders. Demand was met through makeshift, high-cost, company-owned assembly and farmed-out assembly through subcontractors.[12] By the end of 1959 Honda had skyrocketed into first place among Japanese motorcycle manufacturers. Of its total sales that year of 285,000 units, 168,000 were Supercubs.[13] The time seemed appropriate to build an automated plant with a 30,000-unit-per-month capacity. "It wasn't a speculative investment,"

---

[8] Sakiya, "Honda's Founders," Series #11.

[9] Ibid.

[10] Ibid., Series #13; also Sakiya, *Honda Motor*, p. 117.

[11] Sakiya, "Honda's Founders," Series #11.

[12] Pascale, Richard T., Interviews with Honda executives, Tokyo, Japan, September 10, 1982.

[13] Data provided by Honda Motor Company.

3

recalls one executive. "We had the proprietary technology, we had the market, and the demand was enormous."[14] The plant was completed in mid-1960.

Distribution Channels

Fujisawa utilized the Supercub to restructure Honda's channels of distribution. For many years, Honda had rankled under the two-tier distribution system that prevailed in the industry. As noted earlier, these problems had been exacerbated by Honda's being carried as a secondary line by distributors whose loyalties lay with older, established manufacturers. Further weakening Honda's leverage, all manufacturer sales were on a consignment basis.

Fujisawa had characterized the Supercub to Honda's distributors as "something much more like a bicycle than a motorcycle." The traditional channels, to their later regret, agreed. Under amicable terms, Fujisawa began selling the Supercub directly to retailers—and primarily through bicycle shops. Since these shops were small and numerous (approximately 12,000 in Japan), sales on consignment were unthinkable. A cash-on-delivery system was installed—giving Honda significantly more leverage over its dealerships than the other motorcycle manufacturers enjoyed.[15]

Honda Enters U.S. Market

Soichiro Honda's racing conquests in the late 1950s had given substance to his convictions about his abilities. Success fueled his appetite for new and different challenges. Explosive sales of the Supercub in Japan provided the financial base for new quests. The stage was now set for the exploration of the U.S. market.

From the Japanese vantage point, the American market was vast, untapped, and affluent. "We turned toward the United States by a process of deduction," states one executive. "Our experiments with local Southeast Asian markets in 1957 and 1958 had little success. With little disposable income and poor roads, total Asian exports had reached a meager 1,000 units in 1958.[16] The European market, while larger, was heavily dominated by its own name-brand manufacturers, and the popular mopeds dominated the low-price, low-horsepower end."

Two Honda executives—the designated president of American Honda Motor Company, Kihachiro Kawashima, and his assistant—arrived in the United States in late 1958. Their itinerary: San Francisco, Los Angeles, Dallas, New York, and Columbus. Kihachiro Kawashima recounts his impressions:[17]

> My first reaction after traveling across the United States was "How could we have been so stupid to start a war with such a vast and wealthy country!" My second reaction was discomfort. I spoke poor English. We dropped in on motorcycle dealers who treated us discourteously and, in addition, gave the general impression of being motorcycle enthusiasts who, secondarily, were in business. There were only 3,000 motorcycle dealers in the United States at the time, and only 1,000 of them were open five days a week. The remainder were open on nights and on weekends. Inventory was poor, manufacturers sold motorcycles to

---

[14] Pascale interviews.

[15] Ibid.

[16] Ibid.

[17] Ibid.

4

dealers on consignment, the retailers provided consumer financing, and after-sale service was poor. It was discouraging.

My other impression was that everyone in the United States drove an automobile—making it doubtful that motorcycles could ever do very well in the market. However, with 450,000 motorcycle registrations in the United States and 60,000 motorcycles imported from Europe each year it didn't seem unreasonable to shoot for 10% of the import market. I returned to Japan with that report.

In truth, we had no strategy other than the idea of seeing if we could sell something in the United States. It was a new frontier, a new challenge, and it fit the "success against all odds" culture that Mr. Honda had cultivated: I reported my impressions to Fujisawa—including the seat-of-the-pants target of trying, over several years, to attain a 10% share of the U.S. imports. He didn't probe that target quantitatively. We did not discuss profits or deadlines for breakeven. Fujisawa told me if anyone could succeed, I could, and authorized $1 million for the venture.

The next hurdle was to obtain a currency allocation from the Ministry of Finance. They were extraordinarily skeptical. Toyota had launched the Toyopet in the United States in 1958 and had failed miserably. "How could Honda succeed?" they asked. Months went by. We put the project on hold. Suddenly, five months after our application, we were given the go-ahead— but at only a fraction of our expected level of commitment. "You can invest $250,000 in the U.S. market," they said, "but only $110,000 in cash." The remainder of our assets had to be in parts and motorcycle inventory.

We moved into frantic activity as the government, hoping we would give up on the idea, continued to hold us to the July 1959 start-up timetable. Our focus, as mentioned earlier, was to compete with the European exports. We knew our products at the time were good, but not far superior. Mr. Honda was especially confident of the 250cc and the 305cc machines. The shape of the handlebar on these larger machines looked like the eyebrow of Buddha, which he felt was a strong selling point. Thus, after some discussion and with no compelling criteria for selection, we configured our start-up inventory with 25% of each of our four products—the 50cc Supercub and the 125cc, 250cc, and 305cc machines. In dollar-value terms, of course, the inventory was heavily weighted toward the larger bikes.

The stringent monetary controls of the Japanese government together with the unfriendly reception we had received during our 1958 visit caused us to start small. We chose Los Angeles where there was a large second- and third-generation Japanese community, a climate suitable for motorcycle use, and a growing population. We were so strapped for cash that the three of us shared a furnished apartment that rented for $80 per month. Two of us slept on the floor. We obtained a warehouse in a run-down section of the city and waited for the ship to arrive. Not daring to spare our funds for equipment, the three of us stacked the motorcycle crates three-high, by hand; swept the floor; and built and maintained the parts bin.

We were entirely in the dark the first year. We were not aware that the motorcycle business in the United States occurs during a seasonable April-to-August window—and that our timing coincided with the closing of the 1959 season. Our hard-learned experiences with distributorship in Japan convinced us to try to go to the retailers direct. We ran ads in the motorcycle trade magazine for dealers. A few responded. By spring 1960, we had 40 dealers and some of our inventory in their stores— mostly larger bikes. A few of the 250cc and 305cc bikes began to sell. Then disaster struck.

By the first week of April 1960, reports were coming in that our machines were leaking oil and encountering clutch failure. This was our lowest moment. Honda's fragile reputation was being destroyed before it could be established. As it turned out, motorcycles in the United States are driven much farther and much faster than in Japan. We dug deeply into our precious cash reserves to air freight our motorcycles to the Honda testing lab in Japan. Throughout the dark month of April, Pan Am was the only enterprise in the United States that was nice to us. Our testing lab worked 24-hour days bench testing the bikes to try to replicate the failure. Within a month, a redesigned head gasket and clutch spring solved the problem. In the meantime, events had taken a surprising turn.

Throughout our first eight months, following Mr. Honda's and our own instincts, we had not attempted to move the 50cc Supercubs. While they were a smash success in Japan (and manufacturing couldn't keep up with demand there), they seemed wholly unsuitable for the U.S. market where everything was bigger and more luxurious. As a clincher, we had our sights on the import market—and the Europeans, like the American manufacturers, emphasized the larger machines.

We used the Honda 50s ourselves to ride around Los Angeles on errands. They attracted a lot of attention. One day we had a call from a Sears buyer. While persisting in our refusal to sell through an intermediary, we took note of Sears's interest. But we still hesitated to push the 50cc bikes out of fear they might harm our image in a heavily macho market. But when the larger bikes started breaking, we had no choice. We let the 50cc bikes move. And surprisingly, the retailers who wanted to sell them weren't motorcycle dealers; they were sporting goods stores.

The excitement created by Honda Supercub began to gain momentum. Under restrictions from the Japanese government, we were still on a cash basis. Working with our initial cash and inventory, we sold machines, reinvested in inventory, and sunk the profits into additional inventory and advertising. Our advertising tried to straddle the market. While retailers continued to inform us that our Supercub customers were normal everyday Americans, we hesitated to target toward this segment out of fear of alienating the high-margin end of our business—sold through the traditional motorcycle dealers to a more traditional "black leather jacket" customer.

An Advertising Twist

As late as 1963, Honda was still working with its original Los Angeles advertising agency, its ad campaigns straddling all customers so as not to antagonize one market in pursuit of another.

In the spring of 1963, while fulfilling a routine class assignment, an undergraduate advertising major at UCLA submitted an ad campaign for Honda. Its theme was "You Meet the Nicest People On a Honda." Encouraged by his instructor, the student passed his work on to a friend at Grey Advertising. Grey had been soliciting the Honda account—which, with a $5-million-a-year budget, was becoming an attractive potential client. Grey purchased the student's idea—on a tightly kept nondisclosure basis. Grey attempted to sell the idea to Honda.[18]

Interestingly, the Honda management team, which by 1963 had grown to five Japanese executives, was badly split on this advertising decision. The president and treasurer favored another proposal from another agency. The director of sales, however, felt strongly that the Nicest People campaign

---

[18] Ibid.

was the right one—and his commitment eventually held sway. Thus, in 1963, Honda adopted a strategy that directly identified and targeted that large, untapped segment of the marketplace that was to become inseparable from the Honda legend.[19]

The Nicest People campaign drove Honda's U.S. sales at an even greater rate. By 1964 nearly one out of every two motorcycles sold was a Honda. As a result of the influx of medium-income leisure-class consumers, banks and other consumer credit companies began to finance motorcycles—shifting away from dealer credit, which had been the traditional purchasing mechanism available. Honda, seizing the opportunity of soaring demand for its products, took a courageous and seemingly risky position. Late in 1964 it announced that thereafter, it would cease to ship on a consignment basis but would require cash on delivery. Honda braced itself for a revolt that never materialized. While nearly every dealer questioned, appealed, or complained, none relinquished the Honda franchise. In one fell swoop, Honda shifted the power relationship from the dealer to the manufacturer. Within three years, C.O.D. sales would become the pattern for the industry.[20]

Honda's growth on several dimensions is shown in *Exhibit 2*. Automobiles were introduced into the product line in 1963, shifting resources and management attention heavily in that direction in the ensuing years.

25 Years Later

In late 1972, anticipating the company's twenty-fifth anniversary, Fujisawa, 62, raised the issue of retirement. "We are strong dominating individuals," he said. "I must step aside and let the younger men lead our company." Soichiro Honda, 66, also conceded to retire. In September 1973, the two stepped down. States one source: "Fujisawa retired early to provide Mr. Honda with an opportunity to retire, also. It is a reflection of Fujisawa's genuine personal friendship with Mr. Honda."[21]

---

[19] Ibid.

[20] Ibid.

[21] Sakiya, Tetsuo. "The Story of Honda's Founders," *Asahi Evening News*, August 29, 1979.

Exhibit 1   Motorcycle Production in Japan by Japanese Makers

Calendar Year	Honda	Yamaha	Suzuki	Kawasaki	Other	Total
1950	531	-	-	-	6,960	7,491
1951	2,380	-	-	-	21,773	24,153
1952	9,659	-	-	-	69,586	79,245
1953	29,797	-	-	-	131,632	161,429
1954	30,344	-	-	200	133,929	164,473
1955	42,557	2,272	9,079	-	205,487	259,395
1956	55,031	8,743	18,444	5,083	245,459	332,760
1957	77,509	15,811	29,132	6,793	280,819	410,064
1958	117,375	27,184	66,363	7,018	283,392	501,332
1959	285,218	63,657	95,862	10,104	425,788	880,629
1960	649,243	138,153	155,445	9,261	520,982	1,473,084
1961	935,859	129,079	186,392	22,038	531,003	1,804,371
1962	1,009,787	117,908	173,121	31,718	342,391	1,674,925
1963	1,224,695	167,370	271,438	34,954	229,513	1,927,970
1964	1,353,594	221,655	373,871	33,040	128,175	2,110,335
1965	1,465,762	244,058	341,367	48,745	112,852	2,212,784
1966	1,422,949	389,756	448,128	67,959	118,599	2,447,391
1967	1,276,226	406,579	402,438	79,194	77,410	2,241,847
1968	1,349,896	423,039	365,330	78,124	34,946	2,251,335
1969	1,534,882	519,710	398,784	102,406	21,091	2,576,873
1970	1,795,828	574,100	407,538	149,480	20,726	2,947,672
1971	1,927,186	750,510	491,064	208,904	22,838	3,400,502
1972	1,873,893	853,317	594,922	218,058	25,056	3,565,246
1973	1,835,527	1,012,810	641,779	250,099	22,912	3,763,127
1974	2,132,902	1,164,886	839,741	354,615	17,276	4,509,420
1975	1,782,448	1,030,541	686,666	274,022	28,870	3,802,547
1976	1,928,576	1,169,175	831,941	284,478	20,942	4,235,112
1977	2,378,867	1,824,152	1,031,753	335,112	7,475	5,577,359
1978	2,639,588	1,887,311	1,144,488	326,317	2,225	5,999,929
1979	2,437,057	1,653,891	1,100,778	308,191	79	5,499,996
1980	3,087,471	2,241,959	1,551,127	521,846	-	7,402,403
1981	3,587,957	2,792,817	1,764,120	521,333	-	8,666,227

Source: Japan Automobile Manufacturers Association, Inc.

Note: KD sets and scooters are included.

Exhibit 2   Honda's Financial Performance and U.S. Motorcycle Sales

Calendar Year	Gross Sales (million yen)	Honda U.S. Motorcycle Sales (units)	Outside Financing (million yen)	Employees
1948	14.3	-	1	20
1949	34.6	-	2	70
1950	82.8	-	-	90
1951	330.3	-	-	150
1952	2,438	-	15	1,337
1953	7,729	-	60	2,185
1954	5,979	-	-	2,494
1955	5,525	-	120	2,459
1956	7,882	-	-	2,377
1957	9,786	-	360	2,438
1958	14,188	-	720	2,705
1959	26,165	-	1,440	3,355
1960	49,128	1,315	4,320	4,053
1961	57,912	6,052	8,640	5,406
1962	64,552	27,840	9,090	5,798
1963	83,206	65,869	-	6,816
1964	97,936	110,470	-	7,696
1965	123,746	227,308	-	8,481
1966	106,845	272,900	-	9,069
1967	141,179	181,200	-	11,283
1968	193,871	174,706	18,180	13,165
1969	244,895	272,600	-	16,614
1970	316,331	441,200	-	17,511
1971	332,931	656,800	-	18,079
1972	327,702	707,800	-	18,297
1973	366,777	556,300	19,480	18,287
1974	519,897	628,500	24,350	18,455
1975	563,805	343,900	-	18,505
1976	668,677	444,624	25,500	19,069
1977	849,635	439,822	29,600	19,968
1978	922,280	401,114	-	21,316

Note: Above figures are related solely to Honda Motor Co.. Ltd., and are not consolidated with those of its subsidiaries.

HARVARD | BUSINESS | SCHOOL

9-710-414
FEBRUARY 5, 2010

JULIE WULF

SCOTT WAGGONER

Corporate Strategy at Berkshire Partners

"While I don't think private equity firms will go the way of the conglomerates, the coming years will require some careful consideration of how we execute the model (basically how much leverage), how well we are doing versus independent listed companies as opposed to being measured solely as our own asset class, and how we communicate to the broader community who and what we are."[1]

— Carl Ferenbach, Co-Founder and Managing Director of Berkshire Partners

On a Friday afternoon in late 2008, the managing directors (MDs) of Berkshire Partners (Berkshire) assembled in the firm's main conference room, which overlooked Boston's historic Back Bay. That afternoon, they had to finalize the agenda for the following week's annual MD strategy meetings.

The meetings promised to be especially eventful given recent changes at Berkshire. Over the past several years, the MDs sought to institutionalize many of the firm's best practices to support its growth and to address the natural transition and evolution of the firm. For example, the MDs created three new executive oversight committees and built up Berkshire's organization with new centralized corporate functions in such areas as business development, legal, human resources and capital markets. They also recruited personnel to exclusively support the management of portfolio companies.

However, the MDs still wondered if these changes were sufficient to sustain Berkshire's competitive position, motivate Berkshire's future generations of talent, and enable the business to scale while maintaining Berkshire's culture of teamwork, consensus and collaboration. Some of the issues the MDs were considering included: (1) the continued evolution of the firm's governance model; (2) the future challenges regarding professional development given the growth of the firm and advancement of "functional" teams; and (3) retaining Berkshire's culture amidst the expansion. With respect to this last issue, one investment staff member asked, "Are we becoming *too corporate*?"

Another major topic for debate revolved around Stockbridge, Berkshire's recent diversification into public securities investing. Stockbridge was incubated as an internally-financed adjacency and had built a dedicated team and a solid track record. While Berkshire had no experience in marketing a public securities fund to outside investors, the firm had a deep bench of professionals with a successful, long-term background investing in private equity. As for challenges, Stockbridge required material investment of resources, and represented a new business effort that was outside of

Professor Julie Wulf and Research Associate Scott Waggoner prepared this case. We are grateful to Global Research Group Research Associate David Lane for his assistance. HBS cases are developed solely as the basis for class discussion. Cases are not intended to serve as endorsements, sources of primary data, or illustrations of effective or ineffective management.

Berkshire's core private equity business. At the offsite strategy meetings, Berkshire's MDs needed to decide when and how to begin marketing this emerging public securities business to outside investors.

objective → Stockbridge

Snapshot of the Private Equity Industry

Private equity firms formed funds which raised money from investors and invested the fund's money in portfolio companies. Upon sale of the portfolio companies, the funds returned the investors' principal, plus a share of the fund's profits. From an operating perspective, the private equity firm's MDs served as the fund's General Partners (GPs) and were responsible for actively managing investments for the fund's passive outside investors, or Limited Partners (LPs). The typical private equity fund had a ten year lifespan.

Early history of the private equity industry   As the conglomerate business model moved out of favor in the late 1970s, pension funds began to allocate more cash to alternative asset classes such as private equity funds and hedge funds (which invested principally in publicly traded securities). This new source of funding helped finance the formation of private equity firms which specialized in leveraged buyouts (LBOs), including Kohlberg Kravis Roberts & Co., Forstmann Little & Co. and Thomas H. Lee Equity. Carl Ferenbach, who was one of the five founding members of Berkshire Partners in the early 1980s, reflected, "Businesses tend to be rooted in the times of their founding. As we go back to the beginning of leveraged buyouts at the end of the 70s, compensation, governance and ownership in publicly-traded firms were not aligned in any way, shape or form. We thought it made all the sense in the world that they be aligned. . . . Although the conglomerate model was still popular at that time, leveraged buyouts would change the way the world did business globally."[2]

While the private equity industry had only $5 billion[3] in assets under management[a] (AUM) in 1980, the industry grew exponentially during the decade.

1980s leveraged buyout revolution   During the 1980s, the LBO became an increasingly popular method for private equity firms to acquire businesses. In a nutshell, LBOs utilized a small percentage of investor equity and a large percentage of relatively inexpensive debt issued by the portfolio company. This aggressive LBO financing was enabled by the development of high-yield bond markets by investment bankers such as Michael Milken from Drexel Burnham.

LBO debt financing imposed financial discipline on company management to generate sufficient cash flows to cover high levels of debt service. Ideally, following an LBO, the acquired company could pay down the acquisition debt through a combination of operating cash flows and proceeds from asset sales. If the acquired company could not cover its own debt service, it risked moving towards bankruptcy as the portfolio companies of private equity funds generally did not cross-subsidize each other. Private equity firms sought to create additional value by providing portfolio company management teams with significant equity incentives, thereby aligning their interests with those of the fund's investors. Furthermore, private equity firms implemented robust monitoring tools such as separate, value-added boards and transparent financial reporting for each individual portfolio company.

---

[a] Assets Under Management for a private equity firm could be defined as, "Equity value of existing companies currently in the portfolio (plus funds committed by investors) currently available to be called up." (Tim Friedman, ed., *2009 Preqin Global Private Equity Review* (London: Preqin Ltd., 2009), p. 12).

The period's easy credit markets and limited LBO regulation enabled some private equity firms to engage in hostile takeovers of public companies and to break up conglomerates, garnering in the process negative media attention. Some critics complained that the private equity industry was too focused on short-term issues, such as financial engineering and layoffs, and not focused enough on long-term value creation.

KKR's record-breaking $31 billion acquisition of RJR Nabisco in 1989 heralded the end of the first LBO boom as the economy moved towards recession, the market for high-yield bonds dried up and Drexel Burnham was forced out of business. By 1992, the private equity industry had $111 billion in AUM[4] but fundraising and investment activity had slowed dramatically.[5]

1990s industry evolution   In the early 1990s, as high-yield financing remained scarce and governments increased LBO regulations, private equity firms focused on creating value through friendly transactions and helping the management teams of portfolio companies to improve operations through such efforts as revenue growth, margin expansion and synergistic acquisitions. Venture capital investing in emerging technology and biotechnology businesses, which required limited amounts of leverage, became popular in the 1990s, until the technology bubble burst in 2000 and the U.S. economy moved into recession.

Renaissance and diversification in the 2000s   By 2003, global private equity AUM had reached $960 billion[6]; the abundant availability of inexpensive debt and rising asset values set the stage for an industry renaissance. In 2006, global private equity firms raised $538 billion[7] and were involved in 25% of global M&A activity.[8] Over the past 15 years, private equity deals had represented less than 10% of global M&A activity.

As private equity firms grew in size, they migrated to increasingly larger transactions, even eclipsing the groundbreaking deals of the 1980s (see **Exhibit 1** for a summary of the largest private equity transactions). Private equity firms also launched more funds specialized by industry and geography. For example, in 2006, The Carlyle Group (Carlyle) raised separate funds specialized in Asian, European, Japanese, Mexican, early-stage venture, energy and infrastructure opportunities (see **Exhibit 2** for examples of fund specialization). Furthermore, some large private equity firms, such as The Blackstone Group (Blackstone), Carlyle and Bain Capital, diversified into hedge fund activities while some hedge funds, such as Caxton Associates and Fortress Investment Group (Fortress), began to invest in private equity transactions.

Emergence of club deals   So-called club deals, where several private equity firms jointly invested in a target, became popular in the mid-2000s. Club deals, combined with easily accessible debt financing, allowed groups of private equity firms to bid for increasingly larger targets while realizing the benefits of portfolio diversification. From a governance perspective, club deals could be complicated by the differing views of each shareholder with respect to managing the target, future investments and exit timing. While club deals may have increased bidding competition for large transactions by allowing smaller firms to enter into auction processes, the U.S. Department of Justice began investigating potential anti-competitive effects of club deals in 2006.[9]

Founders sell General Partner stakes   In 2007, several alternative investment firms sold stakes in their management companies. For example, Fortress and Blackstone completed initial public offerings (IPOs) for $634 million[10] and $4.1 billion,[11] respectively. In that same year, sovereign wealth funds from Abu Dhabi and China acquired stakes in Apollo Management (Apollo), Blackstone and Carlyle,[12] and Nomura Bank acquired a 15% stake in Fortress for $888 million.[13] While some of the cash raised in these transactions provided the private equity firms with permanent investable capital (reducing the firms' need to continually raise new funds to make future acquisitions), a significant portion of this cash went directly to the firms' founders in exchange for some of their equity. A 2009

Wall Street Journal article reported that 11 executives from Blackstone, Fortress and Apollo, "Took $6 billion in cash off the table" during 2007.[14]

The private equity industry in 2008   By 2008, global private equity AUM had increased to $2.5 trillion[15] (**Exhibit 3** lists the largest private equity firms). However, as asset values collapsed, investment banks Bear Stearns & Co. and Lehman Brothers failed, and the markets for high-yield debt closed down, the global private equity industry dramatically slowed. In 2008, global private equity fundraising came to a near standstill and LBO deal volume dropped by over 70%.[16]

Background of Berkshire Partners

Brad Bloom, Christopher Clifford, Russell Epker, Carl Ferenbach and Richard Lubin formed the first Berkshire private equity fund in 1984. The founding MDs, who had been doing deals together since the late 70s, had previously worked in consulting, corporate operations, investment banking and private equity. Their experience levels ranged from CEO of a turnaround situation to head of M&A at a bulge bracket investment bank to a junior staff member at a private equity firm. Despite the founding MDs' disparate backgrounds and years of experience, they divided the equity in Berkshire equally among themselves. Importantly, the firm viewed itself as investing its own money first, augmenting it with outside capital.

Between 1984 and 2007, Berkshire invested in over 90 companies and by 2008 was still investing its most recent $3.1 billion Berkshire Fund VII (see **Exhibit 4** summarizing Berkshire's funds). Capital for this fund came principally from large institutional investors that had invested in previous Berkshire funds (see **Exhibit 5** for a summary of fund investors). While Fund VII was the largest fund Berkshire had raised to date, it was dwarfed by recent fundraising efforts of several other private equity firms. Managing Director Kevin Callaghan commented that Fund VII was well oversubscribed because Berkshire pursued a "stay small" philosophy, actively managing its growth. "One of the things that drove the size was that we were committed to consistently high investment returns rather than funds under management. So, we've always been an IRR and multiple of money group rather than an AUM group and that's engrained in the Berkshire mentality."[17]

An internal memo summarized Berkshire's investment process, "We don't feel pressure to put money to work and we don't feel pressure to not put money to work. However, we do feel pressure to be looking as hard as we can for excellent opportunities. . . . we will invest in all of those where our diligence confirms that opinion."[18] Berkshire's mission statement emphasized producing top quartile returns, supporting the management teams of portfolio companies, honesty, fairness, ethics, analytical rigor, open debate, teamwork, consensus decision-making and staff support to, "Provide consistently superior returns to our investors"[19] (see **Exhibit 6** for Berkshire's mission statement).

The Investment Process at Berkshire

Sourcing Deals

Deal sourcing was an early step in the investment process and involved identifying potential target companies to add to Berkshire's portfolio. Traditionally, Berkshire received deal leads through the firm's network of investment bankers, consultants, industry executives and the managers of current and former portfolio companies. Berkshire also received a significant number of unsolicited investment opportunities. Berkshire's Managing Directors believed that Berkshire's network and

comp adv.

reputation provided it with access to a variety of target candidates that were not as widely marketed by sellers to Berkshire's competitors for reasons such as confidentiality, partnership fit or need for accelerated timing. These opportunities were highly coveted by the private equity industry because they generally provided better management access, deeper due diligence and potentially better deal pricing than comparable highly marketed deals.

strategy

Berkshire typically targeted companies with enterprise values in the $200 million to $2 billion range, the so-called middle market. Berkshire invested $50 to $500 million of equity capital in a portfolio company and used outside debt financing from banks and other investors to bridge the difference. With respect to debt financing in the LBO industry, Managing Director Brad Bloom elaborated, "We believed that financial engineering was neither unique nor a true driver of value."[20]

While many private equity firms launched funds specialized by sector or region, Berkshire was a generalist equity investor. Nonetheless, Berkshire focused on a few key industries and, on a historical basis, had invested approximately 40% of its funds in retail/consumer sectors, 26% in transportation/industrial sectors and 25% in business services (see **Exhibit 7** for Berkshire's current investment portfolio). Berkshire generally steered away from technology, early stage and debt investment opportunities. Despite the fact that many private equity firms were opening offices around the world and investing a larger share of their funds internationally, all of Berkshire's employees worked in its Boston office and most of its portfolio companies were U.S.-based. Berkshire generally did not participate in club deals.

sector expertise

Berkshire had historically developed sector expertise around actual portfolio investment activity. In an effort to continue to be strategic and proactive when looking for new opportunities, Berkshire evolved its industry ownership responsibilities through its **On POINT** initiative. On POINT's objectives were to continue to formalize and drive Berkshire's best practices in developing relationships within industry verticals, sourcing attractive investment opportunities and positioning the firm in market segments that Berkshire believed had attractive investment attributes. On POINT was structured around six **Sector Teams** that covered opportunities in the consumer/retail, business services, energy, healthcare, transportation/aerospace and wireless telecommunications industries. Each of these represented areas where Berkshire had historically invested. Each Sector Team was led by a principal and senior associate, directed by either one or two MDs and supported by several associates. Sector Teams were responsible for developing key industry trends, pursuing company and management networking, and meeting periodically with the dedicated industry groups at bulge bracket investment banks to improve deal sourcing.

Importantly, while On POINT teams led the outreach effort in their particular sectors, staffing across live deals remained flexible. Berkshire Managing Director Mike Ascione explained, "We believe that it is good for professional development to have exposure to a variety of deals across industries. It also helps retain the quality of the investment decision as there is no deferring to an 'industry team' on any given deal." Managing Director Carl Ferenbach further elaborated on Berkshire's hybrid business model, "One of the things that came out of some recent strategy work was the advantage that industry specialization had at the front-end of the process. We wanted to build a model that enabled us to take advantage of this, but retain the discipline of our investment process on the back-end."[21] While Berkshire was pleased with its On POINT effort to date, the degree of industry specialization the firm needed to be competitive in the future remained a key question.

ONPOINT question

Analyzing Deals

Berkshire's investment process was highly selective. For example, between 1992 and 1998, Berkshire reviewed thousands of investment opportunities, scrutinized over 700 in-depth, but made

↑ strength

fewer than 60 investments. Berkshire's MDs believed that the firm's extensive industry and company due diligence processes helped it to select good companies, consequently providing superior returns to its funds' investors.

π target

Berkshire generally searched for target companies in recession resistant industries, with leading market positions, motivated management teams, solid financial performance and the potential to grow revenues and expand margins in a number of different ways. Ascione added, "We look for companies that have developed really good market positions and will benefit in the future from multiple growth opportunities. We really dig deep to understand the industry dynamics and the range of levers that can be pulled to grow a business. We employ leverage in our deals, but we have a definitive bias towards growth."[22]

process

In a typical deal analysis, after a new investment opportunity arrived at Berkshire, an MD coordinated a preliminary screening. For the most promising opportunities, the MD then contacted Managing Director Jane Brock-Wilson (who had lead responsibility for investment team staffing) to assemble a **deal team** from Berkshire's pool of investment staff.

As deal analysis progressed, the deal team presented increasing amounts of information for discussion during Berkshire's Monday morning **Firm Meetings**. At the Firm Meetings, Berkshire's entire investment staff, which totaled more than 40 people including junior professionals, discussed general firm matters, reviewed current portfolio companies and debated the pros and cons of new deal opportunities. A deal could not progress (even to a preliminary meeting or initial bid) without Monday discussion and subsequent firm approval. Berkshire believed that the benefit of this mechanism was that deal teams knew exactly where the firm stood on any given project, teams could not get "out ahead of themselves" on a given deal, and deal teams could rely on the full commitment and resources of the firm for approved projects. While the Firm Meetings served a valuable function, questions regarding sustainability lingered. Bloom observed, "As the firm gets larger, we need to think about how to maintain the Berkshire culture. How can we keep the consensus model effective with so many people in the room?"[23]

issue
values/ opinion

Regardless, the Firm Meetings remained a centerpiece of Berkshire's culture. Bloom emphasized, "Not only do we expect you to come to the meeting, we expect you to have a point of view."[24] While the MDs at most private equity firms were ultimately responsible for investment decisions, Berkshire's junior professionals were given a strong voice in the process. Berkshire had no separate investment committee; its entire investment staff constituted the committee. Berkshire's MDs also sought out advocates and skeptics to help stir up debate on even the most promising opportunities. However, unlike some private equity models, Berkshire did not have a star-based culture that evolved around the opinions and achievements of individuals. Brock-Wilson noted, "We leveraged the collective wisdom and collective ownership of the staff."[25] — *preach equality*

If Berkshire's investment team agreed to continue forward with a potential deal, Brock-Wilson might add additional resources to the deal team. A large, fully staffed deal team historically included one or two pre-MBA associates, a senior associate and/or a principal and at least two MDs. Due to the team philosophy of the firm, Berkshire's goal in any process was to staff a deal team that would diligence the opportunity appropriately and put the firm in the best position to win a deal. That could often result in an increase or decrease in the number of personnel regardless of professional level. Sometimes three or four MDs worked on a deal together if it was in the best interest of the firm; this was not necessarily typical industry practice.

The MDs closely monitored all deals in the pipeline to ensure that adequate resources were dedicated to promising opportunities. Before acquiring any company, Berkshire required a majority vote by its investment staff. Managing Director Ross Jones noted that Berkshire's consensus-driven culture helped provide balance to investment decisions which tended to help the firm recognize potentially volatile situations, "It saved us from making some big mistakes that others made . . . we also missed certain opportunities."[26]

While Berkshire's culture encouraged constructive debate and consensus, Ferenbach feared that endless unstructured debate, which he called the "tyranny of the minority,"[27] could grind the firm to a standstill. To avoid that risk, most investment decisions were based on majority voting rather than 100% consensus, with a clear preference for substantial or "super majority" of two-thirds to three-fourths of the staff. If the vote were close, the firm might keep analyzing and discussing in order to come to a more definitive decision. Once a decision was made, there was no second guessing without significant new data. The consensus system was not perfect, as Bloom observed, "We had a stretch in 2000-2002 where, in hindsight, we might have been too conservative. The investment decision process can at times be complicated by our size, managing a range of views around risk, and adhering to the consensus culture."[28]

Adding Value to Portfolio Companies

Ex-ante   Berkshire's MDs believed that they added value early in the acquisition process by sourcing good investment opportunities, executing effective due diligence and selecting the best companies to acquire. When bidding for target companies, Berkshire had a reputation for submitting professional bid packages with reliable bank financing, reasonable closing terms and compelling management development programs. Berkshire's MDs believed that the firm's reputation drove a significant amount of unsolicited deal flow, as sellers welcomed reliable buyers. Berkshire believed that its reputation was important in the bidding process when guaranteed financing was difficult to obtain or when several private equity firms submitted bids with similar terms.

From a seller's perspective, strategic buyers, such as conglomerates, generally entered an auction process with several advantages over private equity firms. For example, strategic buyers often had businesses operating in the same or similar industries as the target company, so their management could complete due diligence efficiently. Strategic buyers also had the potential to offer higher bids due to synergies that stand-alone private equity funds might not realize. Additionally, strategic buyers generally used less leverage, so their bids were less dependent on fickle outside financing.

Ex-post   Berkshire strove to differentiate itself by investing significant time and resources to help portfolio companies improve their financial and operating performance. For example, in 2006, Berkshire acquired **N.E.W.**, a Virginia-based leading provider of extended service contracts, buyer protection services and product support for retailers, home service providers, manufacturers, and other consumer-oriented companies. The company offered product replacement programs, retail support services, and extended service and customer care programs for various consumer products. Shortly after completing the acquisition, Berkshire's deal team worked jointly with N.E.W.'s management team to refine their medium-term strategic plan, identify any necessary external resources to help the team achieve the plan, and establish metrics to measure future performance. Berkshire helped strengthen N.E.W.'s board of directors by working with management to recruit two highly experienced operating executives to the company's board. Berkshire also provided support on major organizational, personnel, operational, and investment issues. While Berkshire worked closely with N.E.W.'s management team, Managing Director Chris Hadley emphasized the boundaries of Berkshire's core competencies, "We are not operating managers, and don't intend to be."[29]

Although Berkshire held a controlling interest in N.E.W., Jones described how Berkshire's governance process evolved. "It's not about controlling a majority stake but rather about the right partnership dynamics. We want to create a partnership and positive dynamic with the management team and work with them to drive the company to the next level."[30]

Berkshire used N.E.W. stock and options to align the goals of N.E.W.'s management, Berkshire's investment team, and Berkshire's outside investors. These equity incentives were expected to increase in value as N.E.W. increased its revenues and margins. In many ways, N.E.W.'s management's incentives paralleled those of Berkshire's investment team, which were principally composed of carried interest and a direct 8% ownership stake through Berkshire Fund VII.

In 2008, N.E.W. entered into a combination agreement with Asurion Corporation, the leading provider of value-added subscriber services to the wireless industry, with significant share in the core handset protection business. Berkshire believed the combination of N.E.W. and Asurion presented a compelling opportunity to combine two companies with solid historical performance, leading market positions in their core segments, complimentary product offerings, and attractive growth prospects, both domestically and abroad. Berkshire further believed such a combination would allow these companies to leverage their management talent and resources to better serve existing clients, provide greater value to consumers, share best practices, capitalize on significant synergy opportunities, and more rapidly pursue international product protection opportunities.

Exiting Investments

Berkshire typically held portfolio companies for three to seven years and exited a relatively high proportion of its investments through private sales. To a lesser degree, Berkshire used the public markets to exit portfolio companies via initial public offerings (IPOs). Yet Berkshire's exit activity remained dependent on the capital markets, which helped determine valuation benchmarks and provided debt and equity financing for many potential buyers. Strategic buyers, such as conglomerates, differed from private equity firms in that they were not required to sell the companies they acquired. According to Managing Director Larry Hamelsky, "Our philosophy on exit is fairly simple. If you build really good companies that have and continue to exhibit good growth characteristics, you should be able to create multiple exit strategies. And because of our history and track record, we generally do not feel rushed to have to create a liquidity event."[31] This last point was exemplified in Berkshire's current longest holding, Advanced Drainage Systems, in which the firm had held an investment for over 21 years.

Economics

Private equity funds typically charged their LPs an annual management fee of 2% of AUM,[32] helping to cover the salaries and overhead related to managing the fund. Over time, funds sold their investments and returned cash to fund investors; for many maturing funds, this decline in AUM drove management fees downwards. From a firm wide perspective, Managing Director Richard Lubin noted that, "There is somewhat of a "step function" nature to the annual (management fee) revenue base. Revenues are flat to declining for a period of time as existing funds get invested and near the end of their useful lives, and then step up with a new fund."[33]

While management fees provided a steady revenue stream, carried interest was the principal long-term incentive fee for private equity firms. After a fund returned the LPs' initial investment, GPs and LPs typically split any capital gains 20%/80%, respectively. Some funds in the industry were required to exceed a minimum annual return before earning carried interest; these hurdle rates were typically in the 8% range.

Berkshire's annualized net returns to fund investors after fees (better known as net IRR) were approximately 29% since inception, which, on a gross basis (i.e. before fees), represented a multiple of invested capital[b] of 3.7x. Cambridge Associates LLC, an investment advisor, ranked the performance of Berkshire Funds I-V in the top quartile of LBO funds (see **Exhibits 8** and **9**). Berkshire's track record, and the resulting demand for its funds, enabled the firm to earn carry that was above the market average of 20%. [c]

Organization and Governance at Berkshire

Recruiting, Promotion and Incentives   → Question 2

Recruiting and promotion   Recruiting at Berkshire was highly competitive. To help maintain Berkshire's culture, the firm's recruiting process leveraged their employees' professional and personal contacts to source the best candidates, which they described as, "Good all around athletes with great business analytics who fit with the culture of the firm." For Managing Director Randy Peeler, a key recruiting challenge was that, "We want people who want to win but have a low ego."[34]

Most of Berkshire's investment staff was sourced from top-tier universities, consulting firms and investment banks, with strong representation from Harvard Business School (75% of MDs) and Bain & Co. (25% of MDs). The firm also sought to ensure that a good portion of the investment staff had the opportunity to meet recruiting candidates and had a voice in the new hire decision. Historically, Berkshire had promoted from within its own ranks. However, the firm continually reexamined its approach. Ascione commented, "We want to be careful not to become too 'Berkshirized.' We need to find the right balance between internal promotion and bringing in fresh perspectives."[35]

Berkshire, unlike some of its competitors, generally assigned its investment staff leading a deal to work with the resulting portfolio company for the duration of the firm's investment, from initial due diligence, acquisition, harvesting to final sale. Berkshire's MDs believed that providing project continuity to junior staff helped reinforce good investment decisions. This continuity, coupled with monthly and quarterly firm-wide discussions about the status and progress of each portfolio company, strengthened their firm's model. However, the risk in this approach was that it could stretch the deal staff (balance between sourcing deals and working on the portfolio) and could lead to teams becoming too "entrenched" at a company over time. On occasion, team members might be swapped out or added to ensure a good match of a portfolio company's needs with Berkshire's capacity and skills.

Berkshire's team-oriented, consensus-driven culture was an integral driver of its promotion policy. Berkshire's MDs worked hard to communicate that employees staffed on the most profitable deals did not have an advantage over those staffed on more challenging projects. As Callaghan put it, "We like to say that every deal is the firm's deal, not Chris' or Mike's. Compensation and promotion mirror that, as they are agnostic to the deals you work on. We have been successful in avoiding an "up or out culture" and try hard to create opportunities for great talent to advance within the firm."[36] According to Peeler, "Promotion is based on things like judgment, business analytics and cultural fit. We really try to view how good a person is and if they can they work within the Berkshire culture.

---

[b] Multiple of invested capital could be defined as dollars returned to investors divided by initial dollars invested.

[c] To illustrate simplified carried interest economics, assume that a private equity fund with 20% carry realized capital gains of $1 billion. Approximately $800 million of these gains would be allocated to the LPs and $200 million to the GP.

9

We hope to avoid the politics which can impact decision making and behavior."[37] Historically, the track to MD promotion ranged from 7 to 10 years for post-business school hires.

Incentives   The compensation of Berkshire's junior investment staff included salary, bonus, carried interest and co-investment rights. The firm's goal was to ensure that the investment staff's base salaries were competitive with market rates and that target bonuses were generally between 75% and 100% of base salary, and paid annually. Carried interest awards and direct cash investment (known as co-investment) was made across all deals (there was no "cherry picking"). A snapshot of compensation in the private equity industry is included in **Exhibits 10** and **11**.

Berkshire typically awarded carried interest to its entire post-MBA investment staff, which generally vested over a period of five years. While many private equity firms locked-in an employee's carried interest for the life of each fund, Berkshire's carried interest program was more flexible and helped further motivate and retain staff. Lubin commented, "We review carried interest participation more frequently than just with each fund. Absent a new fund, the carried interest 'pot' is fixed. So dilution occurs to some as a particular individual's carried interest participation increases with professional advancement."[38] Hiring additional investment staff was a sensitive issue in the industry as it effectively diluted everyone if no new funds were raised.

The co-investment philosophy permeated Berkshire. All of Berkshire's employees (both investment staff and support staff) were eligible to directly co-invest personal capital in Berkshire's deals. This was not a trivial benefit given the historic performance of Berkshire's funds, the inability of most outside individuals to access private equity investments and the fact that Berkshire's employees paid no management fees or carried interest on their co-investments. Berkshire expected its investment staff to make meaningful direct investments in Berkshire's funds. To facilitate the investment for junior investment staff, Berkshire often provided credit availability to help fund portions of co-investment obligations.

Berkshire's personnel collectively were the largest investor in their funds. For example, the Berkshire team held an 8% stake, or approximately $250 million, in Fund VII. Industry-wide, *Dow Jones Private Equity Analyst* estimated that GP contributions averaged 3.6% of capital in 2008 LBO funds.[39] Berkshire's MDs believed that Berkshire's successful co-investing program transformed the firm's employees from asset managers to investing partners whose personal wealth was highly correlated with the success or failure of the firm's funds.

Lubin commented on the compensation structure for the MDs at Berkshire and how it differed from that of most private equity firms:

> The MDs each have a unit interest in the firm's profits – both the annual profits and the carried interest. The MDs also have a significant co-investment obligation. Unlike many firms, MD "participation" at Berkshire tends to be flatter and perhaps not as concentrated in a small number of individuals. There may be less spread between a relatively new MD and a senior MD at Berkshire than you would find at most firms. There are also fairly well defined transition plans.[40]

To sustain active involvement of its MDs, Berkshire recently implemented a policy whereby MDs were eligible for three months of sabbatical after five years tenure as MDs. Berkshire believed that this policy would enable seasoned MDs to "recharge" and continue to be actively involved in the firm for longer periods of time.

Berkshire's founding MDs were keenly interested in Berkshire's legacy. To ensure the successful transfer of the firm to the future generations of leaders, the founders had not actively considered an

IPO or outright sale. As a result, from very early days, the founders formalized compensation systems that would not drain Berkshire's resources, and would effectively enable, over time, the transfer of ownership to Berkshire's future leaders. Brock-Wilson commented that, "It's a lot easier to build on a strong foundation. I think the five founding MDs did a phenomenal job of being fair-minded and thoughtful in terms of their approach to structuring the original partnership. All the way along they have been fair-minded about tweaking it to accommodate growth. For the same reasons, their individual names are not on the door. . . . This has helped us manage through generations and build a cohesive team."[41]

Evolution of Organization and Governance

In 2006, as Berkshire was raising its largest fund to date, the MDs reorganized the firm to strengthen functional areas and accommodate future growth. Berkshire's new executive committees and specialist groups helped each MD to supervise more people and manage more assets. They also helped leverage the MDs' time and standardize governance processes and practices throughout the firm.

New corporate functions   To consolidate certain activities that were previously performed by the firm's deal professionals and external consultants, Berkshire created new business development, human resources, general counsel, capital markets and portfolio support groups. Several leading private equity firms, such as Bain Capital, KKR and TPG Capital, also recently had added functional specialists to their organizations.

In 2006, Berkshire hired a Principal to lead **Business Development**, working with the investment staff to help increase the quantity, quality and consistency of Berkshire's deal flow. At times, managers were preoccupied with urgent portfolio management responsibilities and forced to set aside deal generation efforts. Business development helped spearhead visits to investment banks and brokers to help uncover additional investment opportunities which were previously off the firm's radar screen. Jones noted that, "While deal generation responsibilities still resided largely with everyone on the investment staff, Business Development helped increase consistency and depth of the firm's business development."[42] Business Development's role dovetailed with Berkshire's On POINT initiative.

Beyond Brock-Wilson's investment duties as Managing Director, she was also responsible for resource management. Her resource management responsibilities evolved around managing and driving professional development of Berkshire's investment professionals and included recruiting, deal staffing, coaching and performance evaluations. She also was responsible for expanding Berkshire's external networks with outside consultants and executives. As Berkshire grew, its MDs considered recruiting a **Director of Talent Management** from outside the firm. This would allow Brock-Wilson to focus on her investment responsibilities and further professionalize Berkshire's internal management processes. However, some investment professionals were worried about taking certain activities, such as recruiting, staffing and professional development, out of the hands of the MDs.

Additional functional specialization occurred when Berkshire hired a **General Counsel**. The General Counsel's responsibilities included managing deal matters (confidentiality agreements, bid letters and agreements), fund partnership documents and firm legal matters. The General Counsel developed uniform practices regarding deal terms, kept Berkshire's staff current on legal terms and structures and was also a key resource for deal negotiations. In 2007, Berkshire also brought on a **Director of Capital Markets**, who worked alongside deal teams to develop optimal financing alternatives for new deals and to restructure financing packages opportunistically for selected portfolio companies. Historically, individual deal teams were responsible for sourcing and negotiating financing with banks and other financing sources for each acquisition. The Director of Capital Markets became Berkshire's key contact for banking relationships and the firm's expert on current terms, conditions and suppliers in the debt markets. The General Counsel and Director of Capital Markets provided Berkshire with functional depth and the ability to better react to the market's increasingly rapid and complex deal processes. Importantly, deal teams could now focus more of their time on business diligence, management assessment and winning deals. Berkshire believed these functional hires were somewhat unique for mid-market private equity firms.

Historically, Berkshire's investment staff obtained deep operating insights into portfolio target companies during the due diligence process. Post-acquisition, Berkshire often retained external operating specialists and executives to help improve portfolio company operations and financial performance. In 2005, Berkshire evolved its operating strategy to take a more active role in improving the performance of its portfolio companies with its new **Portfolio Support Group** (PSG).

PSG's mission was to create value by working alongside company management and Berkshire's deal teams to address operating opportunities and challenges within portfolio companies. PSG staff was involved in early-stage due diligence and in post-acquisition roles such as project manager, acting executive, crisis management, advisor and analyst. The structure and staffing of Berkshire's PSG continued to evolve with portfolio company needs and the availability of PSG personnel.

New executive committees   Berkshire's MDs set up three executive committees with rotating membership (see **Exhibit 12** for Berkshire's organizational chart). The **Compensation Committee** was responsible for the establishment of compensation policies as well as the evaluation, development and compensation of the firm's Managing Directors. The Compensation Committee was aided in performing its functions by the **Feedback Committee**. A member of the feedback committee sat down with every MD at least once a year to conduct a peer review process.

The **Agenda and Planning Committee** coordinated a number of major processes each year. First, the Committee helped organize Berkshire's annual investment staff offsite, typically held in early December. This was a full day strategy session that involved the entire investment staff, regardless of position. To facilitate the discussion, Berkshire typically collected feedback across a number of topics in advance of the meetings. One form used for this purpose was the firm "scorecard." The scorecards were based on Berkshire's mission, culture and values and addressed approximately 20 issues such as: recruiting great talent, analytical rigor, training programs, proactively sourcing new deal opportunities, leveraging PSG, supporting the management teams of portfolio companies, strengthening culture as the firm grew, consensus, honesty, fairness and work-life balance. Effectively, the scorecard helped assess how the staff thought the firm was performing, and highlighted areas that needed to be addressed going forward.

Second, Berkshire's MDs gathered offsite each winter to discuss strategic issues (often formed from December's firm wide strategy session), estimate resource requirements and develop formalized strategic plans for the coming year and the future. While the entire investment team was not part of the offsite meetings, Ferenbach noted, "The scorecards helped bring everyone's brain into the game."[43] Following the offsite, the Agenda and Planning Committee organized small group meetings with everyone on Berkshire's staff to discuss the new strategic plan and obtain feedback.

Third, the Committee coordinated other strategic activities. For example, in 2007 the MDs embarked on the Vision 2012 exercise to envision strategic, operational, organizational, governance and management challenges the MDs might need to address five years in the future. In 2008, the MDs worked with Bain Consulting to benchmark Berkshire's business model to those of its competitors and, "looked at how deals are sourced, due diligence is undertaken, portfolio company value is added and the extent of specialization others deploy."[44]

Lastly, the Agenda and Planning Committee set the agenda for the semi-monthly MDs' meetings.

Implications of Changes

Berkshire's organizational changes resulted in an increase in the number of positions reporting to its governing body of Managing Directors. At the same time, functional specialists represented a greater proportion of these direct reports. One benefit of these organizational changes was that functional specialists helped to provide additional coordination among Berkshire's investment professionals. And from an operational perspective, the organizational changes helped to leverage the MDs' time and gave them greater ability to govern and control the firm. This leverage could be illustrated quantitatively; in 2004, 10 MDs were investing the $1.7 billion Fund VI with a team of 17 professionals. By 2008, 11 MDs were investing the $3.1 billion Fund VII with a team of nearly 45 professionals (see **Exhibit 13**). Essentially, Berkshire's flattening organizational structure was becoming similar to those used by other professional service firms, including consulting, legal and investment banking. Despite the changes, the MDs were still concerned that they were spending too much of their time on governance and not enough on deal making and driving portfolio value.

The ongoing evolution of Berkshire's organization was not without its challenges. For example, junior investment staff became concerned about their own professional development; with Berkshire's deep team of functional specialists, could the junior staff continue to develop general management skills and gain relevant experience in such areas as deal sourcing, portfolio company support, legal and financing activities? One employee added, "it feels more hierarchical with less interaction between junior staff and MDs." Some also worried that competition for promotion might increase as the investment staff increased in numbers. These issues were important because the MDs believed that a team-oriented environment had been critical to Berkshire's success.

Recent Diversification - Stockbridge ✳ → question 4

In 2005, Berkshire's MDs decided to incubate an internal public securities investment fund. According to Callaghan, "We launched Stockbridge because we thought that we could use a private equity approach to successfully invest in public equities. As in private equity, we performed extensive due diligence around a business, its industry and thought carefully about sustainability. From a firm wide perspective, Stockbridge provided good and useful diversification and was not meaningfully different from Berkshire's core private equity business. We believed it represented a natural adjacency. It also provided an alternative career path to our investment staff who might be interested in the public markets."[45] Stockbridge implemented a consensus-driven, team-oriented investment process similar to that of Berkshire.

Stockbridge's investment strategy was based on a concentrated portfolio of publicly traded (mostly equity) securities in 10 to 20 U.S. firms. Stockbridge's goal was to hold marketable securities in its investment portfolio over a period of 3 to 5 years. The fund was permitted to use leverage, shorting and other hedging strategies opportunistically. Robert Small, Stockbridge's Managing Director, elaborated, "Compared to other investment funds focused on public securities, I believe that we spend more time doing research, so we will drive to a higher level of conviction in our investments. Overall, we aim to invest in the best companies at reasonable valuations but do not consider ourselves to be deep value investors."[46]

As Stockbridge did not engage in the high-volume, short-term trading strategies typical of many hedge funds, Small believed that Stockbridge could effectively leverage Berkshire's operational platform, especially with respect to sharing activities in administration, risk, compliance and technology.

To lead Stockbridge, the MDs chose Small, a 15 year veteran with Berkshire who previously worked at Bain & Co. and Goldman Sachs & Co. Ascione recalled, "Rob was a clear choice to run Stockbridge. He was excited about the project, is a great investor, incredibly intelligent, has market savvy and is a good team builder at Berkshire."[47]

By the end of 2008, Stockbridge had hired four senior professionals, two junior staff members, and had established a solid investment track record. Importantly, three of these individuals had worked at Berkshire previously and, as a result, were familiar with the firm's culture, strategy, and processes. Berkshire's MDs, who had been funding the initiative, were impressed with Stockbridge's progress and discussed the potential to raise capital from outside investors, including LPs who had previously invested in Berkshire's private equity funds.

Preparing for Next Week's Annual MD Strategy Meeting

Returning to Berkshire's main conference room, the MDs began to discuss the evolution of Berkshire's strategic, organizational and governance models. How could the MDs best align the interests of Berkshire's team, Stockbridge's team and their respective fund investors? Did Berkshire's new corporate functions and executive committees effectively address the recent changes in the private equity market, the growth of Berkshire's business, and the transition of its leadership? Had these changes impacted Berkshire's consensus-based, team-oriented culture, and if so, did it matter? Was Berkshire becoming too corporate?

Exhibit 1   Largest Private Equity Transactions (in U.S.$ millions)

Target	Transaction Value	Year	Acquiring Firms
TXU	$43,800	2007	KKR, TPG, Goldman Sachs
Equity Office Properties	38,900	2006	Blackstone
Hospital Corporation of America	32,700	2006	Bain Capital, KKR, Merrill Lynch
RJR Nabisco	31,100	1988	KKR
Clear Channel	27,500	2006	Bain Capital, Thomas H. Lee
Harrah's Entertainment	27,400	2006	Apollo, TPG
Kinder Morgan	21,600	2006	Goldman Sachs, AIG, Carlyle, Riverstone
Freescale Semiconductor	17,600	2006	Blackstone, Carlyle, Permira, TPG
Albertson's	17,400	2006	SuperValu, CVS, Cerberus Capital, Kimco
Hertz	15,000	2005	Carlyle, Clayton Dubilier & Rice, Merrill Lynch

Source: Dealogic sourced from CFO Magazine, The Buyout Binge, http://www.cfo.com/printable/article.cfm/8909971, accessed July 31, 2009, adapted by casewriters.

Exhibit 2   Selected Recently Raised Specialized Private Equity Funds (in U.S.$ millions or Euro millions)

Fund	Investment Type/Geography	Amount
Cerberus Institutional Investors Series 4	Distressed	$7,500
Avenue Special Situations Fund V	Distressed	6,100
Wilbur L Ross Recovery Fund IV	Distressed	4,000
Summit Partners Europe Private Equity Fund	European	E1,050
Blackstone Credit Liquidity Partners	Debt and related	$1,300
Carlyle Infrastructure Partners	Transportation and water infrastructure	1,150
Carlyle Europe Technology Partners II	European technology	E530
Thomas H. Lee Credit Partners	Debt instruments	$500
Levine Leichtman Capital Partners Deep Value Fund	Distressed LBOs	500
Carlyle MENA Partners	Middle Eastern and North African	500
Highland Consumer Fund	Retail	300
Catterton Growth Partners	Consumer growth deals	300
Clarity Partners China Fund I	Chinese	200-400
Allied Capital Senior Debt Fund	Middle-market senior loans	125

Source: Dow Jones Galante's Venture Capital and Private Equity Directory (2009), pp. xiv and xxix, adapted by casewriters.

Exhibit 3   Top U.S.-Headquartered Private Equity Firms Based on Capital Under Management for 1989, 2002 and 2008 (in U.S.$ millions)

Rank	1989	Capital	2002	Capital	2008	Capital
1	Kohlberg Kravis Roberts	$5,600	Bessemer Trust	$38,000	Goldman Sachs Capital Partners	$58,700
2	Forstmann Little	2,500	Kohlberg Kravis Roberts	24,000	Carlyle Group	46,000
3	Morgan Stanley	2,250	Oaktree Capital Management	19,780	Blackstone Group	41,700
4	Merrill Lynch	1,900	Thomas H. Lee	18,000	Kohlberg Kravis Roberts	38,100
5	Acadia Partners	1,600	DLJ Merchant Banking Partners	15,000	Bain Capital	37,000
6	Thomas H. Lee	1,600	Forstmann Little	14,600	TPG	32,500
7	Butler Capital	1,400	Hicks Muse Tate & Furst	14,000	Cerberus Capital Management	25,000
8	Shearson Lehman Hutton	1,300	Carlyle Group	12,500	Warburg Pincus	24,000
9	Robinson-Humphrey	1,250	HarbourVest Partners	11,000	Providence Equity Partners	21,064
10	Wasserstein Perella	1,060	Warburg Pincus	11,000	Apollo Advisors	19,250
11	Clayton Dubilier & Rice	1,000	Welsh Carson Anderson & Stowe	11,000	Hellman & Friedman	16,900
12	Continental Equity	1,000	General Atlantic Partners	10,000	Welsh Carson Anderson & Stowe	16,000
13	First Boston	1,000	Morgan Stanley	10,000	General Atlantic Partners	15,000
14	Manufacturers Hanover	1,000	Blackstone Group	9,000	Angelo Gordon	14,750
15	Welsh Carson Anderson & Stowe	910	Madison Dearborn Partners	8,000	Silver Lake Partners	13,400
16	Blackstone Group	850	Goldman Sachs Capital Partners	7,300	First Reserve	12,700
17	Prudential-Bache Interfunding	800	TPG	7,200	Lexington Partners	12,000
18	DLJ Merchant Banking Partners	750	AIG Capital Partners	7,000	Fortress Investment Group	11,200
19	Charterhouse Group	612	BankAmerica	7,000	Avenue Capital Group	11,150
20	First Chicago	600	Clayton Dubilier & Rice	6,600	Madison Dearborn Partners	10,500
	Subtotals – Top Twenty Firms	**$28,982**		**$260,980**		**$476,914**
	Berkshire Partners	**$184**	**Berkshire Partners (ranked #50)**	**$3,000**	**Berkshire Partners (ranked #49)**	**$6,500**

Source: Corporate Finance (Magazine), December, 1989, "The Top 20 LBO Funds Ranked by Equity Capital" p. 90,
Dow Jones Galante's Venture Capital and Private Equity Directory (2002), "The 500 Largest U.S. Venture Capital & Private Equity Firms" pp.23-24 and
Dow Jones Galante's Venture Capital and Private Equity Directory (2008), "The 500 Largest Venture Capital & Private Equity Firms" pp. xlix-l. Adapted by casewriters.

Exhibit 4   Berkshire Partners' Funds (in U.S.$ millions)

Fund	Investment Type/Geography	Status	Year	Amount
Berkshire Fund VII	LBO / Principally U.S.	Investing	2006	$3,100
Berkshire Fund VI	LBO / Principally U.S.	Fully invested	2002	1,700
Berkshire Fund V	LBO / Principally U.S.	Fully invested	1998	985
Berkshire Fund IV	LBO / Principally U.S.	Fully invested	1996	387
Berkshire Fund III	LBO / Principally U.S.	Fully invested	1992	168
Berkshire Fund II	LBO / Principally U.S.	Fully invested	1986	125
Berkshire Fund I	LBO / Principally U.S.	Fully invested	1984	59

Source: Company.

Exhibit 5 Amount of Capital Invested in Private Equity by Investor Type

	Berkshire Fund VII
University Endowments	30%
Corporate & Public Pensions	17%
Foundations	16%
Non-U.S. Institutions	12%
Financial Institutions	11%
Insurance	7%
Special Relationships	7%
	100%

	Global PE Industry
Public Pension Funds	25%
Private Sector Pension Funds	20%
Insurance Companies	13%
Banks and Investment Banks	11%
Endowment Plans	7%
Family Offices/Foundations	6%
Sovereign Wealth Funds	5%
Corporate Investors	4%
Government Agencies	4%
Investment Companies	4%
Superannuation Schemes	1%
	100%

Excludes capital invested by the employees of private equity firms.

Source: Company and Tim Friedman, ed., 2009 Preqin Global Private Equity Review (London: Preqin Ltd., 2009), p. 78.

Exhibit 6 Berkshire Partners - Mission Statement

- Produce investment returns that consistently rank us in the top quartile of comparable private investment firms.

- Support the management teams of our portfolio companies with the resources needed to realize the full potential of their businesses.

- Strive for honesty and fairness and uphold the highest ethical standards.

- Make decisions based on analytical rigor, open debate, and logic-based judgments.

- Maintain the Firm's culture of teamwork, inclusiveness, and consensus decision-making.

- Support the development of our staff and encourage all our colleagues to seek balance in life through their commitments to family, community service and outside interests.

Source: Company.

Exhibit 7   Berkshire Partners – Current Investments

Investment yr	Company	Description	Industry	Headquarters
2009	Grocery Outlet	Extreme value grocery retailer.	Retail	Berkeley, CA
2009	United BioSource	Develops and globally commercializes medical products in partnership with life sciences companies.	Healthcare	Bethesda, MD
2009	Tower Development Corporation	Acquires and develops wireless infrastructure sites; partnership with Crown Castle.	Telecommunications	Boston, MA
2009	Eyeglass World	Supported existing portfolio company National Vision in acquisition of regional optical retailing chain.	Retail	Atlanta, GA
2008	TransDigm	Designer, producer and supplier of commercial and military aircraft components.	Transportation	Cleveland, OH
2007	MBT	Designer and marketer of functional footwear.	Consumer products	Romanshorn, Switzerland
2007	HMT	Provider of aboveground storage tank maintenance products and services.	Industrial	Houston, TX
2007	Masterplan	Provider of service, maintenance and asset management for medical equipment.	Business services	Chatsworth, CA
2007	AmSafe	Manufacturer of safety and securement systems for aviation, air cargo, military and specialty vehicle markets.	Transportation	Phoenix, AZ
2006	Vi-Jon	Manufacturer of private label personal care products.	Consumer products	St. Louis, MI
2006	Citizens of Humanity	Designer and distributor of premium denim and other apparel.	Consumer products	Huntington Park, CA
2006/2008	N.E.W. Asurion Corporation	Provider of extended service plans, consumer product support and value added wireless subscriber services.	Business services	Sterling, VA Nashville, TN
2005	Electro-Motive Diesel	Manufacturer of freight and passenger diesel-electric locomotives.	Transportation	LaGrange, IL
2005	American Tire Distributors	Tire distributor to replacement market.	Transportation	Huntersville, NC
2005	Aritzia	Canadian retailer of women's apparel and accessories.	Retail	Vancouver, BC
2005	Party City	Retailer of party goods.	Retail	Rockaway, NJ
2005	National Vision	Retail optical company that operates vision centers.	Retail	Lawrenceville, GA
2004	Amscan	Manufacturer of party goods and metallic party balloons.	Consumer products	Elmsford, NY
2004	Bare Escentuals	Marketer of branded cosmetics and skincare products.	Consumer products	San Francisco, CA
2004	Bartlett Nuclear	Provider of radiation protection support personnel and decontamination services to the U.S. nuclear industry.	Business services	Plymouth, MA
2002/1988	Advanced Drainage Systems	Manufacturer of high-density polyethylene pipe.	Industrial	Columbus, OH
1997	Gordon Brothers Group	Advisory firm that assists retailers with asset deployment.	Business services	Boston, MA

Source: Company, http://www.berkshirepartners.com/invest_current.shtml, accessed July 20, 2009, adapted by casewriters.

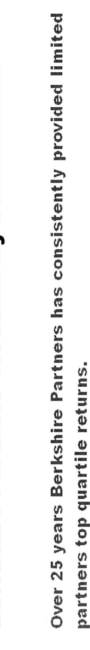

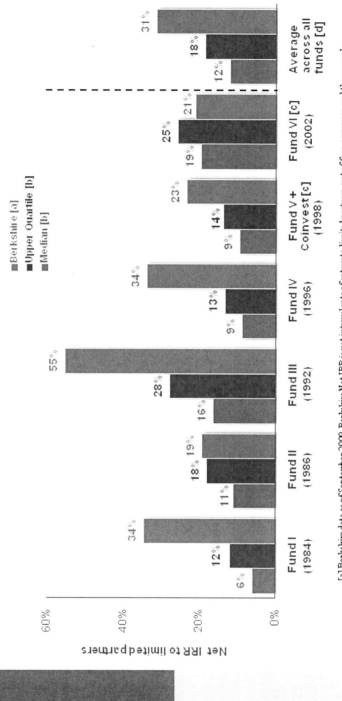

Exhibit 8   Berkshire Partners - Performance Overview (internal rates of return in percentages)

Berkshire Partners vs. industry benchmarks

Over 25 years Berkshire Partners has consistently provided limited partners top quartile returns.

Net IRR to limited partners

- Berkshire [a]
- Upper Quartile [b]
- Median [b]

	Fund I (1984)	Fund II (1986)	Fund III (1992)	Fund IV (1996)	Fund V + Coinvest [c] (1998)	Fund VI [c] (2002)	Average across all funds [d]
Berkshire	34%	18% / 19%	55%	34%	23%	25%	31%
Upper Quartile	12%	11%	28%	13%	14%	21%	18%
Median	6%		16%	9%	9%	19%	12%

[a] Berkshire data as of September 2009. Berkshire Net IRR is net internal rate of return to limited partners, net of fees, expenses, and the general partner's carried interest.

[b] Benchmark data from Cambridge Associates as of June 2009. U.S. Buyout Funds benchmark used unless not available, in which case U.S. Private Equity Funds benchmark is used. Funds I-III compared to U.S. Private Equity Funds. Funds IV-VI compared to U.S. Buyout Funds.

[c] Berkshire Funds V and VI are not yet fully realized funds as of September 2009. Fund V has fully realized sixteen of its twenty-two original holdings. Fund VI has fully realized four of its seventeen original holdings.

[d] Averages on chart are arithmetic averages across all funds and benchmarks shown. Shown this way for comparability purposes. Actual net IRR of Berkshire funds since inception is 29%.

Source: Company.

Exhibit 9   Berkshire Partners - Performance Overview (multiples of invested capital)

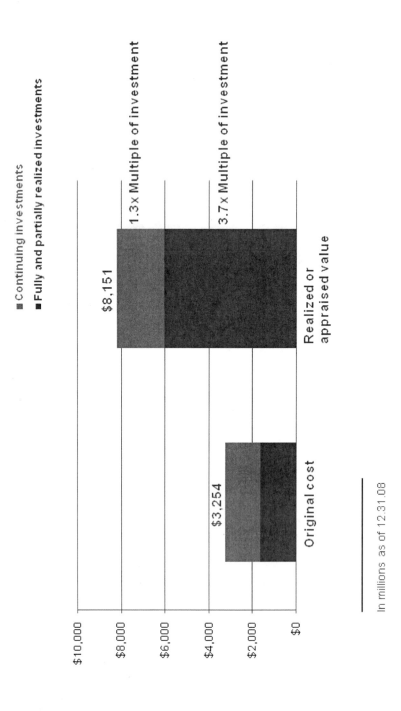

Source: Company.

Exhibit 10 Median LBO Industry Compensation – 2006 (in U.S.$ thousands)

Level	Salary		Bonus[1]		Carried Interest at Work[2]
	25%	75%	25%	75%	
Junior Partner	$250	$350	$135	$253	$6,690
Principal/VP	150	200	86	140	1,450
Senior Associate	110	130	54	89	850
Associate	80	100	50	78	200

(1) For those receiving a bonus.

(2) Carried interest at work was a measurement that helped standardize compensation across the private equity industry. For example, at a $1 billion fund, a total of 20%, or $200 million, carried interest at work might be available for the GP's team. A Principal/VP might have a claim to $1.45 million, or 0.725% of the total available.

Source: Dow Jones, Private Equity Partnership Terms and Conditions, 2007 edition, p. 76, adapted by casewriters.

Exhibit 11 Private Equity Industry Carry Distribution

Level	Historic	Going forward
Managing Partners, General Partners	85%	75.00%
Principals	10%	15.00%
VP/Senior Associate	5%	7.50%
Associates/Analysts	0%	1.25%
COOs, CFOs, CAOs	0%	1.25%
	100%	100%

Data are estimates based on offers and acceptances tracked by Glocap Search as well as recruiter knowledge of compensation trends.
Table represents distribution of the approximately 20% carry available for the GP's team. The remaining 80% would be distributed to LP's.

Source: Investment Benchmark Reports 2009, The 2009 Private Equity Compensation Report, (Thomson Reuters and Glocap Search), p 11. Adapted by casewriters.

Exhibit 12 Berkshire Partners – Organizational Structure c. 2008

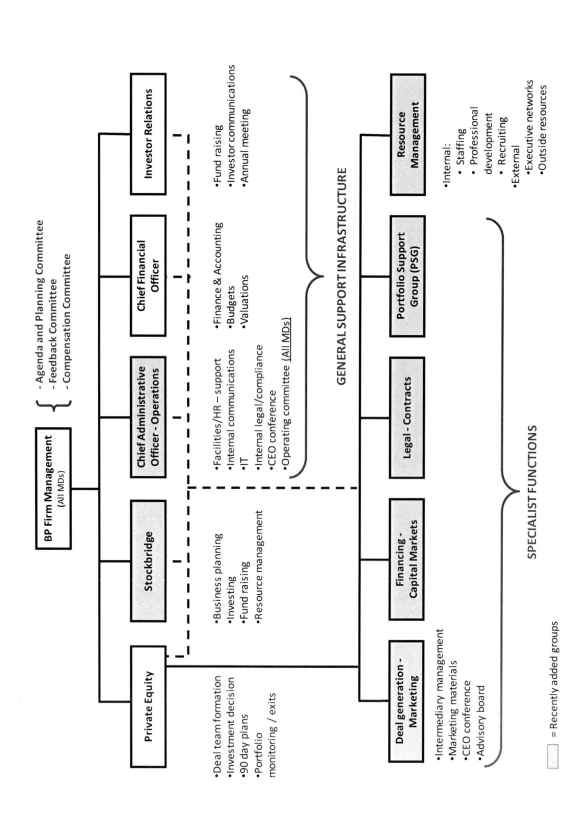

- Agenda and Planning Committee
- Feedback Committee
- Compensation Committee

BP Firm Management
(All MDs)

Stockbridge

- Business planning
- Investing
- Fund raising
- Resource management

Private Equity

- Deal team formation
- Investment decision
- 90 day plans
- Portfolio monitoring / exits

Chief Administrative Officer - Operations

- Facilities/HR – support
- Internal communications
- IT
- Internal legal/compliance
- CEO conference
- Operating committee (All MDs)

Chief Financial Officer

- Finance & Accounting
- Budgets
- Valuations

Investor Relations

- Fund raising
- Investor communications
- Annual meeting

GENERAL SUPPORT INFRASTRUCTURE

Deal generation - Marketing

- Intermediary management
- Marketing materials
- CEO conference
- Advisory board

Financing - Capital Markets

Legal - Contracts

Portfolio Support Group (PSG)

Resource Management

- Internal:
  - Staffing
  - Professional development
  - Recruiting
- External
  - Executive networks
  - Outside resources

SPECIALIST FUNCTIONS

□ = Recently added groups

Source: Company, adapted by casewriters.

208

Exhibit 13   Berkshire Partners - Staff Count History

	At Year-End								
	2001	2002	2003	2004	2005	2006	2007	2008	2009
Associates	5	6	7	7	6	8	9	10	11
Senior Associates and Principals	7	6	6	7	8	8	9	9	11
Total Assoc/SA/Princ	12	12	13	14	14	16	18	19	22
Other investment staff	2	2	3	3	6	9	11	11	12
MDs	10	10	10	10	9	11	12	11	11
Total investment staff	**24**	**24**	**26**	**27**	**29**	**36**	**41**	**41**	**45**
Total non-investment staff				25	21	32	43	45	46
Stockbridge				0	0	1	3	8	10
Grand total				52	50	69	87	94	101

Note: Other investment staff included: business development, general counsel, capital markets, PSG, operations, marketing and the CFO.

Non-investment staff included: executive assistants, information technology, human resources, facilities, finance and accounting.

Stockbridge figures excluded Rob Small; Small is captured in MDs.

Source: Company, adapted by casewriters.

Endnotes

[1] Co-Founder and Managing Director Carl Ferenbach, interview by casewriters, Boston, MA, July 19, 2009.

[2] Co-Founder and Managing Director Carl Ferenbach, interview by casewriters, Boston, MA, July 13, 2009.

[3] Board of Governors of the Federal Reserve System. "The Economics of the Private Equity Market." Board of Governors of the Federal Reserve System Web site, http://www.federalreserve.gov/pubs/staffstudies/1990-99/ss168.pdf, pp. 1-2, accessed November 2, 2009.

[4] Watson Wyatt Worldwide. "Private Equity Explained," August, 2007. Watson Wyatt Worldwide Web site, http://www.watsonwyatt.com, p. 25, accessed July 17, 2009. Based on Merrill Lynch, Somerset Capital Limited and Watson Wyatt estimates.

[5] Friedman, Tim, ed. *2009 Preqin Global Private Equity Review.* London: Preqin Ltd. 2009, p. 12.

[6] Friedman, Tim, ed. *2009 Preqin Global Private Equity Review.* London: Preqin Ltd. 2009, p. 13.

[7] Friedman, Tim, ed. *2009 Preqin Global Private Equity Review.* London: Preqin Ltd. 2009, p. 12.

[8] Bank for International Settlements. Committee on the Global Financial System. *CGFS Papers No. 30 – Private Equity and Leveraged Finance Markets,* July, 2008, p. 5. http://www.bis.org/publ/cgfs30.pdf?noframes=1, accessed November 2, 2009.

[9] Carey, David. "PE Collusion Hard to Prove." *TheDeal.com,* October 11, 2006. http://www.thedeal.com, accessed August 10, 2009.

[10] Yvonne Ball, "Fortress Investment IPO Exceeds Expectations, 3rd Update," Dow Jones News Service, February 9, 2007, via Factiva, accessed August 10, 2009.

[11] Jason Kelly and Jonathan Keehner, "Schwarzman's 'Perfectly Timed' IPO Means Long Wait for Holders." Bloomberg LP, June 20, 2008. http://bloomberg.com/apps/news?pid20670001&sid=ab1Xeq8UM0PA, accessed August 10, 2009.

[12] Michael Flaherty, "Apollo Chief Says Sold Nine Percent of Firm to Abu Dhabi." Reuters, November 7, 2007. http://www.reuters.com/articlePrint?articleID=USN0756534920071107, accessed August 10, 2009.

[13] Nomura Holdings, Inc. December 19, 2006 Form 6-K. Tokyo and New York: Nomura Holdings, Inc., 2006. http://www.sec.gov, accessed November 2, 2009.

[14] Peter Lattman, "Private Equity's Ultimate Buyout." The Wall Street Journal Online, January 23, 2009, via Factiva, accessed November 2, 2009.

[15] Friedman, Tim, ed. *2009 Preqin Global Private Equity Review.* London: Preqin Ltd. 2009, pp 12-13.

[16] Friedman, Tim, ed. *2009 Preqin Global Private Equity Review.* London: Preqin Ltd. 2009, p. 60.

[17] Managing Director Kevin Callaghan, interview by casewriters, Boston, MA, July 13, 2009.

[18] "Bullet Points of Investment Strategy 2009." Berkshire Partners internal memorandum, provided to casewriters by Mike Ascione.

[19] "Mission Statement." Berkshire Partners internal memorandum, provided to casewriters by Mike Ascione.

[20] Co-Founder and Managing Director Brad Bloom, interview by casewriters, Boston, MA, July 13, 2009.

[21] Co-Founder and Managing Director Carl Ferenbach, interview by casewriters, Boston, MA, July 13, 2009.

[22] Managing Director Mike Ascione, interview by casewriters, Boston, MA, June 26, 2009.

[23] Co-Founder and Managing Director Brad Bloom, interview by casewriters, Boston, MA, July 13, 2009.

[24] Co-Founder and Managing Director Brad Bloom, as framed by Carl Ferenbach, interview by casewriters, Boston, MA, July 13, 2009.

[25] Managing Director Jane Brock-Wilson, interview by casewriters, Boston, MA, July 13, 2009.

[26] Managing Director Ross Jones, interview by casewriters, Boston, MA, December 18, 2009.

[27] Co-Founder and Managing Director Carl Ferenbach, interview by casewriters, Boston, MA, July 13, 2009.

[28] Co-Founder and Managing Director Brad Bloom, interview by casewriters, Boston, MA, July 13, 2009.

[29] Managing Director Chris Hadley, interview by casewriters, Boston, MA, December 18, 2009.

[30] Managing Director Ross Jones, interview by casewriters, Boston, MA, December 18, 2009.

[31] Managing Director Larry Hamelsky, interview by casewriters, Boston, MA, July 13, 2009.

[32] Dow Jones. *Private Equity Partnership Terms and Conditions,* 2007 ed., p. 32. Wellesley, MA: Dow Jones, 2007.

[33] "Compensation Outline." Berkshire Partners internal memorandum, provided to casewriters by Richard Lubin.

[34] Managing Director Randy Peeler, interview by casewriters, Boston, MA, July 13, 2009.

[35] Managing Director Mike Ascione, interview by casewriters, Boston, MA, December 18, 2009.

[36] Managing Director Kevin Callaghan, interview by casewriters, Boston, MA, July 13, 2009.

[37] Managing Director Randy Peeler, interview by casewriters, Boston, MA, July 13, 2009.

[38] Co-Founder and Managing Director Richard Lubin, interview by casewriters, Boston, MA, July 13, 2009.

[39] Dow Jones. *Dow Jones Private Equity Analyst,* p. 4. http://img.en25.com/web/dowjonesfis/soc09.pdf, accessed November 2, 2009.

[40] "Compensation Outline." Berkshire Partners internal memorandum, provided to casewriters by Richard Lubin.

[41] Managing Director Jane Brock-Wilson, interview by casewriters, Boston, MA, July 13, 2009.

[42] Managing Director Ross Jones, interview by casewriters, Boston, MA, December 18, 2009, adapted.

[43] Co-Founder and Managing Director Carl Ferenbach, interview by casewriters, Boston, MA, July 13, 2009.

[44] "Our Business Plan For 2009." Berkshire Partners internal memorandum, dated February 10, 2009, provided to casewriters by Mike Ascione.

[45] Managing Director Kevin Callaghan, interview by casewriters, Boston, MA, July 13, 2009, adapted.

[46] Managing Director Rob Small, interview by casewriters, Boston, MA, June 26, 2009.

[47] Managing Director Mike Ascione, interview by casewriters, Boston, MA, July 27, 2009.